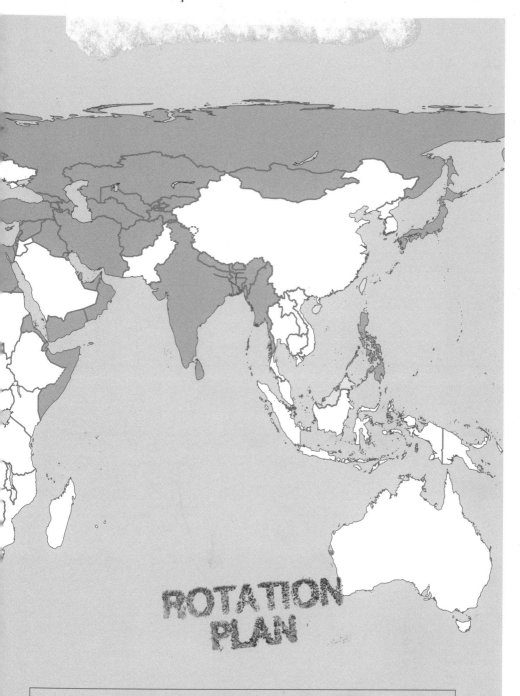

ROTATION
PLAN

THE KEY BATTLEGROUNDS
Shown in white

THE LANDGRABBERS

Also by Fred Pearce

Deep Jungle: journey to the heart of the rainforest

When the Rivers Run Dry: what happens when our water runs out?

The Last Generation: how nature will take her
revenge for climate change

Earth Then and Now: potent visual evidence of our
changing world

Confessions of an Eco Sinner: travels to find where
my stuff comes from

Peoplequake: mass migration, ageing nations and
the coming population crash

The Climate Files: the battle for the truth about climate change

THE LANDGRABBERS

The New Fight over Who Owns the Planet

Fred Pearce

eden project books

TRANSWORLD PUBLISHERS
61–63 Uxbridge Road, London W5 5SA
A Random House Group Company
www.transworldbooks.co.uk

First published in Great Britain
in 2012 by Eden Project Books
an imprint of Transworld Publishers

Copyright © Fred Pearce 2012
Maps by Tom Coulson at Encompass Graphics

Fred Pearce has asserted his right under the Copyright, Designs
and Patents Act 1988 to be identified as the author of this work.

A CIP catalogue record for this book
is available from the British Library.

ISBNs 9781905811731 (hb)
9781905811748 (tpb)

Addresses for Random House Group Ltd companies outside the UK
can be found at: www.randomhouse.co.uk
The Random House Group Ltd Reg. No. 954009

The Random House Group Limited supports the Forest Stewardship Council (FSC®), the
leading international forest-certification organization. Our books carrying the FSC label are
printed on FSC®-certified paper. FSC is the only forest-certification scheme endorsed by
the leading environmental organizations, including Greenpeace. Our paper procurement
policy can be found at www.randomhouse.co.uk/environment.

Typeset in 11.5/16.5pt Berkeley by Falcon Oast Graphic Art Ltd.
Printed and bound in Great Britain by CPI Group (UK) Ltd, Croydon, CR0 4YY

2 4 6 8 10 9 7 5 3 1

CONTENTS

INTRODUCTION

'Buy land. They're not making it any more.'
Mark Twain

Soaring grain prices and fears about future food supplies are triggering a global land grab. Gulf sheikhs, Chinese state corporations, Wall Street speculators, Russian oligarchs, Indian microchip billionaires, doomsday fatalists, Midwestern missionaries and City of London hedge-fund slickers are scouring the globe for cheap land to feed their people, their bottom lines or their consciences. Chunks of land the size of small countries are changing hands for a song. So who precisely are the buyers – and whose land is being taken over?

I spent a year circling the globe to find out, interviewing the grabbers and the grabbed on every continent, from Jeddah, London and Chicago to Sumatra, Paraguay and Liberia. Almost everyone seems to be a landgrabber today. My cast of characters includes super-financier George Soros and super-industrialist Richard Branson; Colombian narco-terrorists and Italian heiresses; an Irish dairy farmer in the Saudi desert and the recent commander of British land forces, now tilling soil in Guinea; gunrunners and the couple who sold the world high fashion with the Patagonia brand before buying the wild lands of the same name.

I discovered how logging concessions in central Africa may have helped elect Nicolas Sarkozy as president of France; what Lord Rothschild and a legendary 1970s asset stripper are doing in the backwoods of Brazil; who is buying Laos and Liberia, and who already owns Swaziland; how Goldman Sachs added tens of millions to the world's starving; the dramatic contrast between Kenya's Happy Valley and Zimbabwe's Hippo Valley; who grabbed a tenth of the new state of South Sudan even before it raised its flag; why Qatar is everywhere; and what links a black-skinned Saudi billionaire to Bill Clinton, Ethiopia's ex-freedom-fighting prime minister and rich cattle pastures at the head of the Nile.

I found an evangelical American ex-prison boss draining bogs on the shores of Lake Victoria; a dapper English banker ploughing up the Brazilian *cerrado* grasslands; Saudi sheikhs in Sudan, extending the world's largest sugar farm; the Moonies seeking 'heavenly life' by grabbing Paraguayan jungles; and Gaddafi's doomed henchmen annexing black earth in Ukraine and yellow sands in Mali. The Kidmans and Windsors and Gettys and Khashoggis and Oppenheimers are in there too – and most likely you, or at least your pension fund, have a slice of the action.

Some regard the term landgrabbers as pejorative. But it is widely used, and the subject of academic conferences. I use it here to describe any contentious acquisition of large-scale land rights by a foreigner or other 'outsider', whatever the legal status of the transaction. It's not all bad, but it all merits attention. And that is the purpose of this book.

I have been in awe at the grabbers' sheer ambition, and sometimes at their open-hearted altruism too. Some want to save their nations from a coming 'perfect storm' of rising population, changing diets and climate change. Others look forward to making a killing as the storm hits. Many believe they will do good along the way. But I have been appalled at the damage that often results from their actions.

Their hosts share much of the blame for what goes wrong. After years of neglecting their agriculture, African governments are suddenly keen to invest. Their desire for a quick fix to deep-seated problems makes foreign investors, with their big promises, attractive. Many governments ask few questions when investors come calling. They clear the land of existing inhabitants, and often don't even ask for rent. There may be an unspoken cultural cringe, in which foreign is always considered best. The investment, ministers believe, will inevitably bring food and jobs to their people. But such easy assurances rarely work out, for reasons that are social, environmental, economic, geopolitical – and sometimes a toxic mix of all four.

There is much uncertainty about how much land has been 'grabbed', and how firm the grasp of the grabbers is. In 2010, the World Bank came up with a figure of 47 million hectares. The Global Land Project, an international research network, hazarded 63 million hectares. The Land Deal Politics Initiative, another network of researchers that helped organize a conference on land-grabbing in the UK in mid-2011, totted up 80 million hectares. Within weeks, Oxfam, an aid agency, published its own estimate of 227 million hectares. The truth is nobody knows. There is no central register; there is little national transparency. Some of the largest deals I came across were done in secret and unknown even to the most diligent NGOs, while other deals have attracted head-lines but have never come to fruition. I have tried to disentangle the truth about individual projects, but I have not attempted any global figure.

I hope I have reported fairly. I did find new mega-farms with thoughtful managers who make sure to offer secure jobs, food and basic social services to their workers and their families. I found others with vibrant 'outgrower' schemes that supported nearby peasant farmers and bought their produce. I found investors with a long-term view. But I also found poor farmers and cattle herders who woke up to find themselves evicted from their ancestral lands; corporate potentates running enclave fiefdoms oblivious to the country beyond their fences; warlords selling land they don't own to financiers they have never met; hungry nations forced to export their food to the wealthy; and speculators who buy land and then disappear without trace. I was reminded repeatedly of scenes from books like John Steinbeck's *Grapes of Wrath* and Joseph Conrad's *Heart of Darkness*.

This is not about ideology. It is about what works. What will feed the world and what will feed the world's poorest. But what works has to do with human rights and access to natural resources, as well as about maximizing tonnes per hectare. As one agribusiness proponent, James Siggs of Toronto-based Feronia, admitted at an investment conference in 2011, 'Exclusively industrial-scale farming displaces and alienates peoples, creates few jobs and causes social disruption.'

Yet industrial-scale farming is what most landgrabbers have in mind. According to Graham Davies, consultant to the British private equity company Altima Partners, the 'vast majority' of investors in Africa are only interested in commercial Western-style agriculture, 'largely ignoring' the continent's 60 million small farms that grow 80 per cent of sub-Saharan Africa's farm produce.

It is important to know what agribusiness can and cannot deliver. But it is equally important to be angered by the appalling injustice of people having their ancestral land pulled from beneath their feet. And to question the arrogance and ignorance surrounding claims, by home governments and Western investors alike, that huge areas of Africa are 'empty' lands only awaiting the magic of foreign hands and foreign capital. And to baulk at the patina of virtue that often surrounds environmentalists eagerly taking other people's land in the interests of protecting wildlife. What right do 'green grabbers' have to take peasant fields and pastures to grow bio-fuels, cordon off rich pastures for nature conservation, shut up forests as carbon stores, and fence in wilderness as playpens and hunting grounds for rich sponsors. They are cooking up a 'tragedy of the commons' in reverse.

Over the next few decades I believe land-grabbing will matter more, to more of the planet's people, even than climate change. The new land rush looks increasingly like a final enclosure of the planet's wild places, a last round-up on the global commons. Is this the inevitable cost of feeding the world and protecting its surviving wildlife? Must the world's billion or so peasants and pastoralists give up their hinterlands in order to nourish the rest of us? Or is this a new colonialism that should be confronted – the moment when localism and communalism fight back?

I began and ended my journey round the world in the cockpit of the greatest land grab in history – the unfenced plains of Africa, where governments, corporations and peasants seem set to fight for the soil of their continent. I started with a man named Omot.

PART ONE

LAND WARS

The wild lands of Africa – the forests and pastures and wetlands where millions live – are being taken over by agribusiness. We begin in a remote corner of Ethiopia, annexed from its inhabitants by two of the world's richest men, a Saudi and an Indian. Why? On the trading floors of Chicago and in the oil-rich deserts of Arabia, the financial and geopolitical forces behind soaring food prices and the rush for farmland are exposed. And back in Africa, in the world's newest nation, cowboy speculators are sowing the seeds of corruption rather than corn.

1

GAMBELLA, ETHIOPIA

Tragedy in the commons

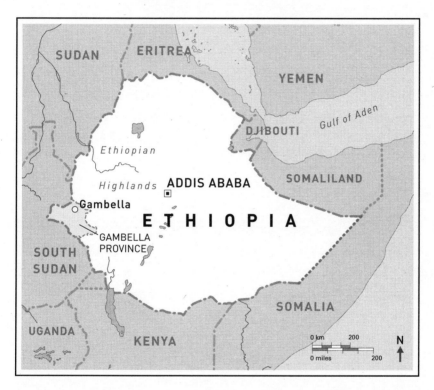

Omot Ochan was sitting in a remnant of forest on an old waterbuck skin, and eating maize from a calabash gourd. He was lean and tall, wearing only a pair of combat pants. Behind him was a straw hut, where bare-breasted women and barefoot children were busy cooking fish on an open fire. A little way off were other huts, the remains of what was once a sizeable village. Omot said he and his family were from the Anuak tribe. They had lived in the forest for ten generations. 'This land belonged to our father. All round here is ours. For two days' walk.' He described the distant tree that marked the boundary with the next village. 'When my father died, he said don't leave the land. We made a promise. We can't give it to the foreigners.'

Our conversation was punctuated by the rumble of trucks passing on a dirt road just 20 metres away. The dust clouds they created wafted into the clearing and rained down on the leaves of the trees. Beyond the road huge earth-diggers were excavating a canal. Omot watched them: 'Two years ago, the company began chopping down the forest and the bees went away. The bees need thick forest. We used to sell honey. We used to hunt with dogs too. But after the farm came, the animals here disappeared. Now we only have fish to sell.' And with the company draining the wetland, the fish will probably be gone soon, too.

Gambella is the poorest province in one of the world's poorest nations – a lowland appendix in the far south-western corner of Ethiopia. Geographically and ethnically, the hot, swampy province feels like part of the new neighbouring state of South Sudan, rather than the cool highlands of the rest of Ethiopia. Indeed, Gambella was effectively in Sudan when it was ruled by the British from Khartoum, until they left in 1956. For the half-century since, the government in Addis Ababa has ruled here, but it has invested little and cared even less for its Nilotic tribal inhabitants, whose jet-black skin and tall, elegant physique mark them out from the lighter-skinned and shorter highlanders. The livestock-herding Nuer, who frequently cross the border into South Sudan, and the Anuak, who are farmers and fishers, are peripheral to highland Ethiopia in every sense.

Only three flights a week go to the small provincial capital, also called Gambella. When you get there, there are no taxis, because there is no demand. The road from the airport is a dirt track through an empty landscape. Gambella town is a shambles. Its population of 30,000 has no waste collection system, so garbage piles up. The drains don't work, public water supplies are sporadic and electricity is occasional. There are few public latrines. The couple of paved roads are heavily pot-holed and give out before the town limits. My billet, the Norwegian-built guest house at the Bethel Synod church, was probably the dirtiest, bleakest and most ill-kempt building in which I have ever rested my head. The only vehicle in town for hire was a 40-year-old Toyota minibus of dubious roadworthiness, with a crew of three. I took it.

Of late, the central government in Addis Ababa has stopped pretending that the province of Gambella doesn't exist. It now seems intent on taming a populace that might prefer rule from Juba, the capital of South Sudan. In practice, that means bringing in foreign agribusiness and collecting the province's dispersed population in state-designated villages, while their forests, fields and hunting grounds are handed over to outsiders. In the service of capitalism, the Gambella 'villagization' programme will relocate a domestic population much in the manner of Stalin, Mao and Pol Pot.

I set out along the only road south from Gambella town to find the landgrabbers. On the outskirts, as we hit the dirt, my driver decided to pick up a dozen hitchhikers. From then on, we were the local bus service. To an outsider, much of the province looks deserted. Its expanses of lowland forests and bush, grassland and marsh are wide open to wildlife migrations, passing cattle herders and occasional shifting cultivators. For miles, the only obvious sign of human activity was the odd mobile-phone mast, usually with a generator to power it and a resident native guard. But there were hidden villages in the bush. Their members would sit by the roadside trying to sell mangoes and other fruit to any vehicles that passed. Mangoes cost less than three cents each, and the price had halved by late afternoon.

Soon after the small town of Abobo, the road passed through a landscape of ash, smoke and charred trees. This was land newly acquired by my first landgrabber – Sheikh Mohammed Hussein Ali Al Amoudi, a Saudi oil billionaire with large holdings in Ethiopian plantations, mines and real estate. In 2011, *Fortune* magazine put his personal wealth at more than $12 billion. Ethiopian-born, he is often described as the world's richest black man. He is a million-dollar donor to the Clinton Foundation, and also a close confidant of Ethiopia's prime minister, Meles Zenawi, and his ruling party, which had granted a 60-year concession on 10,000 hectares of Gambella to Al Amoudi's company, Saudi Star.

Al Amoudi has been eyeing agriculture since the world food price spike in 2008 sent Saudi Arabia into a spin about its future food supplies. He is intent on shipping most of his intended produce, including in excess of a million tonnes of rice a year, to Saudi Arabia. There he has been fêted by the king for making investments abroad to keep the kingdom fed. To smooth the wheels of commerce, Al Amoudi has recruited one of Zenawi's former ministers, Haile Assegdie, as chief executive of Saudi Star.

Saudi Star's concession is based around the Alwero dam, built in the 1980s to irrigate a state cotton farm that never happened. The dam's rusting sign still advertises the consulting services of Soviet engineers Selkhozpromexport. Al Amoudi is digging a 30-kilometre canal from the dam to irrigate rice paddies. Once the old state farm is watered, he wants to expand to at least 250,000 hectares, to grow sunflowers and maize.

At the gate of the Saudi Star compound, I watched soldiers usher in giant Volvo trucks and Massey Ferguson tractors, and workmen starting to replace the temporary buildings with new permanent structures. Close by, they were laying an airstrip in a recently made clearing in the forest. Nobody at the company here or in Gambella town would talk to me. Perhaps they thought there was nothing to add to their boss's recent media statement that 'land-grabbing poses no harm on the environment or on the local community'.

Our next hitchhikers, outside the company gate, were a couple of schoolgirls who wanted a lift back to their home two kilometres away. It was there, in a small clearing in a forest by the road, that we found Omot Ochan in his combat pants on his waterbuck skin, describing how Al Amoudi and his company were destroying his world. Hearing his testimony of ancestral connection with this patch of forest, and his determination to keep it, I was struck by how most Westerners have lost any sense of place and attachment to the land. I move around all the time, and buy and sell houses without feeling ties to the soil. But here in Gambella, their land is like their blood. It is everything. And to lose it would be to lose their identity.

Omot insisted Saudi Star had no right to be in his forest. The company had not even told the villagers that it was going to dig a canal across their land. 'Nobody came to tell us what was happening.' He did remember officials from the 'villagization' programme dropping by to say the families should go to the new village at Pokedi, across the River Alwedo from Saudi Star's compound. But that was all. Omot had no doubt that the purpose of the new village was to clear them and others off land taken from them to give to Saudi Star. So far, his family and their neighbours had refused to go, even though their children walked to the school at Pokedi on a Monday morning and didn't return until Friday evening.

'In our culture, going to a different place is unusual. You get different people and there is quarrelling,' he told me, as his children gathered round and grabbed the remaining maize. 'We should remain in our own area. We won't go unless we are forced. God gave us this land.' Another truck rumbled past, spraying dust over the tiny forest community – a community that has found itself ostracized by its own government and under siege from a Saudi billionaire. After the truck had gone, I noticed a large, dead stork in the road. One of the women headed off down the road with a bucket, on a long walk to find water.

Saudi Star's farm looked huge, extending for miles along the road. But it was nothing compared to what I saw the next day, driving west on the other road out of Gambella town. At another roadside farm complex, most of the way to the border with South Sudan, I dropped in unannounced on Karmjeet Sekhon, an Indian agriculturalist recently arrived in Ethiopia. He took a parasol to shade himself from the fierce sun as we met at the gate of his compound, then settled into his air-conditioned mobile cabin.

Resplendent in his turban and tweaking his long moustache, Sekhon said he could not believe his luck at being in charge of this land. In 2009, the Ethiopian agriculture ministry gave his company, Bangalore-based Karuturi Global, a 50-year lease on 100,000 hectares, either side of the only road through the north of the province. It promised 200,000 hectares more if he cleared the first tranche within two years. He was well on the way.

Sekhon had a long career as a dairy man in India, where the options for expansion are constrained by more than a billion people. But here he had an area twenty times the size of Manhattan to do anything he wanted – with an option on sixty Manhattans. 'The soil is excellent. It is virgin land,' he told me. 'You can grow anything here; the climate is ideal. We have no land like this in India. There we are lucky to get 1 per cent of organic matter in the soil. Here it is more than 5 per cent. We don't even need fertilizer.' All for an annual rent of about a dollar a hectare.

Outside the cool cabin, Gambella's dry season was ending, and smoke plumes dotted the horizon. Sekhon's men were burning the bush to drive out snakes. He said he would soon have put in 600 kilometres of private roads, more than all the tarred public roads in the province. A South African remote sensing company had mapped every half-metre of the concession for him. Fifteen huge 475-horse-power John Deere tractors were clearing and levelling 500 hectares every day. Drainage ditches and irrigation canals were being dug, and irrigation kit was being shipped in from Israel and India. He had storage for 50,000 litres of diesel, mainly to run the pumps.

Soon, Sekhon would be planting. He had half a million oil-palm seedlings growing in a nursery. Within a year, he intended to be growing 20,000 hectares of oil palm, 15,000 hectares of sugar cane, 25,000 hectares of rice, and 10,000 hectares each of maize and sorghum. Contractors would soon be on site building process-ing works to extract palm oil, crush sugar cane and mill rice. Then they would start work on the townships, with schools and hospitals, shopping centres and housing for up to 50,000 people.

The company had hired two tugboats to pull barges carrying its harvests from the banks of the Baro River, a tributary of the Nile that ran through the mega-farm, upstream to Uganda and Lake Victoria, and downstream to Khartoum and beyond. The boats would follow the same route that British river traders took a century ago to export to the world Ethiopian coffee that they bought in Gambella town. The echoes of a new imperialism were strong.

I asked Sekhon whether locals would get jobs. He said most of his technical people would be Indian or Ethiopians from the high-lands. He had absorbed the Ethiopian ethos that the local tribespeople from the Gambella lowlands were lazy. 'But labourers will be from the villages whose land has been allotted to us. About 85 per cent of our drivers are from local tribes,' he assured me. Several dozen women from the nearby village of Iliya, which woke in 2009 to find itself surrounded by the Karuturi concession, now earn a dollar a day tending the oil-palm nursery rather than their own fields. Iliya is the home village of Nyikaw Ochalla, an exile I met in Reading, England. 'All the land round Iliya has been taken,' he told me. 'People have to work for the Indian company. They have no real choice.'

Karuturi Global is owned by Sai Ramakrishna Karuturi, an Indian engineer in his forties. Starting from scratch, he has become the world's largest owner of greenhouses, many of them in Ethiopia. Under glass roofs, he has created the world's largest rose-growing business, selling 650 million stems a year. This is a stunning 10 per cent of the global market. He employs 10,000 people in Africa alone. But Karuturi reckons he cannot sell any more roses. The market is sated. So he is moving into mainstream agriculture. 'I want to be among the top four or five integrated agri-product companies in the world. And I will implement this vision out of Africa,' he says. He plans on having a million hectares of land under his ploughs in Africa – a third of them in Ethiopia and, he suggested in late 2011, another third in Tanzania.

Karuturi promises to invest a billion dollars in the virgin fields of Gambella alone. Flash floods from the River Baro obliterated thousands of hectares of the first maize harvest in late 2011, but his response was to bring in Dutch consultants to prevent a repetition. He means business. His investment should see handsome returns both for him and for his US private equity investors, including Bethesda-based Monsoon Capital and Boston-based Sandstone Capital. The investment seems set to create Africa's largest privately owned farm, and make Karuturi one of the world's largest producers of a range of foodstuffs, able to take on long-standing US and European commodity giants like Cargill, ADM and Dreyfus.

But will promise become reality? Sekhon and his Indian lieutenants are a long way from home. They have little experience of Africa or Africans, and know little of the people whose land they are now tilling. Nor, it seemed, did they know about the anger caused by the land grab: the tales of government intimidation, of massacres, of vanishing livelihoods and wildlife, and the mutterings I heard in huts and clearings across the province about arming the tribal youth to reclaim their land.

Most of the millions of hectares of land being bought up across the plains of Africa, the paddy fields of Southeast Asia, the forests of South America and the steppes of Russia is ostensibly sold or leased as undeveloped land without owners. But in reality very little land in the world today is unclaimed or unused. When men like Karuturi and Al Amoudi call the land they are occupying 'empty' and 'virgin', they are as misguided as the colonial adventurers who came this way a century before. To the locals, every inch of the land is owned.

The biggest prize is known to geographers as the Guinea Savannah Zone: a great expanse of grasslands half the size of the United States, occupying a huge arc of 25 countries between the rainforest and the deserts – through West Africa to Sudan, then south through Kenya and Ethiopia to Zambia and Mozambique in the south. The World Bank calls these four million square kilometres 'the world's last large reserves of underused land'. Yet these lands are also the home of 600 million African peasant farmers and herders, approaching a tenth of the world's population. They are among the world's poorest people. They badly need economic development. The question is whether the new colonialists are there to develop Africa or ransack its resources. Will they feed the world – or just the bottom line?

For the moment, Africa's leaders seem convinced that foreign investment in mechanized big farming is the way forward. If they can turn their bush into American-style prairie, they will. The ambition of Karuturi and Al Amoudi in Gambella is matched by that of Ethiopian prime minister Zenawi. He has now been in post for 16 years. In that time his political philosophy has shifted from Marxism to capitalism. Under his rule, his country has not suffered a repeat of famines on the scale that blighted it in the 1970s and 1980s. But he has grown exasperated by its failure to energize smallholders to feed Ethiopia's fast-growing population.

Zenawi is now offering outsiders the chance to invest in its soil. The government's current five-year plan promises to lease 3 million hectares for large-scale mechanized agriculture by 2015, much of it in the rebellious tribal border lands of Gambella. Ironically, it is only because of Ethiopia's socialist past, in which all land was nationalized, that the foreign capitalists will be able to move in.

In Gambella, as in much of rural Africa, traditional customary land rights are still recognized by the people. But Ethiopian governments have a long history of moving people around, from state to state and into villages where none existed before. Gambella is scattered with communities of Zenawi's compatriot Tigrayans who were given land here after the great famine in the 1980s. Near Abobo, I saw one Tigrayan-owned farm growing 4,000 hectares of cotton. Along the road were power lines – a rare sight in Gambella. Other highlanders have come too, setting up businesses and taking land. In all, highlanders now make up nearly half of the 300,000 inhabitants of Gambella province. They are much resented, by the Anuak in particular.

Now the government is moving the locals too – out of the bush and their tiny settlements and into larger centralized villages. The federal affairs minister, Shiferaw Teklemariam, announced in late 2010 that the 'villagization' programme would resettle 180,000 people in 49 villages between 2011 and 2013. That is more than half of the entire population of Gambella, and will include the great majority of those living outside Gambella town.

Villagization had just begun when I visited. It seemed to be a rush job, done with little or no local consultation, and certainly no regard for the wishes of those being moved off their traditional lands. One foreign aid worker I spoke to remembered being called, not long before, to a meeting with the Gambella president, Omod

Obong, 'at which he suddenly said that he'd drawn up a villagiz-ation plan for the province. It was the first time we had heard about the plan. Yet he said he had done all the awareness raising with the people. Now he was ready to go ahead, and he wanted the aid agencies to pay for it. It was crazy.' They refused to help, but he went ahead anyway.

The publicly declared purpose of the villagization seems con-tradictory. Officials say it is to allow the provision of basic services such as boreholes, clinics and primary schools in centralized places in a region where flooding cuts off many people during the long wet season. The plan promises 19 schools, 25 health posts, 18 veteri-nary clinics, 41 flour mills and 195 kilometres of new rural roads. Yet communities that do not suffer floods, and which already have services like boreholes and schools and clinics and roads, are also being moved.

Locals have no doubt that the real purpose is to reduce their freedom, to take their land and to give it to landgrabbers. The government insists that it is 'a coincidence' that the mass removals are happening at the same time as the arrival of foreign mega-farmers. And it says that nobody is forced to move. But aid workers and villagers I met said that, while not forced, many had been put under strong pressure to move, with threats of crop burnings, the shutting of schools and the like.

I might have found such stories of intimidation hard to believe if I hadn't read the concessions contracts that the government signed with the foreign companies. The Karuturi contract, for instance, stipulates that the land must be provided with 'vacant possession', and that the government 'shall ensure during the period of the lease, the lessee [Karuturi] shall enjoy peaceful and trouble-free possession of the premises [with] adequate security free of cost . . . against any riot, disturbance or other turbulent time as and when requested by the lessee'.

I visited several of the new villages, picking up and decanting hitchhikers as I went. I began to realize that the people we were carrying were often trying to farm their old land while satisfying the government by living in the new villages. I heard mixed reactions to the villagization. The Nuer, traditionally semi-nomadic pastoralists who migrate across the plains between Ethiopia and Sudan, seemed more at ease than the Anuak. A large crowd of Nuer assembled at a brand new village named Bildak, close to the western boundary of the Karuturi farm, the men with their ornamental parallel scars carved across their foreheads, the children with braided hair, and the women in their long brightly coloured slip dresses, smoking long slender white-stemmed pipes.

The new village's ranks of identical round Nuer-style straw huts with their distinctive conical roofs contained an estimated thousand people. More were arriving all the time. The government had promised each household 'up to' four hectares near the new village, and to provide grain and cooking oil for up to eight months. But the villagers grumbled that there were only three boreholes and no electricity generator, grain store or school. The Nuer claimed, as they assembled for a picture, that 'We are all happy.' Though that might have been because the village was also home to some 30 policemen, who were taking an interest in our conversation. I also noticed small padlocks on the doors to their new houses, something I only saw in Gambella in the new government settlements. Surely that was a sign of a new insecurity.

The Anuak were more forthright in their opposition than the Nuer. As farmers and fishers, they are much more territorial. Villagization and land-grabbing threaten their identity. 'This land is owned by our kings and chiefs, through whom all the community have user rights,' said Oman Agwa Udola, an Anuak working in Gambella for a Swiss evangelical humanitarian NGO named Hilfswerk der Evangelischen Kirchen Schweiz. 'The government talks about developing empty land, but there is no land that is empty in our culture. If you go anywhere, the people will tell you who owns any bit of land. The land is our supermarket and our game reserve.' This is not just rhetoric. Much of what Karuturi calls virgin land is simply fallow, part of the cycle of shifting cultivation traditionally practised by the Anuak. The high quality of the soils is testimony to their farming skill.

Driving across the province with the Anuak, I heard about their often violent cultural landscape. I was told of killing fields where they had shed blood in battles with Nuer pastoralists, Tigrayan farmers and government troops; of the clearing, draining and occupation of their land by foreign farmers; of the sacred hill in Gambella town where highlanders had built an Orthodox church; and an ancestral cemetery near Iliya that had been ploughed up by Karuturi. But what almost any Anuak wants to talk about most urgently is their experience of 'the massacre'.

On 13 December 2003, highlanders and government troops went hunting Anuak. Literally. They targeted and killed teachers, government officials and church pastors – many of them easily identifiable by the Anuak tradition of removing their front lower teeth. Human Rights Watch estimates some 420 people were killed that day, and many homes destroyed. Those running for their lives often took shelter in the grounds of the Bethel Synod church in Gambella town. By the time they dared to come out, the military had buried many of their fellows in mass graves.

The killings were provoked; armed Anuak had attacked highlanders working for a relief agency looking for land to house refugees from the Sudan civil war. But Human Rights Watch accused the Ethiopian military of engaging in collective summary punishment of the entire Anuak community for the actions of a few.

The massacre has shattered the Anuak community. Many subsequently left for Addis, for refugee camps in Sudan or to join tribal elders in the Kenyan capital Nairobi. The fear continues. One local told me during my visit to Gambella: 'Just on Friday we heard that my cousin was going to be arrested on Monday. So we put him on a bus to a distant border village, from where he went into Sudan on a bike. He is now living in a refugee camp at Pochalla.' My informant continued: 'I am staying behind. If we leave we have surrendered. We will never be able to return.' (Later, I met Anuak in England who refused to come to London because they feared being spotted by government agents.)

The Anuak believe they are the victims of slow genocide. But the fear is in danger of becoming self-fulfilling. One aid worker told me: 'In recent years they have forgotten how to farm. They used to grow tomatoes and okra and sell them in the markets. Now most of the food in the markets is imported from the highlands.' Efforts to stimulate business through micro-finance have faltered. 'They are not greedy. The opposite really. They tend to share the money out and not to invest.'

A UNICEF study in 2005 concluded that even before the foreign land grabs and villagization programme, Gambella was characterized by a 'climate of fear' in which 'the deracination of indigenous people in rural areas of Gambella is extreme. It is very likely that Anuak culture will completely disappear in the not-so-distant future.' I saw much evidence that the bleak prognosis was being accelerated by the land grabs.

South of the Saudi Star farm, we went in search of several isolated groups in the woods – but all had disappeared. We moved to the base of another landgrabber. Ruchi Soya is a billion-dollar edible-oils giant from India that sells its products across Asia. It has a 25,000-hectare foothold in the virgin soils of Gambella. But there wasn't much to see yet. Two managers told me that the first test harvest of soya beans was completed. They were guarded by a man with a flower protruding from the barrel of a rifle. Other Indian companies nibbling at Gambella include tea-growers Verdanta Harvests, which has a 50-year lease on 3,000 hectares of forest claimed by the Majangir people, and Sannati Agro Farm Enterprise, which has 10,000 hectares in the far south of the province, to grow rice for export to the US.

My next destination was a new village called Gok Pipach. We drove past a World Food Programme food store and a refugee camp, through denser bush where there were signs of shifting cultivation still being practised. But the settlement itself was a product of the recent villagization process. The people here had been moved from land now needed by the landgrabbers. Before they moved, they had been 'a big community', said one of the elders, wearing an American baseball shirt as we drank tea in the shade of a huge mango tree. 'We had our own grinding mill and a savings account that we used to help the poor and send students to seminary school.' But they had been much diminished: 'Before the massacre there were a thousand of us. Now there are about 300.'

Bitterly, the elder related how, during the massacre, the army had destroyed the school and clinic in their old village. He laughed. Now the government required them to move so they could get back the services the army had previously destroyed. 'The government propaganda says the people are moving willingly. But it's not true,' he said. Worse, the government broke its promises. 'They promised us a borehole, but it is not deep enough and it isn't functioning any more. They promised us food but they only came once, and then brought only wheat. They said we could keep our old farms, but then when we got here they said we couldn't go back.'

The conversation turned again to land, the touchstone of everything for the Anuak. 'We have decided, each of us, that in the rainy season we will go back and cultivate our ancestral land,' he said. 'It is only an hour away, and it is better land than here. If they try and stop us, conflict will start. We will fight for our land.' Maybe this was bravado, but there was no mistaking the gravity he intended when he concluded: 'We are poor. If you are poor and a rich man comes and offers help, you will accept. But if he doesn't keep his promise, he will become your enemy.'

There is another side to the land grab. An environmental tragedy is unfolding in this remote corner of Africa, one I saw repeatedly in my journeys. While traditional land uses such as shifting cultivation and pastoralism can often coexist with wildlife, there is simply no room for wild animals when intensive mechanized farming moves in. And here in Gambella, the giant foreign-owned farms imperil the second-largest mammal migration on the African continent. Most of us know about Africa's largest migration, the millions of wildebeest and their attendant predators that race across the Serengeti plains of East Africa in search of water each year. It is the stuff of hundreds of TV natural history programmes. But how many have heard of the second-largest migration?

As I drove through the bush beyond Karuturi's base at Iliya, the track ahead was suddenly alive with large animals. It soon became clear they were antelope. As we drew closer, their numbers grew, and they began running. They numbered many thousands, with warthogs in among them, darting through the tall wet grass between a series of ponds and heading towards the Baro River. Mesmerized, I did not notice for a while that, not far away on the horizon, there were bulldozers and plumes of smoke. The Karuturi farm was advancing. Someone else wanted this rich grassland and its water. This bush would soon be transformed – and the future of the great migration in grave doubt.

The antelope were white-eared kob. Most of them came from South Sudan, travelling across the bush at the end of the dry season in search of Gambella's open water and wetlands. More than a million of them are estimated to come this way each year. Along with a scattering of elephants, another endangered antelope called the Nile lechwe and the giant shoebill stork, they were the main reason for the announcement back in 1974 of the Gambella National Park.

The park, which also hosts hundreds of baboons, bushbucks, duikers, hartebeest, waterbucks, buffalo, reedbuck and roan, is a huge region of swamp, woodland and wet grassland, stretching from the Baro River in the north to the Gilo in the south. It occupies much of central Gambella. But, while the park has a handful of rangers, it is little more than a mark on a map. It has no management plan and has never been formally declared. Its northern boundary includes much of the Karuturi concession. Within its borders too are the Alwero dam and the old state farm recently reallocated to Saudi Star, plus much of the land that the company anticipates taking over soon. Yet neither company has conducted so much as an assessment of the environmental impact of their activities in the park. I asked Karuturi's Sekhon about the wildlife. Yes, he said, the animals on his land were a 'problem'. But he said he knew of no rules that prevented Karuturi from cultivating its concession.

Some 18,000 cattle and more than 25,000 people live in the park, mostly along the river banks and roads. Park rangers sporadically chase Anuak hunters through the swamp grasses, which can grow up to three metres high. On the road to Nyininyang, near the South Sudan border, I spotted a small gang with dogs, rifles and a couple of chestnut-coloured kob slung over their shoulders. They had set a fire that sent dense smoke and flames across the road. Back in Gambella town in the evening, I spoke to a park official. He took note of my report on the hunters. He would send his people out in the morning to check if they were still there, he said. But on the subject of the landgrabbers – the real threat to wildlife in the park – he could only shrug his shoulders. It wasn't his business. As a spokesman for the Ethiopian Wildlife Conservation Authority, which oversees the parks, said: 'We have a conflict with the agriculture department. We both want different things. We will see what happens.'

This is tragic. Properly managed, the wildlife could provide economic development for Gambella through tourism, while allowing the people to maintain their ways of life. Sanne van Aarst of the Horn of Africa Regional Environment Centre at Addis Ababa University says that, as the home of the second-largest wildlife migration in Africa, Gambella has the same tourist potential as the Serengeti. But mechanized agriculture is the only item on the government's development agenda.

The government has asked the conservation authority to 're-demarcate' the park's boundaries to make way for the new farms. There are three options, according to the conservation authority's Cherie Enawgaw. Each involves moving the park boundaries south and west by several tens of kilometres. But his own maps of wildlife sightings, produced to help with the demarcation, show that all three options will block migration paths and allow 'wildlife core areas' to be ploughed up.

After my visit, Ethiopia's prime minister was dining with his Indian counterpart in Addis. Lauding the Karuturi investment, he said: 'I am often accused of being too pro-India. My answer is: guilty as charged.' He went on: 'We want to develop our land to feed ourselves rather than admire the beauty of fallow fields while we starve.' His UK ambassador, Berhanu Kebede, wrote within days in the *Guardian* newspaper in London that Karuturi and the other new farms 'bring huge benefits. Not just the jobs, houses, schools, clinics and other infrastructure, but knowledge transfer, skills training, tax revenue and other benefits to the workers and to the country as a whole.'

I saw none of these benefits. But, even if they happen, the

questions raised are huge. Is it ethical for a country such as Ethiopia, repeatedly hit by famine, to give up thousands of square kilometres of its best farmland to foreigners, with the promise that they can take the produce back home or sell it round the world? Is the concentration of land in fewer hands an essential part of the economic development that the poor world so desperately needs? Or will it create a new underclass of pauperized landless peasants?

Arriving home in London, I noticed on my bookshelf a book about the Irish famine of the 1840s. It was about a time when absentee British landlords annexed a country to grow food for their own nation's needs – and continued to export that food while a million of the Irish starved. They told themselves all the while that the market would deliver food for the famished. It did not.

2

CHICAGO, USA

The price of food

In the visitors' centre of the Chicago Board of Trade, you can play the markets. Nominate yourself as a trader, and for two minutes you buy and sell a commodity. Mine was timber, but it could as well have been maize, pork bellies or soya. The idea is to make your trades, as a moving graph on the display in front of you rolls out price changes, in response to news headlines broadcast from a speaker.

I was mesmerized. I didn't give a thought to the logged landscapes and dislocated lives I was causing as I bought and sold. I didn't even listen much to the news of bumper harvests, consumer booms or natural disasters. I only knew dimly how these events might influence prices. It was the chase I loved. I just looked at the prices graph. I bought as prices bounced off a bottom and looked like they were recovering. I sold as they came off a peak. It worked. After my two minutes of trading, the screen said I had come out $180 up. I felt like a successful speculator.

The Chicago Board of Trade's 200-metre art deco building at the foot of LaSalle Street, with its marble floors and gleaming mirrors, is a monument to markets and what they can achieve. Before playing the trading game, I had been reading the PR. Since its establishment in 1848, to serve the prairies of the American Midwest, the institution has been the world's premier trading house for maize and the other grains that feed the world. This is where they invented the futures market. In 1851, the first 'forward contract' for 3,000 bushels of maize was made. The idea was to allow farmers to sell their crops ahead of time, ensuring their income whatever the weather. The forward contracts also gave them collateral to invest in seeds, fertilizer or equipment.

CBOT prospered. It had the largest trading floor in the world, covering 5,500 square metres. Tickertape was invented here to speed news of price changes round the world. The first skyscrapers were built in Chicago in the 1880s, and tickertape parades were held in the LaSalle Street 'canyon'. Overseeing it all today is a ten-metre aluminium statue of Ceres, the Roman goddess of grain crops, perched on the roof of the CBOT building, waving a sheaf of wheat and a bag of maize.

Some trades, like rye and potato futures, have disappeared. Others, like soya beans and ethanol, have replaced them. CBOT has a derivatives exchange, where they even buy and sell weather futures. On the trading floor, boards with chalked-up prices have been replaced by electronic flashing numbers in red and yellow and green. The traditional hand signals of the traders (palms out for sellers and palms in for buyers) are augmented, but not replaced, by headsets and microphones.

The exchange retains its noble ambitions. 'The CBOT is committed to operating a global marketplace for risk management and price discovery,' its mission statement says. Or as the display boards in the visitors' centre put it, 'to bringing buyers and sellers together to ensure a fair price, create a more stable market, and ultimately a better price for your morning bowl of cornflakes'. Books in the foyer have titles like *My Word Is My Bond – Voices from inside the Chicago Board of Trade*.

A more stable market? A lower price for consumers? Was that what I was creating as I played the trading game? Did my buying and selling bring down prices, reduce risk and keep a box of corn-flakes cheap? Placing my bets in the visitors' centre felt the way it looked on the trading floor – like speculating in a market to make a profit. It also felt more like what has been going on in the real world in the past five years, as market prices for maize and rice, vegetable oil and coffee, wheat and sugar have yo-yoed like the stakes in some demented game. Perhaps I had misunderstood the hidden hand of the market, and my own hidden altruism? I hoped to find out more in the displays about the illustrious history of CBOT. But, strange to say, the timeline stopped just before some of the biggest events in this place's history – the 2008 food price spike, the subsequent crash following the credit crunch, and the new surge in prices that was roaring as I toured the exchange in late 2010.

I left confused and decided to go for a McDonald's. I figured that, even more than the bowl of cornflakes, a Big Mac was now the ultimate modern consumer expression of the trading I had just watched. But, outside the exchange, my eye was caught by *Harper's* magazine on a news-stand. The cover story was entitled 'The Food Bubble – How Goldman Sachs and Wall Street Starved Millions and Got Away with It'. I read it over my burger. This was food for the brain. I was filled with a sense of recognition. This, perhaps, was what I had really been doing when I played the commodities game.

They first noticed the food price bubble in early 2007 in Mexico. The price of tortillas, the staple food of the Mexican poor, quad-rupled in two months. Around 70,000 Mexicans marched through the capital in protest, waving maize flatbreads as they went. Angry mobs of housewives besieged President Felipe Calderón.

In subsequent months, there were food riots across North and West Africa. In Cameroon, where 40 people died; in Burkina Faso, Senegal, Guinea, Mozambique, Mauritania, Morocco and Côte d'Ivoire. For the world's poorest people in the poorest countries, food is by far the biggest household expense, taking up to 80 per cent of income. Those who ate rice, or bread made from wheat, or tortillas made from maize, seemed equally affected. They were hungry, and angry.

In Egypt, the world's largest wheat importer, bread prices tripled. There were all-night queues outside bakeries. As we shall see later, some Arab analysts say this was the beginning of the anger that brought down Hosni Mubarak three years later. In the Philippines, the world's largest rice importer, rice prices doubled. In Bangladesh, hundreds of thousands of women working for a dollar a day in the garment sweatshops of Dhaka put aside their sewing machines to protest.

In those panicky months, fears of long-term food shortages returned for the first time in almost half a century. It was the moment when people realized that markets might not always deliver their daily bread. In the Gulf, the authorities began hoarding food. Oman bought up two years' rice reserves and put it into warehouses. Even rich European countries began to wonder whether they would always be able to buy the food their people needed. British food secretary Hilary Benn said that 'with rising prices and increasing demand across the globe, we cannot take our food supply for granted'. In a call for food self-sufficiency not seen since the Second World War, when besieged Britons were urged to 'dig for victory', his government proposed consumption of more home-grown food.

The UN began to talk about a new kind of famine – urban famine. In the past, it was people in the countryside who died when their crops failed. Now, in the cities, 'we are seeing more urban hunger than ever before. We are seeing food on the shelves but people unable to afford it,' said Josette Sheeran, the director of the World Food Programme. When rural people starve, they head for relief stations. But when urban people starve, they start riots. In April 2008, UN peacekeepers in Haiti fired at people looting shops

25

in Port au Prince. Four died. Days later, the prime minister was toppled. The UN's emergency relief coordinator, John Holmes, warned that rising food prices threatened global security.

What had happened? What had caused the simultaneous surges in prices of maize, wheat and rice, the world's three major grains? Some said the population bomb was finally exploding. In the 1960s, with world population doubling in a generation, mega-famines seemed inevitable. 'The battle to feed the world is over,' said Paul Ehrlich in his book *The Population Bomb*. 'Billions will die in the 1980s.' This Malthusian nightmare was prevented by the green revolution. A major investment in new high-yield varieties of all the major grain crops doubled food production even faster than human numbers. But that led to complacency. As granaries filled, world grain prices slumped for a generation, agricultural research slackened and foreign aid spent on agriculture fell from a fifth of total aid to less than 3 per cent. The price spike looked like the reckoning.

There were other long-term drivers as well, such as the growing diversion of grain to feed livestock and supply the rising demand for meat in developing countries like China. A cow needs to consume eight calories of grain to produce one calorie of meat. By the start of the twenty-first century, more than a third of the world's grain was feeding livestock rather than people. Rising demand, low prices and slackening investment eventually brought down world grain reserves. Rice stores were emptier than at any time since 1976. Wheat stocks were the lowest for 20 years – and half of the world's wheat stocks turned out to be in China.

But these long-term trends were accentuated by more immediate market influences. Maize stocks were being consumed by a boom in biofuels. In 2007, the US earmarked more than a third of its maize harvest to making ethanol for the nation's automobiles, diverting surpluses from export markets. Wheat was hit by droughts. Maybe this was climate change kicking in. In any event, poor rains hit two major wheat-exporting countries. Shipments from Australia fell by 60 per cent, and from Ukraine by 75 per cent, pushing up demand for US wheat in particular.

What of rice? Its prices rose more than either maize or wheat. Rice production round the world had flat-lined for a decade, but so had consumption, because many Asians had been eating less rice and more bread and meat. However, when bread prices surged at the end of 2007, many Asians switched back to rice, pushing up demand in a tight market. Then oil prices soared to almost $150 a barrel during mid-2008, feeding into food prices through the cost of everything from chemical fertilizer to fuelling tractors to getting food to market.

The world food summit met in June 2008 at the UN Food and Agriculture Organization's Rome headquarters. By then, the International Monetary Fund had recorded an 80 per cent rise in the world's food prices since the start of 2007. Nations agreed with the World Bank that biofuels were mostly to blame. That the disruption they caused to the maize market had spilled over into the wider grain market. But there were doubts. For while biofuels certainly pushed up international demand for grains, overall the global harvest for the big three grains also broke records in 2007. At 2.1 billion tonnes, it was 5 per cent up on the previous year.

It didn't seem obvious that supply and demand in the grain markets could have caused the price surge. So did something else trigger it, by amplifying modest price signals into a full-blown crisis?

World Bank president Robert Zoellick pointed the finger at old-fashioned protectionism. As prices rose, major food-exporting countries such as Brazil, Thailand, Vietnam, Pakistan and India had been understandably anxious to keep feeding their own people, and to maintain low prices at home. So they shut their ports and banned some food exports – pushing international prices yet higher.

This was the worst possible response, Zoellick said. What was needed was freer markets.

For a while it looked like Zoellick was right. The 2008 grain harvest turned out to be a record. In the second half of 2008, food prices fell back. Long-time observers of commodity markets swiftly concluded that 2007–08 was a once-in-a-generation blip. Don't worry, they said. High prices encourage more planting, the market is correcting itself, and all will be well. At a conference on the future of world agriculture I attended in London in June 2010, Ron Trostle of the US Department of Agriculture echoed the common view of experts that 'This kind of price spike happens only once in every three decades or so. It's highly unlikely a price spike will be repeated, especially in the next four to five years.' Around the same time, the UN's food trade guru, Hafez Ghanem, insisted that 'the market fundamentals are sound and very different from 2007–2008 . . . We don't believe we are headed for a new food crisis.'

But by the end of the year, prices were surging all over again.

So if the 'market fundamentals' were sound, what was the problem? Perhaps it was the markets themselves. For a while, some economists had been arguing that the freer markets that Zoellick saw as the solution to high food prices were in fact part of the problem. They were saying that speculation had played a big role in the price spikes of 2008. A group of 18 leading US economists wrote to the US Congress saying that deregulation of financial markets had 'encouraged hyper-speculative activities by market players who had no interest in the underlying physical commodities being traded. This produced severe price swings.'

This talk was sacrilege, and remains so in many quarters. But read the words of the traders themselves rather than the economic theorists, and there is a lot of support for the view that it was speculators who turned a supply-and-demand problem into a full-blown crisis – one in which, as the UN's special rapporteur on the right to food, Olivier De Schutter, noted in 2011, an extra 40 million people have been made chronically hungry.

The investment bank Goldman Sachs concluded in a research report in 2008 that 'without question, increased fund flow into commodities has boosted prices'. Its take was that the speculators were simply anticipating events in the real world. But to many it looked more like the speculators were creating those events. And to some that looked unacceptable. In the summer of 2008, financier George Soros told the German magazine *Stern* that speculators were distorting prices in a way that 'is like hoarding food in the midst of a famine'. At US Senate hearings around the same time, hedge fund manager Michael Masters said: 'It's not like real estate and stocks – when food prices double, people starve.'

There was a new narrative emerging. It said that food futures – previously a rather humdrum business that helped fund farmers and keep prices stable – had been taken over by speculators in the finance markets, and in the process had been turned into a dangerous beast that bankrupted farmers and caused worsening price volatility. It said that the same kind of forces that had overwhelmed the world's banks in 2008 were disrupting food markets too. And there was an extra wrinkle. It appeared that, as the banking crisis escalated, investors seeking a safe haven were buying into commodities and, by 2010, were driving up food prices once more.

The argument, in essence, is this. Until the 1980s, there was a mutually supportive relationship between farmers and market traders – a relationship that had existed since the mid-nineteenth century, thanks to the futures contracts system invented at the Chicago Board of Trade. But the deregulation of financial institutions in the 1980s undermined that relationship, by creating new forms of financial products that allowed speculators who knew nothing about farming or the food trade to muscle in on the food futures business. New kinds of financial derivatives were created, somewhat analogous to those behind the sub-prime mortgage business, whose collapse triggered the 2008 banking crisis.

Traditional futures are themselves a form of derivative, of course. But the new forms began in 1991, when Goldman Sachs packaged up commodities futures of all sorts (from coffee and maize to oil and copper) into the Goldman Sachs Commodity Index. It then sold stakes in index funds. By buying them, investors were betting on the future price of a basket of commodities. The first index funds bumped along for years without attracting too much attention. Then in 2005, three things happened that suddenly made them extremely attractive to investors.

First, real food prices started to push up after a long period of decline. Second, it started to look like investing in some of the other derivatives markets beloved by speculators, like sub-prime mortgages, might not be so clever. And third, with fear in the financial air, some influential research suggested that commodities were sure-fire winners in bad times. This, argued Frederick Kaufman, the author of the *Harper's* piece on the food bubble, was when the commodity funds took off and the food bubble started to inflate. Soon, the price of food futures began to depend less on the balance between supply and demand for the crops themselves, and more on what was happening elsewhere in the financial system. And that – if you cared about feeding the world rather than turning a profit – began to look dangerous.

Between 2005 and 2008, speculators piled into commodities index funds. The funds swiftly came to dominate key US markets in maize, wheat and soya. A report from Morgan Stanley estimated that the number of contracts in maize futures increased five-fold between 2003 and 2008. The distinguished Indian economist Jayati Ghosh said later: 'From about late 2006, a lot of financial firms realized that there was really no more profit to be made in the US housing market.' They switched to commodities and began pushing up prices 'so that what was a trickle in late 2006 becomes a flood from early 2007'.

As the prices of shares, real estate and other former wealth generators fell during the credit crunch of 2008, the prices of commodities index funds continued to rise, as investors poured in. This accelerated as governments in the US and Europe tried to save the world banking system by pumping in new money – quantitative easing. Much of this new money, we now know, went straight into commodities. In 2003, there had been $13 billion in agricultural commodity funds. But by 2008, many commentators put the figure at over $300 billion.

In his Senate testimony that year, Michael Masters reported that financial speculators accounted for two-thirds of the futures market, and they were crashing the system. Lou Munden, whose Munden Project analyses complex market systems, says 'price booms are a symptom of an excess of capital. What happened in 2007 and 2008 wasn't much to do with supply and demand for food. It was people getting out of the sub-prime market and looking for somewhere to put their capital.' Franz Fischler, a former European Union agriculture commissioner, later told me he reckoned that the volume of trade in the agricultural derivatives market had reached 15 times the size of the real agricultural economy. 'This is nothing to do with the futures market. We need that. It is pure speculation.'

The prices that speculators were paying for food futures inevitably fed back into the real price of wheat and rice and maize being bought and sold on world markets. Even in 2011, many traders doggedly denied any influence, at least in public. But the UN trade body UNCTAD did not believe them. It said in June 2011 that 'the financialization of commodity markets' had 'accelerated and amplified price movements'. In the old days, futures prices were tethered to the real prices of commodities. Now it was the other way round.

Anti-capitalists were quick to claim that Wall Street was fuelling global hunger. Deborah Doane, the director of the World Development Movement, attacked the financiers at a Barclays Bank annual general meeting in 2011: 'Allowing gambling on hunger in financial markets is dangerous, immoral and indefensible. And it needs to be stopped before any more people suffer to satisfy the greed of the banks.' You don't have to subscribe to her dim view of capitalism to believe that the system requires control in the name of feeding the world.

Let's be clear. Speculation did not on its own trigger the soaring food prices of recent years. The background imbalances of supply and demand, including both droughts and the boom in biofuels, began the process. But everyone from market traders to their biggest critics believes that the speculation massively amplified the price signal. Most critically, the new-style futures markets for the world's basic foodstuffs were creating instability where once, as the Chicago Board of Trade has argued for decades, commodities markets had created stability.

Through late 2010 and 2011 prices soared once again. Heat waves and fires across Russia's grain belt cut the wheat harvest by 40 per cent. Rain and tornadoes put wheat crops in jeopardy in the US and Canadian prairies, and La Niña messed with the harvests in Argentina and Brazil. But a bad situation was again made worse by rampant speculation. After the US federal reserve chairman Ben Bernanke pumped another $600 billion of 'quantitative easing' into the US economy in November 2010, Barclays Capital said speculators were pushing record amounts into index funds, in the hope of tapping more profits as prices rose. Investment in commodity index funds in the US alone was reported at above $400 billion. The bubble inflated. Back in the real world, by mid-2011, wheat was up 98 per cent on the previous May, beef 32 per cent, sugar 48 per cent, cocoa 80 per cent, cooking oils 53 per cent and rice 33 per cent. Food prices overall had tripled since 2004.

It is becoming clear things have gone badly wrong. A system of buying and selling food futures is no longer stabilizing prices. Instead it is creating price instability, and the kinds of price spikes that leave poor people starving. Speculators are no longer oiling the wheels of the global food supply engine. They are in charge of a runaway train. The crisis in the world's banking system was bad enough. A similar seizure in the world food system has the potential to be even more devastating for the world's poor. For hundreds of millions of people around the world, the majority of their cash goes to buy food. As Masters put it: when food markets fail, people starve.

This book is about land-grabbing rather than the functioning of the food markets. But, as we shall see, speculation in commodities is now leading to speculation in the farmland that can secure supplies of those commodities. What damage will it inflict this time?

3

SAUDI ARABIA

Ploughing in the petrodollars

Fly over Saudi Arabia today and you will see that the desert sands are dotted with huge circles of green. They were not there 30 years ago. These geometric oases are man-made, the result of a $40 billion national effort to create giant farms in the desert to irrigate fields of wheat, fruit and fodder crops. Look down carefully, and you may also see giant sheds holding tens of thousands of cattle in the desert.

The Tabuk plain in the northwest of the country, close to

Jordan, gets an average of just six centimetres of rain a year. Yet it is a prairie of wheat fields. Fortunes are being made here. The biggest farm – covering 36,000 hectares, or eight Manhattans – is run by the Tabuk Agricultural Development Company (TADCO). Its irrigation pumps extract up to one cubic kilometre of water each year from beneath the sands.

TADCO is part of the vast business empire of the al-Rajhi brothers – Sulaiman, Saleh, Abdullah and Mohammed. As *The Economist* put it, they have made 'one fortune from money brokering and another from farming'. Each brother became a billionaire as they turned a small money-changing business servicing migrant workers in Saudi Arabia into the world's largest Islamic bank, the Al-Rajhi Bank. Then they joined the country's 1980s cropping boom which, for a while, made Saudi Arabia self-sufficient in wheat.

But Saudis don't live by bread alone. Dairy farming is the other big domestic agricultural business. Raising cows in the desert seems even odder than growing wheat. But in the centre of the country, near the capital, Riyadh, the late Prince Abdullah al-Faisal, eldest son of the former King Faisal, established the world's largest dairy farm. At the heart of the Al Safi farm are six giant sheds, where 30,000 Holstein cows from Europe produce around 160 million litres of milk a year, sold under the Danone brand. To keep their udders productive, the cows are cooled by a constantly circulating mist of water. Surrounding the sheds are 3,000 hectares of fields, where dozens of pivots, each up to half a kilometre long, irrigate alfalfa, sorghum and hay destined for the cows' feedlots. This too takes prodigious amounts of water, pumped from two kilometres below the sand.

Not far away, Almarai, a food conglomerate also owned by the Saudi royal family, has five dairy farms with 36,000 cows. This giant was established in 1976 by racehorse-breeding Prince Sultan bin Mohammed bin Saud Al Kabeer and a colourful Irish dairy magnate named Alastair McGuckian. In semi-retirement today, back home in Dublin, the jovial piano-playing McGuckian now writes musicals. He still oversees an agricultural empire that extends from the bogs of Ireland to China, Egypt, Germany, Thailand, the US, the UK, Russia, Romania and Zambia, where he grows marigolds. But his enterprise amid the singing Saudi sands is still his biggest.

There is a madness about farming in the desert. Especially when temperatures are above 40 degrees, there isn't a river for hundreds of miles and the only water is more than a mile underground. The technological bravado is breathtaking, but Saudis are slowly realizing that it cannot go on. That their dream of turning oil wealth into food self-sufficiency is doomed, and they will have to get food from elsewhere. I heard this at a conference on the country's changing attitude to water, held at the Jeddah Hilton in 2009. Outwardly everything looked normal – normal at any rate for the commercial capital of a super-rich petro-kingdom. There were flowers and fountains in the atrium, nineties-style lifts zooming up and down in glass shafts, and limousines outside delivering ministers and industrialists. Not far away a huge desalination plant was making the waters of the Red Sea drinkable for the city.

Saudi Arabians have grown colossally rich on the country's oil reserves. They have grown used to the idea that petrodollars can buy them anything. But Saudis are waking up to the fact that all their wealth will count for nothing if they have nothing to eat. And – despite the conference tables heaving with French, Persian, American and Arab cuisine – that is a growing threat. 'If we want our grandchildren to live as we are, we need to change now, or we will be like an African country in 50 years, asking for aid,' Adil Bushnak, a former member of the Saudi Supreme Economic Council, told me during a conference session I was chairing.

The desert farms are magnificent twentieth-century

monuments to unsustainable agriculture. They were created in the aftermath of the oil crisis of 1973. Back then, the OPEC oil-producing states, headed by Saudi Arabia, held the world to ransom over oil supplies, causing fuel rationing and lines at petrol stations round the world. As anger grew, the US threatened to organize retaliatory food sanctions. OPEC got its way, restricting oil supplies. The world has paid much higher oil prices ever since. But in the aftermath, the Saudis took that American threat to heart. And with the huge new wealth that the oil revenues were generating for them, they set about insulating themselves against any future food embargo by farming the desert. Even the Saudis cannot use sea water to irrigate fields, so they are pumping up underground water reserves from beneath the desert.

By the 1990s, with $85 billion invested, Saudi Arabia was one of the world's largest wheat exporters. Like the dairy business, the wheat crop was vastly subsidized. Money was no object. The government paid its farmers five times the international price for wheat – not just for the wheat the nation wanted, but for any wheat the farmers cared to produce. Riyadh charged nothing for the water pumped from beneath the desert, and virtually nothing for the fuel needed to pump it. This deluge of largesse generated full granaries but staggering inefficiency, not least in the use of water. Every tonne of wheat required between 3,000 and 6,000 tonnes of water – three to six times the global average.

Why such hydrological madness? Saudis thought they had water to waste because beneath the Arabian sands lay one of the world's largest underground reservoirs of water. In the late 1970s, when pumping started, the pores of the sandstone rocks contained around 500 cubic kilometres of water, enough to fill Lake Erie. The water had percolated underground during the last ice age, when Arabia was wet. So it is not being replaced. It is fossil water – and like Saudi oil, once it is gone it will be gone for good. And that time is now coming. In recent years, the Saudis have been pumping up the underground reserves of water at a rate of 20 cubic kilometres a year. Hydrologists estimate that only a fifth of the reserve remains, and it could be gone before the decade is out.

It took years for the truth to sink in. But in 2008, the Saudi government announced it would end wheat subsidies, with the aim of phasing out all production by 2016. Instead, it would import wheat to make Saudi bread. It decided to keep the cowsheds, but reduce their water needs by feeding the animals on foreign fodder. Then, just as the Saudis abandoned their former goal of food self-sufficiency, came the first world food price spike. A bit of food inflation didn't worry the Saudis much. Almost any world price for grains was cheaper than growing them at home. What did scare the Saudis was when their key grain suppliers started banning exports to protect their home consumers. This eventuality, after all, was the nightmare that pushed the Saudis into attempting self-sufficiency in the first place.

So, finding it impossible to feed itself, and unwilling to rely on international food markets, Saudi Arabia came up with Plan C. Under the King Abdullah Initiative for Saudi Agricultural Investment Abroad, announced in 2008 in the wake of the global food crisis, the sheikhs decided to buy up farmland in foreign countries. The king called in his country's agribusiness billionaires, including the al-Rajhi brothers and a number of royal princes. He offered to underwrite the creation of a series of giant consortia to find and cultivate foreign fields, and bring the food home. Soon, the commerce ministry had identified 27 countries that might appreciate Saudi investment in their farms; the ministry of agriculture opened diplomatic doors; the Saudi Industrial Development Fund granted credit; and the government put up $800 million.

For those who had got rich emptying the country's water reserves, but who now had farms running on empty, it was manna from Allah. Now they could double their money by going on a subsidized global land grab. So the desert cattle-raiser Prince Sultan Al Kabeer bought a 48-year lease to grow wheat on 8,900 irrigated hectares on the banks of the Nile, north of Khartoum in Sudan. Meanwhile his dairy rival, TADCO supremo Mohammed al-Rajhi, took charge of two royalty-backed land-grabbing consortia. One was Jannat Agricultural Investment, looking for 215,000 hectares to grow wheat in Egypt and Sudan. The other was Far East Agricultural Investment, which by late 2010 had negotiated leases to grow rice in Cambodia, Vietnam, Pakistan and the Philippines.

Saudi Arabia is the world's second-largest importer of rice. Securing rice supplies had become a key concern of Saudis, since India and Pakistan cut rice exports in 2008. The majority of its land grabs have been to grow rice, usually in fellow Muslim countries in Asia or North Africa.

Sometimes the deals have found local acceptance. In the Catholic Philippines, rice-hunting al-Rajhi's Far East Agricultural Investment homed in on the mainly Muslim island of Mindanao. The island is poor but fertile – and rebellious. The Moro Islamic Liberation Front controls parts of the island. Al-Rajhi signed up local chiefs for a scheme to plant rice, pineapples, bananas and maize on up to 78,000 hectares of communally owned land across Mindanao. The national government was in favour, and so too was the leader of the liberation front. Far from opposing foreign land grabs, he backed the deal 'because it is coming from our Muslim brothers'.

But the path has not always been smooth. The Bin Laden Group – an 80-year-old Saudi family industrial conglomerate with an infamous black-sheep son – led a consortium to grow rice on half a million hectares in the Indonesian province of Papua. At one swoop, it gave the Saudis a third of the Merauke Integrated Food and Energy Estate, a $5-billion mega-project being developed by the

Indonesian government. But, while Indonesia is a Muslim nation, Papua is unruly, and much of it is not Muslim. In mid-2010, the Merauke project was put on hold by its director after opposition from local tribal animists and Christians reluctant to give up their land to Muslims from either Jakarta or Jeddah.

The Bin Laden Group is also behind a scheme to grow rice in Africa. The other main backer is Sheikh Saleh Kamel, a veteran Saudi billionaire who runs a satellite TV group. The AgroGlobe project aims to produce seven million tonnes of rice a year within seven years on 700,000 hectares of irrigated land in the West African Muslim states of Mali, Senegal, Sudan, Mauritania and Niger, and in northern Nigeria. It promises to recruit Thai rice experts to help West Africa cut its rice imports while simultaneously supplying the Saudis. But these plans too seem destined to create domestic strife among the hosts.

The Senegalese government is keen. 'We are offering Saudi Arabia 400,000 hectares of farmland,' a senior official said in late 2010. Most of the land is on the banks of the River Senegal, which will provide the water for irrigation in an arid land. Contracts say that 70 per cent of the rice would be destined for Saudi mouths, and only 30 per cent for locals. So this is a water grab as well as a land grab. The government says existing rice farmers there 'have no problems with these lease deals'. But traditional farmers do object, and local cattle herders will lose vital dry-season pastures near the river.

Saudi rice farmers could also get an angry reception in neighbouring Mauritania, where the president has promised them 40,000 hectares of land on its northern bank of the River Senegal. Just over 20 years ago, the Koranic scholars and land barons who run the secretive Saharan state presided over a pogrom against black Mauritanians, who lived there. It happened during a war with Senegal which began with a dispute over grazing rights along the banks of the River Senegal. Hundreds died and some 100,000 black

Mauritanians fled to Senegal. As they have slowly returned since, many have found their former land taken for irrigated rice crops. Now it looks like the black Mauritanians may lose more of their land to the Saudis.

A sign of the power of Saudi landgrabbers in fellow Muslim countries could be seen at a curious ceremony at the Saudi King Abdullah's royal palace in Mecca in September 2010. In attendance were the king himself and the UN Food and Agriculture Organization's director general, the Senegalese diplomat Jacques Diouf. Diouf was on record a couple of years before as condemning international land-grabbing as 'neo-colonialism'. But now he was in Mecca to award the king, Saudi Arabia's landgrabber-in-chief, his organization's Agricola Medal 'in recognition of his support for improving world food security'. It was an ignominious retreat for the world's top food official.

Saudi Arabia is just one of the Gulf petro-states. The other super-rich emirates were as panicked by the 2008 price spike as the Saudis. They face the same triple whammy of concerns. Demand for food is soaring as the arrival of millions of foreign workers sets them on course to double their populations by 2030. The emptying of water reserves is making food production at home impossible. And the emirs are losing faith in global markets to provide future food.

So, like the Saudi sheikhs, they have gone on a buying spree for farmland, calling on their Muslim brothers to open up their borders to Gulf landgrabbers. One assessment at the end of 2009 found that Saudi Arabia and the other Gulf states were responsible for a third of the land purchased, leased or under offer to foreigners by poorer countries.

The United Arab Emirates (UAE), a federation of seven Gulf emirates headed by Abu Dhabi and Dubai, took the lead. The Gulf's largest private equity company, Dubai-based Abraaj Capital,

said in 2008 that it had acquired 320,000 hectares of 'barren' farmland to grow rice and wheat in the Pakistani provinces of Punjab,
Sindh and Baluchistan. Others securing land in the Punjab,
Pakistan's bread basket, included the Emirates Investment Group, a
private group in Sharjah, and Abu Dhabi-based Al Qudra Holding.
If even a fraction of this goes ahead, the implications could be grim
for small Pakistani farmers, most of whom are sharecropping
tenants of feudal families with vast landholdings, who dominate
Pakistani politics as well as the military. They will lose control of
their plots of land, and will probably not even find regular work as
labourers on the new mechanized farms. UAE officials also said its
companies had acquired 280,000 hectares of Sudan, paying
virtually nothing, on condition only that they invest. But, as in
Pakistan, details of these deals remain sketchy. There have been lots
of promises and pledges, but few statements detail specific projects
and there is even less activity on the ground.

Other Gulf states have been almost as busy. The Kuwaiti
government has followed the Saudis in doing deals to grow rice in
Southeast Asian countries such as the Philippines, Burma, Laos and
Cambodia. But the most dramatic dealing has been from the tiny
island state of Qatar. The more I learned about Qatar's exploits in the
world land markets the more extraordinary they appear. There is
nowhere on the planet like Qatar, and its tentacles are everywhere.

Qatar is a small thumb-shaped peninsula of desert sticking
out into the Persian Gulf from Saudi Arabia. It is half the size of
Wales, with a population the same as Birmingham. It was a poverty-
stricken community of pearl divers until the development of oil
reserves in the 1950s. Then came the discovery, just offshore, of vast
reserves of natural gas. Today, Qatar is the world's largest exporter of
natural gas (250 billion cubic metres a year, for anyone who is
counting). It is super-rich even by Gulf standards. The 800,000
Qataris have both the highest average income and the largest

per-capita carbon footprint on the planet. Its capital, Doha, is planning on being the next Dubai.

Qatar is an absolute monarchy. It has been dominated for more than a century by the Al Thani family, a Bedouin clan originally from Arabia. The current all-powerful emir, Sheikh Hamad bin Khalifa Al Thani, took power from his father in a palace coup in 1995. He has since secured his power by locking up a cousin, allegedly for using state funds to go on a billion-dollar shopping spree in the world's art auction rooms. A curious amalgam of modernity and tradition, the emir funds the al-Jazeera TV network, which helped fan the flames of the Arab Spring, and has bought the right to hold the football World Cup in 2022. In 2011, he appeared to be trying to gain control of Manchester United, the world's richest football club.

Nobody knows quite where the state's wealth ends and the emir's wealth begins. For now, they amount to the same thing. And Qatar has been spending this money all over the world in a way that is surely unmatched for any small nation. In 2011, it was the world's largest investor in overseas real estate. Much of that was spent in cities. In London alone, it spent billions buying the top-people's store, Harrods, and the vacated US Embassy in Grosvenor Square, while redeveloping the billion-dollar Chelsea Barracks site and building Europe's tallest tower, the glass 'Shard' near London Bridge. It also owns almost half of the Canary Wharf financial district.

But there has been no shortage of cash for farmland. The emir's vehicle for farm grabs is a company called Hassad Food. It is the agricultural arm of the Qatar Investment Authority and thus effectively the property of the emir. It has done deals for land in Vietnam, Cambodia, Uzbekistan, Senegal, Kenya, Argentina, Ukraine and Turkey. It has set up partnerships with cattle ranches in Tajikistan, and bought 150,000 hectares of sheep ranches across three states of Australia. In Brazil, it is developing a 25-million-tonne-a-year sugar scheme, and a poultry project that will supply most of Qatar's chicken and eggs. Hassad says it has secured 100,000 hectares in the Philippines to grow rice. For a while, the Qatar government promised to build a billion-dollar freight port at Lamu island on the coast of Kenya, in return for 40,000 hectares of irrigable land in the nearby Tana River delta – though that deal now seems to be off.

The pace has been astounding. It is hard to be sure, but it looks like the country has control of more land in other countries than at home. And while some projects, like many from the Saudis and the UAE, will probably never happen, the Al Thanis do seem bent on spending their treasure chest.

There are plenty of takers for this Arab largesse. A constant stream of leaders from round the world has flown to the Gulf, offering land in return for investment. Indonesia's agriculture minister, Suswono, went wooing Gulf states in 2010, offering 7.7 million hectares of 'sleeping land' for agribusiness investment. The veteran chief minister of Sarawak, the Borneo province of Malaysia, was looking for Gulf investment in his 'Halal hub', 77,000 hectares of former rainforest being turned into farms for him by a Taiwanese company. Abdul Taib Mahmud, who is old enough to remember the Japanese landing in Borneo during the Second World War, was undaunted by fears of a new land invasion. He returned with a promise of a billion dollars from Perigon Advisory, an investment fund based in Bahrain.

For a while in 2009, Gulf investors showed signs of getting cold feet, as the credit crunch created the debt crisis that almost engulfed the region's most visible totem of wealth, the desert mega-city of Dubai. Some deals were quietly put on hold or dropped. Abu Dhabi's Al Qudra Holding had promised in 2008 to acquire 400,000 hectares in a host of countries from Australia to Eritrea, Croatia to Thailand and Ukraine to Pakistan. The first harvests, said CEO

Mahmood Ebrahim Al Mahmood, would be shipped during 2011. But in 2011 there were no firm sightings of either land or harvest. Likewise, there was no subsequent trace of Qatar's plan to buy the Pakistani government's giant Kollurkar farm in Punjab, which farmers' leaders said threatened the homes of 25,000 people.

Eckart Woertz, director of economic studies at the Gulf Research Center, a privately funded think tank based in Dubai, said in June 2010: 'Investment in land was flavour of the month in 2008, but they are far away from building actual farm developments and overcoming political disagreements.' Agricultural expertise was often lacking. Financiers were sitting in their offices with wads of cash but not an engineer on their books, wondering what to do next.

But by late 2010, enthusiasm had revived with food prices. There were more grand declarations. This time, the Abu Dhabi Declaration on Food Security for Gulf Cooperation Council Countries took pride of place. And some investors at least were taking out their chequebooks again. But there were also signs of a new realism, with investors seeking out the expertise needed to turn their pipedreams into reality.

They were turning to the Egyptians, for instance. In 2010, Gulf money was paying for Sudan to bring in Egyptians to revamp its large but dilapidated Gezira irrigation project – originally built by the British in the 1920s. Gezira grows cotton, sorghum, wheat and groundnuts across a million hectares of rich alluvial soil close to where the Blue and White Niles join. Weeks later, Khartoum and Islamabad were in discussions about shipping in Pakistanis to work the new farms.

And they were turning to Americans. The Pharos Finance Group, a Dubai-based hedge fund, is paying up to $100 million for an American pig farmer to start transforming part of Tanzania into a replica of the American Midwest. Bruce Rastetter's plan is to take

45

a 99-year lease on three huge refugee camps in southwest Tanzania that have housed escapees from the brutal conflicts in central Africa, including the Rwanda massacres of 1994. By late 2011, the Tanzanian government had emptied the first camp, the 25,000-hectare Lugufu camp, which had been home to 100,000 people. Rastetter's team, Agrisol, told me they would soon be growing maize and soya and raising poultry there, initially for sale within Tanzania. Pharos promises worker training, community development funds and a system to buy produce from outgrowers, but the heart of the scheme will be a vast expanse of commercialized, high-tech agriculture – Iowa in Tanzania.

Rastetter, who back home in the US is known as a philanthropist and staunch Republican Party funder, told the local *Des Moines Register* that the project is 'the farthest thing from a land grab that could exist'. But I would bet that if you are sitting in a camp in Tanzania, where you have lived your entire life, hearing reports of Arabs paying for fleets of John Deere tractors and truck-loads of Monsanto seeds to come in from Iowa to take over your kitchen garden, you might not agree.

Whatever one feels about such projects, the Gulf governments were certainly right to be alarmed about the possible impact of rising food prices on their people. Perhaps more than they knew. By early 2011, the Middle East and North Africa were erupting with the Arab Spring. While the Western media concentrated on the politics of reform, many on the streets were protesting as much about bread prices as corruption. They were waving baguettes as they marched into Cairo's Tahrir Square and Tunis's November 7 Square (now renamed Mohamed Bouazizi Square, after the vegetable seller whose suicide sparked the revolution). In Yemen they turned on their leaders with chapattis strapped to their temples.

The only Gulf state directly impacted by the uprising was

Bahrain. But this was uncomfortably close for many of the region's autocrats. Bahrain is connected by a causeway to Saudi Arabia. Governments reacted to shore up their popularity. Saudi Arabia increased food subsidies twice. Kuwait promised 14 months of free food rations. Bahrain simply handed out cash as the people rioted against the ruling Al Khalifa royal family. The politics of food is now a serious issue for the princes of petroleum. And right now, cultivating foreign soil seems like their only salvation.

4

SOUTH SUDAN

Up the Nile with the capitalists of chaos

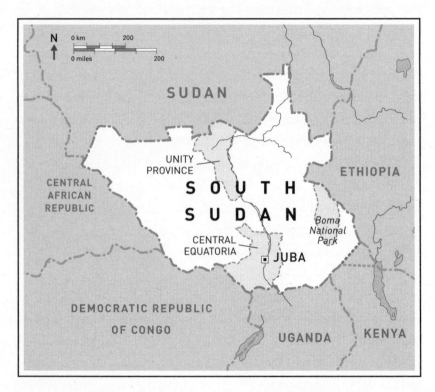

The home page of the website for Jarch Capital has a map of the world with Africa picked out in bright orange. Beneath it is the slogan 'Because it is YOUR land. YOUR Natural Resources!' What can this mean? Jarch's business is in South Sudan, the world's newest state. The website implies that the bosses of Jarch have in mind a collaborative arrangement with the people who live on the 800,000 hectares of South Sudan for which Jarch claims to have a 50-year lease. The company 'believes in the empowerment of the populations who actually own the resources'. It goes on to mention 'self-determination . . . mutually beneficial agreements . . . social programmes . . . strict environmental codes . . . 10 per cent of profits returned . . .' But it also talks about 'contract terms that will be extremely aggressive . . .' An enigma, then.

Jarch is chaired by a self-styled wild man of Wall Street named Philippe Heilberg. The son of a coffee trader, he now plies his trade in midtown Manhattan, where Jarch has its offices on the corner of Park Avenue and Fifty-seventh Street, surrounded by branches of Tiffany's, Chanel and Gucci. But the company's only known assets are in South Sudan's Unity province, formerly the Western Upper Nile, a remote flood-prone grassland with a few nondescript towns and a lot of oil, exported down a pipeline to the Red Sea.

There, Heilberg is buddies with a local warlord named General Paulino Matip, and his son Gabriel. Father and son Matip may not be the most savoury or reliable of friends. Amnesty International reported in 1999 that the general's private militia had torched villages, raped women and executed men to clear land in Unity province for oil drilling. During South Sudan's long war for independence from Khartoum, the general was an unreliable ally. For a while, he supported the Sudanese government based in Khartoum. Then in 2006 he changed sides and took his militia to join the South Sudan Liberation Movement. He became the movement's deputy commander-in-chief. In mid-2011, this group became the government of South Sudan.

Gabriel Matip claimed to own 400,000 hectares of land in Mayom county, amid the oilfields of Unity province, close to the River Nile and the border with Sudan. In 2008, at a time when all kinds of buccaneer entrepreneurs were showing up in the prospective new country looking for deals with the interim administration, he and Heilberg formed an alliance. Jarch gained a 50-year lease on Matip's land by buying control of a company called LEAC that he owned. In return, Matip joined the advisory board of Jarch, and took with him some mates from his Nuer tribe. In 2009, Heilberg said he was negotiating to double his land stake in South Sudan. If the second deal is completed, the company will control, in theory at least, an area 170 times the size of Manhattan.

But what value will this land have? Mayom county is hundreds of miles from anywhere, on a roadless savannah plain where land disputes are at the heart of many lethal conflicts. In early 2010, the Matips' Nuer people from Mayom attacked cattle camps in nearby Kock county inhabited by their rivals for supremacy in the new nation, the Dinka. Reportedly, they killed more than a hundred people, and there were reprisals. Battles continued in Mayom through 2011. A rebel group opposed to Juba rule was based there.

There is a further problem with Heilberg's mega-land deal. Nobody has yet come up with any convincing evidence that the land was ever legally Matip's to lease. Unity province's governor told David Deng, a researcher from New York University on leave at the South Sudan Law Society, that it was not Matip's land. Moreover, the governor said he had never heard of Jarch, even though it was supposedly the largest landowner in his province. He regarded any deal as without legal validity.

Now the governor, Taban Deng Gai, is a Dinka. And his personal forces clashed with those of General Matip in 2009. But, according to David Deng, the local commissioner of Mayom county at the time the land deal was struck claims to be equally in the dark. So do the people living on the land in question. There might be a legal document somewhere. But even so, the chairman of the Southern Sudan Land Commission, Robert Lado, told Reuters in 2009 that 'our land is communal. An individual can only sell it when there is consensus among members of that community.' The country's new Land Act says that 'customary land rights . . . shall have equal force and effect in law with freehold or leasehold rights.'

Deng concludes that 'Despite the media attention devoted to this investment, there is little evidence that the lease between Heilberg and Matip is anything more than an agreement between two companies, neither of which appears to be the legal owner of the land.' But in the badlands of Mayom county, the force of the general may matter more than the niceties of law. That looks like Heilberg's view. He told *Fortune* magazine in 2009: 'As long as General Matip is alive, my contract is good.' Probably the outcome of the continuing tribal dispute – which if anything has been inflamed by the end of the civil war – will determine whether Heilberg gets his hands on the land he claims.

Heilberg is the landgrabbers' landgrabber. He operates in a universe where, if you believe his own rhetoric, law comes from the barrel of a gun. He told *Rolling Stone* magazine: 'This is Africa. The whole place is like one big mafia – and I'm like a mafia head.' He believes we live in a post-state world, the nightmare of mayhem encapsulated by Robert Kaplan in his famous essay, 'The Coming Anarchy'. 'When food becomes scarce, the investor needs a weak state that does not force him to abide by any rules,' says Heilberg. He obviously likes this kind of stuff. But the reality doesn't seem so different. *Rolling Stone* dubbed him the 'capitalist of chaos'.

The capitalist of chaos has big-hitting friends in the US. His vice-chairman and guide through African politics has been Joseph C. Wilson, a former Clinton ambassador in six African countries, who fell out with the CIA after denouncing the agency's claim that Saddam Hussein had obtained uranium from Niger. Other members of the Jarch board have included Gwyneth Todd, another Pentagon adviser on the region in the Clinton days; Larry Johnson, an ex-CIA operative and prolific blogger at his site *NoQuarterUSA* on security and his dislike of Barack Obama; and J. Peter Pham, a prominent neo-conservative commentator on global issues, who pronounced at the birth of South Sudan that it was 'already on the brink of failure'.

Heilberg believes that 'we are seeing the death knell of the financial instrument – of the paper world. We're going to see the rise of the commodity.' But which commodity is he really after? He talks now of introducing mechanized prairie-style agriculture to his piece of South Sudan. Perhaps bringing in Israeli technocrats. But as recently as 2008, Jarch described plans to 'lift the light sweet crude . . . once South Sudan secedes from Khartoum'. Some say that remains his real aim. Certainly there is no sign of him actually breaking the ground in Mayom, let alone doing any farming.

I did try to learn more, but his office told me that 'too many writers and editors use their creative licences with a bit of excess', so Heilberg was no longer talking to them. That's a shame. Because I still want to ask him who he has in mind when he talks about 'YOUR land' and 'YOUR natural resources'.

For many of us with a smattering of geography, the name Sudan conjures up a picture of an arid land, with searing heat, endless sand dunes, drought and occasional famine. Much of the north of Sudan is like that. But the south – which became a state in 2011 when the black Christians and animists of the south formally seceded from the Arab Muslims of the north – is different, geographically as well as culturally and ethnically. It is washed by myriad tributaries of the White Nile, many of them running out of the highlands of Ethiopia. Along the main stream of the Nile lies the Sudd, one of the world's last great untamed wetlands. Flying over South Sudan reveals a huge area of rich, well-watered pasture. It is rather like the Ethiopian lowland province of Gambella, which it borders.

Given its lushness, South Sudan is also surprisingly empty. It is the size of France but has only an eighth as many people. They are mostly exceedingly poor. Only a quarter of the adult population is literate. Grabbing land in South Sudan must look to some as easy as stealing candy from a baby. Certainly, its government has been enthusiastically selling long leases on prodigious amounts of land to people with dubious track records, and no obvious agricultural pedigree. A study by the NGO Norwegian People's Aid concluded that, at independence, it had already parcelled out to foreign investors 5.7 million hectares, or 9 per cent of the new state. A quarter of the country's 'green belt' around the capital Juba, which has the richest soils and best rains, has been allocated.

Almost as mysterious as the Jarch cowboys are two white Western men in their 70s, Leonard Henry Thatcher and Howard Eugene Douglas. They are respectively the chairman of Nile Trading and Development and the managing director of its affiliate, Kinyeti Development, named after South Sudan's highest mountain, on the border with Uganda. Both companies are based in Texas. Douglas was an 'ambassador at large' and coordinator of refugee affairs for President Ronald Reagan in the 1980s, a time when Sudan was producing plenty of refugees. Thatcher is a British investment banker, who claims 'special familiarity and contacts in southern Sudan'. In 2008, Thatcher negotiated a 49-year lease on 600,000 hectares in the state of Central Equatoria. Since he became sick, his friend Douglas has taken over trying to turn the deal into some kind of reality on the ground.

Why do these two men want this huge tract of land, slightly larger than Lincolnshire? Well, it is strategically placed. Central Equatoria is in South Sudan's prized green belt. Thatcher told the governor there that he would grow oil palms, hardwood trees and the biofuel jatropha. Douglas says both men also share a philanthropic belief that South Sudan can only become a free, stable and uncorrupt nation by creating a property-owning middle class of 'yeoman farmers'. He says that is his real purpose, and he is angry that members of the South Sudanese diaspora in the US, and their friends among NGOs, ascribe venal motives to their investment.

There is, if anything, even more confusion about what land Douglas and Thatcher might actually have a real claim to than there is with Heilberg in the oilfields of Mayom county. For a start, the agreement says the 600,000 hectares to which they have a lease is all in the county of Lainya. That's difficult. Lainya covers only 340,000 hectares in total. When I asked Douglas about this, he said it was a technicality that could be resolved. 'The size of the land leased to us came from the Sudanese side. It wasn't a scientific figure, not well-defined. For me it's not consequential whether it is really 600,000 hectares or 200,000 hectares. We can renegotiate if necessary.' Douglas says the whole contract is 'subject to survey', and the necessary aerial surveys and mapping have not yet been done.

This is all weird. Who exactly were the Sudanese people handing over land without even a map to say what land it was? And what did the 90,000 people of Lainya think about losing their entire county to a couple of Western grey-hairs? The deal was done, Douglas says, with an organization named the Mukaya Payam Cooperative. But NGOs who have investigated the deal claim the cooperative is fictitious, and that its three signatories on the contract were Scopas Loduo, the chief of Mukaya, a sub-county covering about a sixth of Lainya, and two members of his family.

I put it to Douglas that he may have done a deal with charlatans. He accepted that it was not clear what rights these three, or any cooperative, had over the land. There was a meeting, he said, at which many people were present. 'We couldn't demand to know if we had the right chiefs. It was always presented to us that they had sufficient authority. Nobody in the two and a half years since the signing ever raised this issue to us, or called the bona fides of the Mukaya Payam into question – not the county commissioner, not the police, not the generals and not the signatories themselves.'

This, surely, shows a lack of what lawyers would call 'due

diligence' on the part of Thatcher and Douglas. There are four traditional chiefs in Lainya county, all of whom should have signed to make the deal in any way valid.

Confusion was increased when, in a BBC interview broadcast in July 2011, chief Scopas claimed he too had been duped. He said provincial officials 'came and said sign here. I signed. But I didn't know what it said.' He said it was only afterwards that he was told he had signed a 49-year lease on his community's land. 'I was deceived.' Douglas is bemused by the chief's response. 'The chief met us several times. I don't understand his concerns.'

Maybe money played a part in the confusion. Douglas says no cash has yet changed hands, apart from fees for registering the land deal. But local officials say they expect Nile Trading eventually to pay the community up to a million dollars as compensation for taking the land. The Mukaya Payam Cooperative will take a share of any profits. Those are substantial incentives. Douglas is adamant that, once business gets going, he will set up a proper body to administer funds and ensure the communities are paid. But many other people may believe they can prosper along the way.

I spoke to Douglas in late 2011, shortly after an angry public meeting in Mukaya attended by local parliamentarians, chiefs and officials had rejected the lease, saying it had been done by 'influential natives' but 'in the absence of the community'. It was unclear whether they were opposed in principle, or whether they wanted a share of the anticipated rewards. Douglas was due to return to South Sudan to try and save the deal. But he feared for his safety in 'an increasingly hostile environment. You can't guard against walk-up shootings in Africa.' He blamed irresponsible NGOs for 'stirring up trouble in a highly charged tribal environment', inciting greed and envy. If they persist, he said, Thatcher's financial backers won't proceed, and nobody will get anything.

Equally, one might argue that the arrival of rich Westerners asking to buy up huge chunks of communal land, in a newly independent country with no clear land laws, was itself 'stirring up trouble'. This clash of cultures seems unlikely to end well.

A further odd aspect of the deal is that the Nile Trading concession appears to overlap two other concessions in Lainya county. The largest, covering 50,000 hectares in Lainya and neighbouring Yei county, is owned by Central Equatoria Teak, a plantation company specializing in the prized hardwood that has grown in the region since the 1940s. Central Equatoria Teak was set up as a joint venture of the British government's Department for International Development, through its commercial investment arm the CDC Group, and Finland's Finnfund. It signed a lease in 2008 for 50,000 hectares of natural forest in the two counties.

Thus between them, Nile Trading and Central Equatoria claim concessions covering as much as 650,000 hectares in Lainya – a county of just 340,000 hectares. When I asked CDC about this, its spokesman admitted that Central Equatoria Teak's agreement with the government of South Sudan contained 'no maps or plans' of the concession area. As with Nile Trading, no survey had actually been done yet. 'The area of natural forest to be included within the 50,000 hectares would be selected at a later date,' the spokesman said. Strange deals, indeed.

Most of the land deals I investigated in South Sudan became tantalizing mysteries. Who had sold what to whom was rarely clear. Here is a third mystery, again involving huge areas of the new country. An organization from Abu Dhabi called Al Ain National Wildlife has bought a 30-year concession to conduct high-roller tourism in Boma National Park, which is one of Africa's largest and least spoilt parks, an ecological gem. The park covers 2.3 million hectares, an area slightly larger than Wales, on the border with Ethiopia.

Boma was largely forgotten by environmentalists during

Sudan's long civil war. But they woke up to its worth in 2007, when the New York-based Wildlife Conservation Society conducted an aerial survey. It reported that Boma's woodlands, swamps and grasslands were home to some of Africa's largest herds of giraffes, elephants and buffalo. It was, moreover, a hub of wildlife migration, from which white-eared kob and Nile lechwe travelled into Gambella in Ethiopia, and other animals went west into the vast Sudd wetland on the Nile.

Naturally, South Sudan is interested in both conserving this unique resource and exploiting its economic potential. Al Ain National Wildlife offered both. The 2009 deal with the provisional South Sudan ministry of wildlife gave the company control of most of the park. Before the year was out, the company was acting like it owned the place, flying in and out without restriction aboard planes registered in the United Arab Emirates, building a resort camp and laying a network of roads, apparently without the approval of the government.

So far, with security in South Sudan still dodgy at best, there are no tourists. But the big mystery is who owns Al Ain National Wildlife. I asked a number of conservationists, administrators, lawyers and others in both South Sudan and Abu Dhabi. Nobody admitted to knowing. The Al Ain Wildlife Park and Resort outside Abu Dhabi, which is owned by the Abu Dhabi royal family, denies any link. 'There are very wealthy people behind it, but the truth is complex,' was the nearest I got. The only known official is the chairman, Falah al Ahbabi, a civil servant who is also the general manager of the Abu Dhabi Urban Planning Council. His day job is to 'green' the city, a centrepiece of which is the expansion of the existing wildlife park into a 900-hectare complex with thousands more animals and 'themed African, Arabian and Asian safari encampments'. There are those who fear – on the basis of what has happened at other wildlife reserves elsewhere in Africa operated by mysterious people from the Gulf emirates – that some of Boma's animals may end up in the new wildlife park. Frankly, I share those fears. I think Al Ain National Wildlife should break cover and tell us its plans.

Other land investors in South Sudan include a Canadian charity that is growing vegetables on a former government plantation outside Juba, and 'teaching the Sudanese how to plant, grow and harvest larger crops to feed their families'. South African drinks combine SAB Miller, the world's second-biggest brewer, wants to help 2,000 smallholders grow cassava to brew its popular White Bull lager in Juba. And a Norwegian forestry company, Green Resources, has plans to plant teak forests on 179,000 hectares of Central Equatoria.

But potentially the biggest player here is Egypt. An Egyptian private equity firm named Citadel Capital, one of Egypt's most high-profile land investors, has won 100,000 hectares of farmland in Unity province near the capital, Bentiu. If the country stabilizes, this will be prime agricultural real estate on the Nile, with full rights to abstract water and a river port to send the crops downstream to Egypt. Citadel plans to grow sugar, maize, sorghum and vegetables. Its local boss, Australian Peter Schuurs, told the *Financial Times* he anticipated returns of 40–50 per cent: 'The name of the game is to get there first and to do it first.'

The scheme forms part of an Egyptian strategy to secure food supplies by accessing well-irrigated land in neighbouring countries. But Egypt also wants South Sudan's help in delivering more water down the Nile to Egypt itself. The idea is to revive an engineering mega-project to dig a giant canal that would allow the Nile to bypass the giant Sudd swamp in South Sudan. The waters of the White Nile spend almost a year meandering through this wetland. During that time, roughly half the water evaporates. The Egyptians reckon that, by bypassing the swamp, the river could deliver an extra five cubic kilometres of water down to Egypt.

But the Sudd wetland is one of the wildlife gems of Africa. It is the world's second-largest swamp. Some years it is as big as England. Its myriad channels contain an ever-shifting maze of papyrus islands, some thick enough to carry herds of elephants and hippos. It has the world's largest wild crocodile population. White-eared kob migrate from here to Gambella. It is one of Africa's top bird sanctuaries. The canal would kill it, and most of its wildlife. It would be an environmental disaster. It would also wreck Dinka pastures.

The canal is no engineers' pipedream. It was two-thirds completed in the 1980s. Work was abandoned only after an armed raid by one of the founders of the South Sudan independence movement, US-educated John Garang – who had written a doctoral thesis on the swamp. The giant machine, known as the 'bucketwheel', that was carrying out the excavation is still there, a little rusted but ready to resume work. Garang, who died in an air accident in 2005, was vehemently opposed to the canal because he said it would steal South Sudan's water. But now that the war is over, the new country's government may have its price for allowing Egypt to grab its water.

What a tragedy. With the ink still wet on its registration as the 193rd member of the United Nations, South Sudan is handing over its most vital resources to neighbours and silver-tongued 'investors'. The fertile soils of the green belt, the precious waters of the Nile and the rich heritage of wildlife in Boma National Park and the incomparable Sudd wetland – all are in danger of slipping into foreign hands. Handing over a tenth of your country on day one does not look like an auspicious start for a new nation.

PART TWO

WHITE MEN IN AFRICA

It's boom time across the continent. Some land-grabbers are on a mission. Calvin Burgess from Oklahoma ploughs a Kenyan swamp beneath a large white cross. Others are carpetbaggers taking the spoils after civil wars. In foreign hands, are Liberia's rich forest resources a source of future wealth or a resource curse? Here and elsewhere, Asian planters want to use foreign soil for oil palm. Meanwhile, the financiers of the City of London bail out of the rotten edifices of capitalism to find something real: land.

5

YALA SWAMP, KENYA

One man's dominion

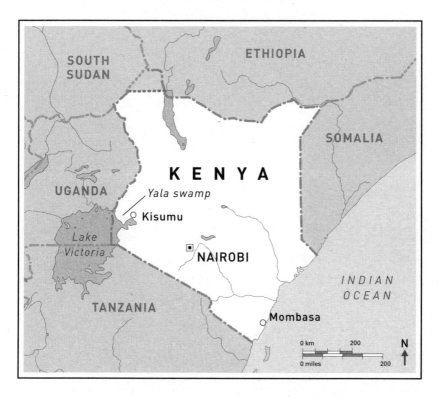

On top of a small green hill, in the midst of what was once Kenya's largest papyrus swamp, stands a large white cross. Ten metres high, it is visible for miles in every direction. Calvin Burgess, the American agricultural entrepreneur who erected it, is a Christian evangelist. He has come to Africa to save souls and to grow rice in the swamp.

The local people watch through a fence in bemusement as his

fleet of green John Deere equipment rips up the papyrus, digs drains to dry out waterlogged soils and dykes the river. They scratch their heads and dodge the dust as trucks ship out thousands of tonnes of Burgess's rice. And, brooding over that cross, erected on a hill where they once performed animist rituals, they talk darkly of living beneath a crucifixion scene. Is this a land grab for God?

Burgess made his millions running private prisons for state governments in the US. He came to East Africa to drain the swamp, purge its people of pagan rituals and transform a place where 'desperation, hunger and corruption reigned and life was hopeless,' as he puts it in the *Kenya Monitor*, a local magazine. 'I had been blessed and now it was my turn to bless. But did I have it in me? I really had no idea of what was in store as I made the decision to take on Africa.'

Speaking from his base in Guthrie, Oklahoma, Burgess told me he wanted 'to make a drastic improvement to the worst place in Kenya, with the poorest of the poor. By the time we're done, I want to take a million people out of poverty.' He writes heartfelt blogs describing his passion for his work and the love that the locals express for him and his farm. On the final morning of a trip to Africa in late 2010, he wrote: 'I walked through the village with all the children running along behind. Their hope is in Dominion Farms, for a future without hunger.'

Burgess called his farm Dominion. It gave the sense of a Christian taming nature and creating order in the world. Some have called him an advocate of dominionism, the belief that Christian values should be made central to all public activity. It is not a term he uses about either himself or his farm. But like many missionaries before him, Burgess has found that the subjects of his philanthropy don't always seem too keen on his Dominion. Many locals I spoke to said they found the name Dominion to be domineering. They don't like his drains or his bulldozers or his fences. They don't like the reservoir that floods their pastures. Most of all, they don't like losing their swamp. For Burgess the swamp is useless, empty boggy land; for them it is a valuable resource. The differing views about the swamp are a powerful metaphor for what goes wrong when people like Burgess head for Africa.

Burgess arranged for me to tour the farm with his two deputies: Chris Abir, who runs community relations, and Ronald Boone, a farm manager from the American south. They made quite a contrast. Abir is young, dapper in a business suit, and soft-spoken. He is a member of the Luo tribe that dominates the area round Lake Victoria, a former missionary and teacher from the country's big Luo city, Kisumu. On his desk sat a book of psalms and a DVD of *The Cross – The Story of Arthur Blessitt*, a biopic about a man who spent 12 years walking around the planet with a four-metre cross on his back. Behind him was a sack of Prime Harvest Rice, the main product of Dominion Farms.

Boone was louder and less dapper, one of life's buccaneers. He wore cowboy boots rather than soft shoes. 'I grew up in Louisiana, draining swamps and growing rice, and that's what I am doing here in Africa,' he said as we piled into his jeep and headed out across the farm. 'I hooked up with Calvin in 2004 when I was broke and needed a job. I left and then he invited me back, and that's why I'm here now.'

My first impression was that the farm was a slightly chaotic operation. The jeep ran out of gas and we had to radio for someone to come out and fill the tank. But around the farm, Boone was constantly waving at his labourers, checking out the work, giving lifts and collecting news about their families. It was a routine, but he was good at it. We were stopped by a farm worker who wanted 'Mr Ronald' to loan him 200 Kenyan shillings (a couple of dollars, or about a day's pay). Just for a week; till he got his wages. Boone happily handed over the cash and wrote a note of the transaction in a little black book.

Evidently this happened a lot, and the loans and bonhomie made him popular. But the day after my visit, Boone was gone. Back to Louisiana. Burgess said he left of his own accord. The workers said he was fired. I had no sense of an impending crisis as we toured the farm, even when discussing his future and that of the farm. Maybe there was just a sudden disagreement with the boss. It was evident the two didn't always see eye to eye. In any event, the next day 150 women workers demonstrated outside the offices demanding his return. It made the local paper.

The Yala swamp is, or rather was, a huge mass of dense papyrus standing four metres high and covering 17,000 hectares of soggy ground where the Yala River empties into Lake Victoria, Africa's largest lake. Impenetrable except by boat down its narrow meandering water channels, the swamp is, or rather was, rich in wildlife. It had hippos, crocodiles, leopards, hyenas, several species of buck and rare birds such as the papyrus yellow warbler. It still hides a number of islands and a small lake, Lake Kanyaboli. Conservationists call the lake a 'living museum', because its reedy waters are a last refuge for fish species that have disappeared from the giant Lake Victoria. Workers on the farm say they occasionally see a critically endangered Sitatonga antelope in the swamp. Out there somewhere too is a village of about a thousand people, on an island covering some tens of hectares. But Burgess's drainage engineers are advancing through the swamp. According to local activists, the reclusive island inhabitants say they will fight to the death, should the invaders get that far.

A lot of nonsense has been talked about the swamp since Burgess arrived. One NGO claims it has 'a population of about half a million'. That is untrue. Burgess, on the other hand, says nobody lived there before or made use of its resources. 'Whatever the locals say, they didn't use the swamp. They couldn't get in. Now they want to go there of course, because we are drying it out. But they didn't before.' Likewise, nonsense. There are 700,000 people living within 15 kilometres of the swamp, and until recently many of them did harvest its fish, wild game and papyrus, and used its drier spots for grazing and growing vegetables.

Engineers and agriculturalists have had their eyes on the swamp for years. Three times, they tried to drain its waters and clear the papyrus for cultivation. Some 2,300 hectares were cleared and drained in the 1970s. A weir was installed on the river. Dutch engineers drew up plans to drain a further 9,200 hectares. But the fields flooded after a dyke failed, and the plans were shelved.

Enter Burgess. A driven businessman, he was looking for a new and godly cause after selling his prisons business. At the suggestion of a missionary pastor back home, he turned up on the shores of Lake Victoria. Several local businessmen and religious folk pleaded with him to take on the failed farm project. He says he made up his mind on Christmas Day 1999, and signed a 25-year deal with two local councils, since extended to 45 years, to lease not just the failed project area but a much wider section of the swamp. Burgess says he has permission to drain much of the swamp and take 70 per cent of the water flowing down the River Yala for irrigating rice.

He has always thought big. His intention is 'the conversion of 17,050 acres of swampland into a modern irrigated farm capable of producing rice, rotation crops, tilapia fish and a number of by-products in a vertically integrated, independent operation'. He also wants to plant bananas and soya beans, and even establish training centres and a radio station.

Locals say they were happy for him to take on the existing failed project, but not to wade ever deeper into the swamp. But he was impatient. Without always waiting to go through bureaucratic hoops, he raised the weir by almost two metres, dug more dykes and canals, levelled the land and divided Lake Kanyaboli in two with a causeway. When conservationists from the Kenya Wetlands Forum visited in 2005, they said the company should be 'compelled to stop immediately all activities . . . as they are in clear breach of the law'. Dominion finally obtained an environment licence for its plans in June 2006 and ploughed on.

Boone took me out to the swamp frontier, where the cleared rice fields meet the papyrus. 'We cut up the papyrus and then burn it,' he said. 'We clear a thousand acres a year,' which should mean 4,000 acres being cultivated by the end of 2011. Yet that wasn't enough. 'Calvin has to get to 9,000 acres for this to be an effective rice enterprise,' he said. But, besides the economic and environmental issues, it is the social challenges that look the greatest. The Wetlands Forum's inspectors reported a 'strong feeling of betrayal . . . the company is implementing its activities without the interests of the community being considered'. Ignoring, that is, the interests of the very people Burgess says he has as his first concern.

After touring the farm, I went to see the neighbours outside the company fence. Close to Gendro, a shabby village of mud huts and tin-roofed shacks, I talked to two women doing their washing. A hand-powered pump brought water three metres from the dirty canal inside the fence to their stone slab just outside. Jennifer Acheng, a strong woman who wore a torn pink T-shirt emblazoned with the words Mighty Mom, remembered: 'Calvin came to see us when they started. We were so happy. We sang for him then. We called him "rain: the father of food". But in the end he brought us hunger.'

The women looked through the fence at a sign saying 'No Trespassing' in English, Swahili and Luo. Beyond it were Dominion's rice-processing plant and the rice fields. 'That land was grazing pasture for our cattle,' Acheng said. 'Even the poorest families had at least 20 cattle, for meat and milk. We used to go right across that land to the swamp. We cut the papyrus to make mats and baskets and thatch for our huts.' She pointed to a mango tree on the other side of the fence. 'That used to be ours, too. The farm took our land. Most people have no cattle now. And the water is dirty. The company said it would give us clean water, but the pumps only deliver dirty canal water.' She went back to her washing.

Sitting under a tree in the village, wearing a yellow shirt and peaked baseball cap, 74-year-old Dalmas told me: 'We used to live right in the swamp. My 17 brothers and sisters and I were born there. My grandfather died there. We had a hundred cattle then.' Most of the village's adults said they were born inside the swamp. Now, 1,500 of them are huddled together like squatters round the edge of the farm.

Dalmas also remembered Burgess visiting them at the beginning. He came with his fellow American director Barbara Waterson and a young local pastor named Ken Nyagudi, who encouraged Dominion to set up here and later became a member of parliament in Kisumu. 'They told us God would bring an answer to our problems,' he said. 'We would get four acres each and we would all have jobs. But there are no jobs. They are laying people off now.'

At the start, the farm employed many people. Gangs of local men did the backbreaking work of clearing the land and digging the dykes. But Boone told me that when he arrived, he advised Burgess to change course. 'There were more than 700 workers here, not properly controlled. There was virtually no equipment. I told him to cut the staff and get in equipment to clear, drain and level the land properly.' As a result, the workforce is now down to 150 full-timers and varying numbers of women working seasonally, mostly standing in the fields to scare birds and clearing weeds.

Burgess insists the women are delighted to be working for him. His December 2010 blog said: '450 women grace our fields daily . . . they are thankful for the work and the pay check. They start each morning early with prayer and singing, then attack the fields. They toil away bent over for nine hours a day and then walk home full of smiles . . . Some walk two hours a day just to get to work and then do it again to get home.' When Waterson joined the women in the fields, they were 'hugging and holding on to her, expressing their love and appreciation for their changed lives'. A German film crew in attendance was 'touched so much that composure was all but lost'.

But outside the fence, I heard a different story. I heard anger that the women, many of them single parents, had to accept such hard labour. As I saw for myself, conditions for the women were rudimentary. There were no buses to get them to work; no shelters from the rain; no canteens; no toilets. At lunchtime, come rain or shine, they gathered on the dykes to eat food that they had brought themselves.

Burgess paid his workers $2 a day – less than the average rate for prisoners in his old US penitentiaries. Boone defended this. 'We employ the women to weed the fields because it is cheaper than spraying herbicides. If we had to pay them more, it would not be cheaper. They need to remember that.'

Soon we were joined in Gendro by a group of men headed by a bald narrow-shouldered man in a white raincoat with a small purse round his neck advertising Manchester United. John Akieno Ongwek was chairman of the liaison committee that met monthly with Dominion's Chris Abir. He looked angrily over the fence. 'They only want women,' he said. 'I want them to employ our boys as well, to avoid their idleness. They said no.' He pointed to a youngster in the group. 'The farm terminated his work. This guy has a wife and three children, but they just sacked him for no reason.' Ongwek picked out another man, who had a mutilated thumb. 'It was chopped off while he was cutting papyrus for the company. But they said it was an accident and he got no compensation.' John suddenly looked shrunken and bewildered. 'We want them to be friendly to us, not treat us like this.'

On the other side of the farm, beyond a large reservoir created by Burgess, they were seething at the loss of several hundred hectares of fields and pastures. When it raised the weir on the river to create the reservoir, Dominion had offered compensation and rehousing to around 90 families. Those in a village that disappeared beneath the waters took the cash. But farmers further up the slope refused. They prefer to plant crops and graze animals as and when they can, taking their chances with the abrupt rise and fall of the reservoir water level.

In 2007, there was a flood and all the grazing land was inundated. Some homes were swept away. It was a traumatic time. The locals blame Dominion. Dominion blames heavy rains and insists the farm was 'in no way responsible'. But the truth is that its weir and sluice gates can only handle river flows of up to 300 cubic metres a second, which was exceeded during the heavy rains. Prevented from escaping into the swamp, the water backed up and flooded the fields.

'Before they built the weir, we had plenty of grazing land and we also used the swamp for making charcoal and for cutting papyrus to make mats,' Jackson Oware told me as we stood outside his hut. He still had a scrap of land to plant maize and beans, though he never knew when the floods might come. He kept goats in a shed and grazed a much reduced herd of 32 cattle inside the swamp when he could.

But the presence of the farm now meant that the waters brought hippos and crocodiles almost to his front door. 'Because of the weir, they can't get to the lake. They stay in the bush right here,' he told me. 'A friend of mine was attacked by a crocodile while he was fishing.' His wife, his aged mother and the young daughter clinging to his hand all stayed indoors at night now. 'I'm not against Dominion, and if they had stuck to their initial plan we wouldn't have all these problems. We tried to negotiate, but instead they

71

started saying NGOs were inciting us to object. They are not developing the land; they are making us poor. Nothing good is coming, and we've lost so much livestock.' Even so, he told me: 'I don't want compensation; I want my land. I won't move.'

Up the hill, safe from the floods, I met Erasto Odindo, who has lived here for many years. He was comparatively well off, with a satellite TV, a generator, a shed full of dairy goats and his own bore-hole. But he was no less angry. 'When Dominion took over we thought it would be good. But in 2005 they started to encroach on people's private land, demanding our common grazing land, and taking over the river. They told us we had to change; to stop raising cattle. Their tractors ran over our crops. We went to court. But the farm told us they didn't need to consult with us because we didn't have title deeds.' I remembered something Boone said on the farm the previous day: 'I told Calvin we don't need to negotiate with them if they haven't got title. We should just get on.'

Another bone of contention is farm chemicals. Burgess has repeatedly and flatly denied that his company uses dangerous pesticides of any sort. But he admits that the Kenyan government's crop-spraying planes do take off from his airstrip when they blitz the quelea bird, a voracious crop-eater. And Burgess himself does spray some herbicides. He noted in his blog in 2009, after intro-ducing his new pilot: 'We must be careful where we spray, especially near the perimeter of the farm and around our gardens, fish farm, and aquatic ponds.' Indeed so. The locals told me they blamed wind-blown spray for killing 60 hectares of kale, and said several people had died after their stomachs swelled after spraying, some-thing that had never happened here before. The deaths may have nothing to do with Dominion, of course, but the locals believe they do. And Odindo said: 'If you get sick and rush to Dominion, they'll pay you a thousand shillings to shut up.'

*

There is a new player in the battle for Yala swamp. The Kenya Wildlife Service, a powerful government agency, has declared part of the swamp a conservation area. There were hopes that might stall further expansion of the farm. It should. A draft conservation plan, drawn up by scientists from the British government's Darwin Initiative to help Kenya meet its obligations for the swamp under international law, called for a cessation of further drainage for agriculture. Drains had 'eroded the ecological and socio-economic values and services derived from Yala swamp'. The researchers called instead for 'restoration and rehabilitation', noting that 'traditional uses that are less destructive allowed the wetland a chance to thrive, but this is no longer possible given the advent of mechanized agriculture'.

So far, however, the Wildlife Service has not heeded this, and is drawing up its own conservation plan with Dominion. 'They want to drain half the swamp and turn the rest into a game park,' Ongwek told me. It looks like the final indignity for the locals. The theft of their swamp will be complete.

Rather than curbing Dominion's annexation of the swamp, the Wildlife Service has been dispatching police to apprehend locals. A few days before I visited, they had arrested Charles Nyango for cultivating a piece of swamp near the Lake Kanyaboli causeway. Ongwek took me to meet Nyango at the crime scene. 'We were beaten and taken to the police station. We were charged with burning papyrus and resisting arrest,' he said. 'Yes, we were cultivating a protected area,' he agreed. But then he pointed down the road. We were standing only a couple of hundred metres from where Dominion's green-liveried John Deere heavy equipment was at that moment clearing land. There was no sign of Dominion employees being arrested. It was plain injustice, he said. 'We've been farming here a long time. Who is doing the real damage? Who is burning hundreds of acres of papyrus here? Dominion.'

Ongwek had one more thing to show me before we left. He pulled from his raincoat a sheet of paper, with an official-looking stamp. It was a permit he had obtained the day before from Yaswa Security Services, which works for Dominion. The permit read: 'To whom it may concern. Allow John Atieno [Ongwek], the community chairman Siaya district, to pass along with visitors to Daraja and back today, the 15th February 2011. This has been authorized by the farm manager Mr Ronald.' The road looked to me like a public road. It was outside the farm fence. I had been driving freely down it. But Ongwek said the local villagers needed written permission to go there. It seemed more like one of Burgess's old prisons than the plains of Africa.

Clearly there are winners and losers from the American's evangelistic land grab. Burgess is impatient to do good. His blogs are full of his virtuous deeds, whether showering beneficence on his farm employees, feeding orphans or recruiting prostitutes as rice saleswomen in Nairobi and Kampala. The company can claim that its investment is in some degree helping to create some of the new wealth visible in nearby towns. There are more bicycles and tin roofs. Siaya has new banks and a shopping complex. Some locals have been offered the chance to sell products from the farm. 'Poverty levels are down – from 85 per cent to 60 per cent because of the money we are putting into the economy,' says Burgess.

But clearly too, other income from harvesting the swamp's natural resources has been lost. People need money now to buy the things the swamp can no longer provide. And this is not just about money, it is about land and identity and dignity. Enos Were, one of Burgess's local office staff, told me that 'some people who moved from their flooded area left their hearts there. But we compensated them. The people are better off. They were barefoot before Calvin came.'

That doesn't cut much ice with Chris Owalla, a Kisumu sociologist who had recently helped form a network of NGOs, the Friends of Yala Swamp, that wants people to map and claim their ancestral lands. 'How do you measure the value of land to people?' he asked. 'In any case, you can't just say that if people don't take the compensation you will come with the police and flood their land. People have rights, whether or not they have title. They should draw up their own plans for the swamp – with or without Dominion.'

In law, the swamp is held in trust for the communities that live there by the two county councils in the area, Siaya and Bondo. But, so far as I could see, the counties did not consult the locals about their needs, and were only interested in extracting rent from the farm. Over the first 25 years, that should amount to 15 million Kenyan shillings, or $175,000. But, because of boundary disputes, the councils can't agree who should get what. Perhaps embittered by this, Bondo county clerk Silas Odhiambo told me almost before I had sat down in his office: 'Dominion should shut down. They don't consult. They just do their own things.'

Bondo council also claims that some of the rent due to Siaya went into a bank account in Kisumu, which mysteriously emptied. It is hard to know the truth of these stories. But Dominion says it paid the cash, and the Siaya administration says it never received it.

Siaya's officials could not find anyone to talk to me, but I met their councillor for much of the swamp and its part of Dominion farm, Leonard Oriaro. He was new and becoming disillusioned. He said his fellow councillors did not take their duties as trustees of the swamp seriously. 'They are looters, and they make problems for me because I am not. Now my electors are getting upset with me because I can't change anything. I don't think I will get elected again.'

The story of Yala swamp shows how even outsiders with the best of intentions can create severe problems. Dominion Farms is not engaged in a crude corporate takeover of the land, as imagined by some NGOs. It is hard-nosed, but also philanthropic in intent. At the start, Burgess received bags of goodwill through his Christian networks and government contacts. Local NGOs were not initially hostile. The extreme local poverty encouraged women in particular to work for him in sometimes distressing conditions. You might say that if Burgess can't make this kind of development work, through sheer force of personality and invoking the will of God, then who can?

Smart locals can see that ultimately the farm can probably only succeed if Burgess and his white managers disappear, and it stands alone as an African project. 'In Africa, there is so much history from the colonial ties,' his black lieutenant Abir told me over lunch before I left, more in sorrow than anger. 'When a white man comes in, it looks like they want to take the land again. People are suspicious. But they also have high expectations. And they expect handouts: an extra dollar from the white man. Then when something goes wrong – which of course it does – they say he is just like the rest and the project will fail.'

Abir told me that he longs for the time when the farm's bosses are Kenyan rather than American. He emailed me a few weeks later to say proudly that Boone's replacement as farm manager was a black African who had worked on the farm for several years. Perhaps it can succeed. Perhaps Burgess will be vindicated and his Dominion will be successfully established. But the scepticism was summed up for me by a bemused local outside the farm fence, who said something I heard many times while researching this book. 'If it all goes wrong, or if they lose interest, they just go home. We have to stay. This is our land.'

A few months later, the situation deteriorated further, when police evicted villagers from a disputed area of the farm. Councillor Leonard Oriaro was arrested for incitement after he took the villagers' side. And when Burgess showed up, angry villagers chased him with knives. He complained to the police that he feared for his life.

Even before then, Burgess had seemed to me less taken with his mission of saving the people of the Yala swamp than he had once proclaimed. When I interviewed him, he was about to head off to the new state of South Sudan to find land. I heard no more about that. But shortly after being chased by the Yala villagers, he popped up in Nigeria. He said he was in the final stages of acquiring 30,000 hectares of a swamp in Taraba state with the blessing of the former Nigerian president, Olusegun Obasanjo. He planned a new rice farm several times the size of the Yala operation.

Like Yala, the swamp land was a moribund former state farm. Local reporters said he told them the Taraba land 'looks more attractive' than his Kenyan dominion. The chief of the local Gassol people said the project would be 'a blessing' to his people. All it needs now is a white cross.

6

LIBERIA

The resource curse

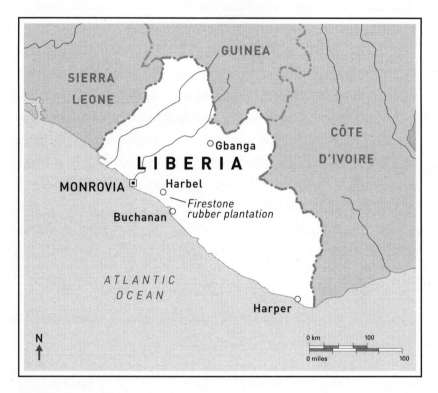

On top of the highest hill in Monrovia, there is a large statue of Joseph Jenkins Roberts, the first president of Liberia, the West African nation created almost two centuries ago as a homeland for freed American slaves. Around the statue is a black frieze showing new arrivals in Africa's land of the free, resplendent in frock coats, and shaking hands with local chiefs in native dress. They are surrounded by trees in what looks like a verdant bush clearing. That is the founding story of Liberia: two groups of noble black men, with different pasts but a shared common future, meeting in peace in an African Garden of Eden. A shame it didn't work out like that.

These days, Roberts looks out on a fractured nation. Over the hill, beyond the bombed-out water reservoir, is 'UN Drive'. Here, a phalanx of international agencies, including the 15,000 peace-keeping soldiers from the United Nations, has been trying to help Liberia recover from 14 years of civil war that wrecked its fragile infrastructure and traumatized its people.

It was a war in which the natives and the elite descendants of the interlopers, still known as Americo-Liberians, mostly took different sides. It was also a war sustained by chopping down many of the trees that shaded their first meeting almost two centuries ago. The Garden of Eden that the freed slaves thought would bring wealth has instead brought trouble. Liberia's recent history, many say, is a prime example of the 'resource curse', in which those who exploit natural riches bring not wealth but conflict, plunder and poverty. It is certainly a salutary warning to those who think foreign investment is a sure-fire winner for distressed African nations.

Liberia is unique in Africa. It is the creation not of European colonialists but of American philanthropists, who formed the American Colonization Society to establish an 'ideal state' for freed slaves in the continent of their ancestors. The first 86 ex-slaves landed on the thinly inhabited 'Pepper Coast' of West Africa in 1820. With some armed threats, they soon succeeded in 'buying' 50 kilometres of the shore from a local chief. Within a few years, some 3,000 of them had colonized the coastal strip and created four settlements. In 1847, they declared the state of Liberia, including everything within 300 kilometres of the coast.

The natives were not consulted and were excluded from citizenship of the new republic. The first land laws said they could not own land until they became civilized. They mostly didn't. They continued to live in the forests, clearing patches for shifting cultivation, orchards and kitchen gardens. Their rebellions against the invaders were short-lived, in part because the natives came from dozens of competing ethnic groups. The Grebo rebelled in 1893 and the Kru in 1915.

Numerically, the colonists were always a tiny minority. Today, their descendants comprise less than 3 per cent of the Liberian population. But for more than a century they ran the country, often treating the natives with disdain. The League of Nations found that during the 1920s, the government forcibly shipped natives to work on Spanish-owned plantations on the West African island of Fernando Po. How strange that freed slaves should be so willing to visit the same abuse on others. But the US provided financial support, and encouraged the settlers' policy of handing over the interior and its resources to foreign companies for extracting timber and minerals, and creating plantations. The king pin of this system was the million-acre land grab by Firestone for a rubber plantation, created in 1926. By the 1950s, Firestone accounted for approaching half the country's cash economy.

This Americo-Liberian hegemony collapsed in 1980 when Samuel Doe, a member of the Krahn people of the interior who had trained with US Army Special Forces, seized power in a coup d'état. He executed President William Tolbert, arrested hundreds of Americo-Liberians, and declared himself the country's first indigenous president. His rule was a disaster. He and his fellow Krahn officers set about seizing the country's precious resources for themselves. In the end, almost everyone bar the Krahn was against him, and he was deposed by his former colleague Charles Taylor.

Taylor proved even worse. He had been sacked by Doe in 1983 for embezzling a million dollars. He fled to the US, where he had banked his lucre. There he was arrested, but escaped while awaiting extradition to Liberia. He claims his escape was with the assistance of the US government. He subsequently fled to Libya, where he was given guerrilla training by Colonel Gaddafi before recruiting a rebel army that crossed into Liberia in 1989. Taylor's takeover triggered a wider conflict that lasted for 14 years, during which half the country fled as ethnic warlords battled for the country's resources as much as the president's palace.

Under Taylor, timber and terror went together. In the early days, he sold logging rights in areas he controlled in return for cash to buy arms. When he had assumed the reins of government, his brother Demetrius ('Bob') Taylor did the same as head of the Forestry Development Authority. A UN study found that 86 per cent of the country's fast-expanding timber production was controlled by arms traders. Landgrabbers turned into gunrunners.

One unlikely forester was a notorious Ukrainian mafia boss, Leonid Minin, whose Exotic Tropical Timber Enterprise also traded in arms and diamonds. Another was Guus van Kouwenhoven, a Dutch adventurer whose colourful past included a 1970s conviction in Los Angeles for trying to sell stolen Rembrandt paintings. He moved to Liberia, where he imported luxury cars and owned the swanky Hotel Africa with its popular casino. Everyone knew him as 'Mr Gus'. By the 1990s, Mr Gus was a confidant of Taylor, and in 1998 he mysteriously became president of a logging company called Oriental Timber.

Oriental Timber had no apparent interest in Liberia until Mr Gus arrived. But, helped no doubt by his seat on the Forestry Development Authority, he turned it into by far Liberia's largest timber operation, with logging rights to more than a million hectares, a quarter of Liberia's forests. The company, which claimed at the time to be Malaysian, brought some 600 loggers from Asia, and even flew in fresh teams of prostitutes every two months.

Oriental Timber shipped hardwood out of Buchanan, a port

with some 30,000 inhabitants that is Liberia's third largest city. The docks, which included an export terminal for upcountry iron mines, covered several square kilometres during those boom years. But today they are a ghost town, with rusting equipment everywhere, including Oriental's old sawmill. Mr Gus's timber went from Buchanan to France and China, and the ships came back loaded with guns. After being cleared of war crimes, and acquitted on appeal of selling weapons to Taylor, van Kouwenhoven is currently awaiting a retrial.

Men like Mr Gus and Minin did very well out of plundering Liberia's precious timber. But so did Taylor, who had stumbled on a system for getting timber companies to fund his warlord economy. Investigators after the war uncovered a cheque for almost $2 billion dated July 2000 from one of Oriental Timber's subsidiaries, Natural Holdings, and made out to Charles G. Taylor's personal bank account.

The NGO Global Witness, which investigated the imbroglio, named other timber companies with Liberian logging concessions at the time. They included the Royal Timber Company, with Mr Gus as a director; the Inland Logging Company, run by Taylor's associates, Maurice and Oscar Cooper; the Mohammed Group of Companies, owned by Mohammed Salamé, who was Taylor's ambassador-at-large in Côte d'Ivoire; and Maryland Wood Processing Industries, owned by a local Lebanese businessman, Abbas Fawaz. Fawaz was required to pay a local commander for 'security', while the commander press-ganged and massacred more than 300 civilians.

The tragedy was that the international community allowed this situation to continue for years. People in the country could see what was going on. A British diplomat told journalists in Monrovia in 2001 that 'it is the timber trade that is keeping Taylor in power'. But the world was reluctant to ban Liberian timber. And as a result, the

UN failed in its efforts to broker a peace in a civil war that by now was often being fought by children.

Only in May 2003 did the UN Security Council impose a trade embargo on Liberia's 'logs of war'. The effect was instant. By August it was all over. Deprived of Taylor's timber revenues, the regime collapsed, the landgrabbers departed, and Taylor fled to Nigeria. With a UN military peacekeeping presence, new elections were held in 2005. They brought to power Harvard-trained and US-backed Ellen Johnson Sirleaf. She won two elections, brought much-needed stability and security, and stemmed the ransacking of the country's resources. But extreme poverty and economic stagnation persisted. Without revenues, government coffers were empty. The dilemma for her administration was that to restart the economy, she needed to tap the country's most saleable resource – the same forests that had sustained a vicious 14-year civil war that left 150,000 dead. Could the resource curse be broken?

Despite the depredations of the civil war, forests still cover 45 per cent of Liberia. They are home to the world's only viable population of pygmy hippos, as well as the indigenous Liberian mongoose, Diana monkey and Jentink's duiker, and West Africa's largest population of forest elephants. The new government has promised to set aside a million hectares for conservation, but it wants the rest to earn its keep.

Sirleaf cautiously began giving out new logging concessions. The old ones, of course, were null and void. In 2011, she signed a deal with the European Union, Liberia's largest market for timber, aimed at placing timber sales on a permanently legal footing. Starting in early 2013, the EU will require companies importing timber from anywhere in the world to demonstrate that the timber has been legally harvested. Liberia plans to achieve that using a unique national timber-tracking system. Every legally harvestable tree and every cut log will carry a barcode, so it can be tracked from stump to port and beyond.

The system is as simple and as foolproof as checking out at the supermarket, says Ivan Muir, a South African forester in charge of the system. He is the local boss of SGS, the Swiss specialists in forest certification systems. In late 2010, when I visited Liberia, some 220,000 trees were being tagged in time for the first wave of exports to Europe. But Muir said it remains to be seen whether the system can defeat pirates smuggling illegally logged timber across the country's notoriously porous borders, for sale outside the EU.

Much will depend on the integrity of the new loggers. Local NGOs suggest that not all of them meet government rules on being open about their backers and associates. One company switched from Korean to Malaysian ownership shortly after winning its concession. Another is accused of links to the North Eastern Logging Corporation, which felled timber under Taylor. And a third turns out to be partly owned by Wael Charafeddine, someone Sirleaf had barred from logging.

Whatever the teething troubles, Liberia is open for business again. The capital, Monrovia, is filling with international investors returning in pursuit of the country's resources. A few never left. I went to see what, for most of the past century, has been the world's largest rubber concession: Firestone's 400,000-hectare world of rubber.

The main plantation is at Harbel, about an hour's drive from Monrovia. The rubber trees stretch for tens of kilometres in all directions close to the US-built Roberts Airport, which gets its electricity courtesy of Firestone's power plant. During the civil war, the plantation was largely abandoned to squatters, militias and charcoal burners. But now it is in operation again. Passing through its gates is like entering a different country. From the ramshackle chaos of roadside shacks and bush outside, it comes as a shock to find roads without potholes, verges mown and junctions signposted.

This is an enclave controlled by a company with many times the resources of the host government. Liberia may be a free state, but Harbel is like a US colony. The dried latex from some eight million rubber trees is trucked down the road to the company's port outside Monrovia, and exported to the US in Firestone ships. The company's senior managers are mostly expats, and judging by the local company magazine, *The Pepper Bird*, most local agreements are signed only when the American managing director shows up from Nashville.

Inside a fenced office compound, I met Rufus Karmorh, the company PR man, who had a Book of Mormon on his desk. Outside was the Kingdom Hall of Jehovah's Witnesses, plus several Methodist churches, and that great secular cathedral of American managerial culture, a golf course. The familiarity was completed by the old yellow US school buses that transport workers around the plantation.

The Firestone fiefdom dates back to 1926. It was established by US rubber baron Harvey Firestone to ensure supplies for his tyre-making factories, which were expanding fast owing to the soaring popularity of motoring in the US. The British chancellor of the day, Winston Churchill, had tried to organize a price cartel to exploit the UK's control of the big rubber plantations in Malaya, which then produced 75 per cent of the world's rubber. Firestone's friend Henry Ford tried to break the cartel with his Fordlandia project to grow rubber trees in the Brazilian Amazon. It failed. But Firestone's operation in the forests of Liberia took root.

His deal with the Liberian government gave Firestone 4 per cent of Liberia's land for 99 years. It made the company the country's largest private employer, responsible for 40 per cent of the Liberian economy by the 1950s. But Firestone was often overbearing, taking over community-run forests, desecrating burial grounds and sacred sites, obliterating water sources and hunting grounds, and clearing villages and farms. Along the way, it exacerbated tensions between Americo-Liberians and natives.

Firestone did good works within its own territory, but its benefit to the national coffers was always small compared to its profits. The annual rent was set in 1926 at a derisory five cents per acre. And the agreement included a notorious 'Clause K' that required the Liberian government to take out a large loan from Firestone. As one expert on the country told me, 'It gave the company control over the country.'

In 2008, the Sirleaf government extended Firestone's franchise until 2041, while reducing its size to closer to the area actually used. Firestone now operates 48,000 hectares, and pays $5 a hectare in rent. Members of the militias who occupied the plantation during Liberia's long civil war are still camped out there in places. 'We have mostly cleared them out,' says Karmorh. 'But the roads through here are public roads, so we have a security issue.' Locals told me the company has employed some old soldiers, known as Gravel Ants, to keep the peace.

Whatever the security concerns, Firestone has 7,000 employees back on the payroll, most of them earning a little over $3 a day, roughly double the national minimum wage. Hundreds of women work in its two larger nurseries, grafting new saplings to replace old trees that no longer yield latex. In the plantation itself, thousands of male tappers daily remove the white fluid that has dripped into red cups attached to the bark of their allotted 750 trees. Then they carry the latex in buckets hung over their shoulders to weigh stations. The central processing plant removes water in a centrifuge and creates great piles of dried latex for shipping. It is a routine virtually unchanged since the plantation began.

Firestone is paternalistic, outwardly confident of its purpose and always ready with a barrage of statistics to defuse any criticism. 'We are doing more than any other private entity for the quality of life in Liberia,' Karmorh said. 'We have 26 schools with 16,000 students. All the children of our employees are educated at no cost to their parents. About 500 get to go to the Senior High as far as 12th grade. We are constructing or renovating 1,900 houses. Our 300-bed hospital has reopened and treats 9,000 patients a month.' The company has its own radio station. I gave them an interview.

The housing compounds I saw were rudimentary. They contained rows of single-storey dwellings, with four rooms but no plumbing. Outside were communal latrines and hand pumps to provide water – typically two for 500 people. At the hospital, most non-emergency services were restricted to employees and their families, though the chief medical officer, Lyndon Mabande, was proud that he allowed any local woman to go there to give birth. He told me he just could not stomach the number of maternal fatalities that happened before in the neighbourhood. Medical hygiene was not all it might have been, I thought. There were bloody sheets on the operating tables. In one room, dirty garbage was stacked right next to a sink where surgical instruments were being washed. We inadvertently opened a door on an amputation under way in an operating room. But for Liberia, this was a good, well-equipped and well-organized hospital.

The company has been accused of polluting local water supplies and of abusive labour policies. Such claims are hard to substantiate. I saw a new water treatment plant – built in response to the complaints – that now cleaned up effluent. The treated water flowed sweetly down a small canal and was extracted by a farmer to irrigate his maize. The water's apparent cleanliness created problems. 'It's not drinking water, and some people think it is,' said Karmorh. Meanwhile, decades of untreated effluent continue to lurk in local wetlands.

What saddened me most on my tour was something probably not in Firestone's control. Dropping by the library in the Firestone high school, I wondered what books they had about Liberia. None. They did have a pile of old *Glencoe World Geography* textbooks. They had one sentence on Liberia, describing how it was 'a colony of former slaves'. The natives, who make up the great majority of the country and most of the school's students, didn't get a mention.

I turned right out of the Firestone plantation, forsaking the cut lawns, golf course clubhouse and yellow buses for the African hinterland. If Firestone's enclave is having an improving effect on the community at large, I thought, it should be here. I drove past a new Lonestar mobile-phone mast, one of hundreds that dot the landscape in a country without a functioning landline system. But I saw little else that suggested outside investment. The nearby village of Glarkon looked especially forlorn with its dilapidated school, unusable soccer pitch, abandoned church and gutted industrial unit.

Goll's Town was no better. The people moved here long ago, after their old community at Korweleh had been obliterated by Firestone's development. But Goll's Town, named after the first settler on the new site, had also lost most of its forest land to Firestone. The village had a Baptist church and a hand pump, but no latrines or bath house. The nearest public school was two hours' walk away. The nearest clinic was on the Firestone plantation. Villagers said they had to pay US$25 as a 'non-refundable gate fee' to go in, with more due in return for any treatment they received. Some families in Goll's Town live by selling latex from rubber trees grown on their own patches, while others turn old trees into charcoal. Many send their youth to Monrovia in search of jobs.

Firestone is a very large, visible and American target for political activists. Fair enough. But conditions are often worse on other rubber plantations. Down the road closer to Buchanan, I passed the 12,000-hectare concession run by the Liberian Agriculture Company (LAC). The land was originally given to a construction company in 1959 in payment for building the road from Monrovia to Harbel and Buchanan. LAC briefly came under the wings of two US companies – Uniroyal of Greenville, South Carolina, and Keene Industries of Ukiah, California. But it is now owned by the Luxembourg-based Socfin group, which specializes in growing rubber and oil palm.

The LAC concession has expanded into the Bassa people's tribal reserve. According to a UN report in 2006, the expansion destroyed 75 villages, with crops burned and houses demolished, before compensation terms had been agreed with the government. It concluded there had been 'serious human rights violations' there.

Before long my driver got stuck behind a truck shedding small pieces of chipped timber. I recognized it as belonging to Buchanan Renewables, based in the town I was headed for – Mr Gus's old stronghold of Buchanan. The company had a contract to chip old, unproductive rubber trees on the Firestone plantation and export the chips to fuel power stations back in Europe.

Buchanan Renewables was started by a Canadian hedge-fund entrepreneur named Joel Strickland, who scouted Liberia in 2006 as peace broke out, looking for business opportunities. He reckoned there were 200,000 hectares of rubber trees that had ceased to be productive during the civil war. He figured they could become a source of timber instead. He went into partnership with John McCall MacBain, a Canadian billionaire who founded the *Auto Trader* publishing empire.

Their first plan was to put the lights back on in war-torn Liberia. The men wanted to harvest the old rubber trees from small farms and burn the chips in power stations across the country. The farmers would be recompensed with new rubber saplings. But the focus has shifted.

When I visited, most of the trees being chipped were owned by Firestone and LAC, rather than small farmers. It was cheaper and quicker to harvest from large plantations. And quicker mattered, because there was a big new shareholder in the company. The Swedish government's energy company, Vattenfall, had bought a fifth of Buchanan and wanted to burn the chips in its European power stations. That required two million tonnes delivered annually to Europe by 2017. The company's general manager in Liberia, Irishman Liam Hickey, told me that required clearing up to 12,000 hectares of rubber trees a year. Though even at that rate, he assured me, the country had more than 20 years' supply.

But what about the promised local electricity? Monrovia was still full of billboards advertising Buchanan Renewables with the slogan 'Light up Liberia'. In three years since chipping began, the promised power plant had not been built. Hickey blamed local bureaucracy, and told me he hoped to break ground on the project in September 2011. But the deadline slipped again and critics were beginning to say that, like logs and latex, the wood chips were just another Liberian natural resource being hijacked by foreigners and shipped out of the country at the earliest opportunity.

Some environmentalists are surprisingly optimistic about Liberia's future. They believe it can break the resource curse. Frank Hawkins, the Africa head of Conservation International, told me the country's rebirth gives it a chance to become the poster child for a new green economy in Africa. 'They start from a fresh place. Liberia has an opportunity to show the world how it is done.' His lobbying in Liberia is part-funded by a foundation set up by Buchanan Renewables' MacBain, and he sees the potential for foreign concession holders to spread their influence in a manner good for both the Liberian people and the environment. 'They have the money and land to do good stuff.'

But even Hawkins admits that the perils of the resource curse remain. 'In Liberia the spectre of private sector asset strippers is clearly very real. There are people with very large chequebooks,' able and willing to bribe government officials so they can ransack the country. 'The short-term temptations are so large, and the people involved are so unscrupulous.'

That is all too clear. Liberia discovered in 2011 that a third of US food aid was being stolen by corrupt staff at the local office of World Vision. They had been allocating containers full of aid to towns that did not exist, and pilfering the contents on the road to nowhere. It was also common knowledge that a hundred cars donated by the mining company ArcelorMittall to help government officials get around the country had ended up instead, through no fault of ArcelorMittall, in the garages of the legislators who had signed off on a deal that gave the company mining rights in the north of the country.

Even by African standards, Liberia is in a bad way. More than 80 per cent of the population live on less than $1.25 a day. Only a quarter have access to clean drinking water. Of every thousand babies born in the country, 76 die before their first birthday. A whole generation has missed out on education, and almost half of all adults are illiterate. The country produces fewer than 40 agriculture graduates, 80 medical graduates, and 60 teachers a year. It has virtually no trained secondary school teachers, and only one doctor for every 25,000 people. 'Even finding mechanics is hard,' said Hickey at Buchanan. When I told the boss of one of the plantations that I had found a reliable driver, he immediately called him up and booked him for a week taking VIPs around.

Most of Liberia's feeble infrastructure was wrecked in the long civil war. Locals say only two factories survived – those producing Coca-Cola and Club Beer. Putting the place back together again has barely started. Monrovia's fire station had three vehicles, one out of commission with its front end dragging on the ground. The main hydroelectric power plant at Mount Coffee, which was destroyed by Charles Taylor in 1990, is still derelict.

'Doing business here is hard,' Hickey said. 'It's not 20 per cent more expensive; it's 150 per cent more expensive.' And what does work is frighteningly dependent on foreigners. The UN and the wider international community dominate the economy of Monrovia – the bars, new apartment blocks, restaurants and prostitutes. UN purchases inflate local prices for everything from real estate to avocados. The main construction projects are embassies, with the Chinese and Americans competing to build the biggest.

Communications are precarious. Even on the country's main coastal road, safe driving stops at Firestone. It is so difficult to get fresh food from the countryside to Monrovian stores that, despite the country's rich soils, the city sells mostly rice from Niger, peppers from Guinea and Mali, and cabbages from the Netherlands. Liberia is the only country in the world without a functioning landline phone system. During my visit, it had just two ATM machines that accepted international cards.

Liberia badly needs enterprises that do not depend on foreign agencies, governments and concessionaires. Some bottom-up development. Aid agencies have been trying to set up small businesses to meet obvious needs. In Monrovia's West Point beach-side slum, Oxfam has given sewing machines to seamstresses to make school uniforms. It has also obtained 30 hectares of country-side north of Monrovia, where a group of war widows are growing cucumbers, cabbages and watermelons.

I met Rebecca Sumo, a computer-science graduate who heads the 50-strong Gbalin women's cooperative, as she was tending rows of cabbages in a small nursery. 'This was empty land before,' she said. 'Nobody was using it till Oxfam bought it for us from the local villagers.' The widows, mostly from Monrovia, employ local men to do the hard labour in the fields. At lunch, they watched appreciatively as the men, stripped to the waist, hoed the fields before breaking off to barbecue a pile of freshly caught field rats and a snake.

To me, this felt more like a sustainable future for Liberia than any number of American-owned rubber plantations or Malaysian-backed logging operations. More sustainable, certainly, than the 10,000-hectare Libyan rice farm near the border with Guinea that wrecked existing village paddy fields, but ran out of funds and collapsed in late 2010.

Making the Gbalin project work will be hard, however. The women said there were not enough local markets for their goods, and without refrigeration the fresh produce swiftly rotted. Some members hadn't been tending their plots recently. But Rebecca had high hopes for making hot peppers a hot sale. As we sheltered from the rain, she showed me a stack drying in the co-op's farmhouse. 'Everyone in Liberia uses hot peppers in their cooking every day,' she said. It was a start.

I was surprised at how peaceful Liberia was in 2011. You could walk the streets safely. But things could change quickly. Ordinary indigenous Liberians told me that, under Sirleaf and her Unity Party, the country and its natural resources had been grabbed back by the Americo-Liberian elite. They saw the civil war, at least in retrospect, as a rebellion against that rule. However disastrous Doe and Taylor had been, the natives had unfinished business.

That certainly was the message I got in the heart of downtown Monrovia, from Alfred Brownell, the stern-faced and bullish boss of Green Advocates, an environmental law NGO. We spoke in the semi-darkness of a power outage in his cramped second-floor offices opposite the Crown Hill Cinema. His staff sat around, sweating, till the power revived their computer screens.

Brownell told me that for the Americo-Liberian elite 'the civil war was a tragic aberration. They see the return of peace as simply a chance to return to business as usual. The government is giving out large areas of land and throwing the people a few crumbs.' He estimated that $16 billion worth of investment had come into Liberia from abroad since 2005, but most of it was linked to exploiting natural resources – to land grabs. 'Ministers are drunk with the idea that multinational investment will bring economic recovery. But it won't. The multinationals just take our resources.'

Letting land to foreign concessions had 'produced a small, reliable stream of government revenue, a large number of poorly paid jobs, and not much else in the way of development'. Firestone had been growing rubber in the country for eight decades and had 'never manufactured so much as a rubber band here'. He fixed me with a stare in the gloom. 'To question the government's priorities is to be accused of being anti-development. But it is not. The big commercial model is not sustainable.'

Land is the central issue, the biggest threat to stability. Every week conflicts over land are reported in the papers. Land is being concentrated in ever fewer hands. Brownell argued for a revival of communal control of the country's land and forests – something the government has sometimes seemed to encourage, but has failed to deliver. Its compromise has seen communities able to claim ownership of their soil, but not the trees that grow on it or the minerals beneath it. What use was that?

The multinationals, of course, see things differently. Karmorh at Firestone said simply: 'I understand the significance of communal land. But you have to have private ownership to get investment.' Hickey at Buchanan Renewables went further. He said communally owned lands had failed the people. 'This land could grow anything. It's so fertile and the climate is good. They don't even suffer from natural disasters like hurricanes or droughts. Everything is going for them. Yet they are hungry and poor. At some point this country has got to deal with the tribal lands issue,' he said. By 'deal with' he meant take them over. Give them to the landgrabbers. But if that happens, Brownell believes, 'things will explode again. The peace here remains fragile, threatened by the unresolved issue of who will exploit and who will benefit from Liberia's natural resources.' The resource curse, complicated by the social divide between natives and Americo-Liberians, persists.

It is possible to overplay the rigidity of this divide. The civil war did not have such neat battle lines, and nor does the peace. Doe was a native Krahn, it is true. But Taylor's father was an Americo-Liberian. Sirleaf is half Gola, a quarter German and a quarter Krahn. And the civil war has changed things. A third of the rural population moved to Monrovia. They came as refugees but want to stay, work, buy mobile phones and watch TV. There is fanatical support for European soccer teams that have provided a good living for a handful of West Africans, most notably Liberian George Weah, who traded his celebrity gained at Chelsea, Manchester City and AC Milan for a career in politics and almost won the 2005 presidential election.

Does this cultural confusion – between old tribal loyalties and soccer-mad street-wise modernism – mean trouble ahead? I began to think so. A leading candidate in the 2011 presidential election was a senator called Prince Johnson. He was famous during the civil war for his brutality and sadism. A widely distributed video shot in 1990 shows him sipping a Budweiser as his men cut off the ear of Doe, prior to killing him. By 2011, he claimed to be a born-again Christian and threw his lot in with Sirleaf in the second round of the election, to ensure her victory. But his presence at the top table was disturbing nonetheless.

Liberia looked to me like the sort of place that other African countries could become, if they succumb to the landgrabbers. Its foreign corporations run enclave economies that provide a modicum of order and basic services for their staff and families, but suck the life out of the rest of the country. They take big profits but fail to pay enough taxes to allow the wider society to benefit from their presence. They don't buy local services or produce, and take their own produce out of the country as swiftly as they can.

This is understandable. The chaos around these foreign enclaves encourages their isolation. But, as the fences are raised and the isolation increases, the chaos outside only intensifies. The companies are making money under siege. They are monopoly users of the country's natural resources, and an impediment to its social, economic and political development. This may not be inevitable. But those who argue that the arrival of foreign investment, of land-grabbers, can hardly fail to improve local economies in Africa and elsewhere should take a close look at the reality of Liberia today.

At the airport, round the corner from Firestone's headquarters, there was an executive jet on the tarmac. It was waiting to whisk away Tony Blair, who was in Monrovia as part of his African Governance Initiative. According to the *Daily Observer* he had come to 'renew his commitment to the country's progress'. When my flight took off, we climbed over a large military area where no fewer than 12 UN helicopters were parked. Their crews too were foreigners intent on preserving peace and bringing prosperity. But I had Brownell's words ringing in my ears. What price progress when not a single rubber band has been made here in eight decades of foreign presence. Not a single condom or tyre or rubber band with a 'Made in Liberia' label.

7

PALM BAY, LIBERIA

Return of the oil palm

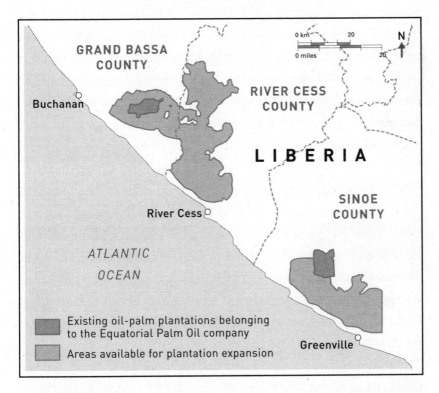

I met Peter Bayliss in the bar of the Sparks Hotel in downtown Buchanan. Bald, British and garrulous, he began with a bit of name-dropping. He got the Gettys and the Rockefellers into the first sentence. His company, London-based Equatorial Palm Oil (EPO), had acquired a lease on 169,000 hectares of Liberia to grow oil palm. Much of the land had been in foreign hands before. The Rockefellers ran a cattle ranch here, he said, and the Getty family had an old oil-palm plantation that Bayliss was now in charge of reviving and extending, after two decades of civil war.

I liked Bayliss. And, by comparison with most other big plantations that I visited, I liked his operation. 'As good as it gets', I wrote in my notebook the next day, after touring his main operation near Buchanan at Palm Bay. Bayliss is an old hand in the oil-palm business. He worked for many years for the Malaysian-owned New Britain Palm Oil company, which has 77,000 hectares of plantations, mostly on the island of New Britain off Papua New Guinea. He went home to run a livestock co-op in Cornwall, but was enticed out to Liberia by Michael Frayne, the London-based chairman of EPO, to become managing director. 'I couldn't turn it down. It was a chance to develop my own plantation,' Bayliss said as we ordered a second Club Beer.

How did a start-up company in London manage to get its hands on two big chunks of West Africa? To some extent, they were the spoils of the civil war. The Getty family pulled out of Palm Bay in 1990, when the armed gangs moved in. They subsequently sold to LIBINCO, a company set up by a local Lebanese called Joseph Jaoudi, whose career also involved both working as an engineer on the Apollo moon programme in the US and running his family's chain of supermarkets in Liberia. Jaoudi in turn sold to EPO, where he remains a shareholder and director.

EPO's second chunk of Liberia, the Butaw concession, is down the coast near the port of Greenville. It had been a government-owned oil-palm plantation. During the war, it was overrun by illegal diamond miners. In 2005, the Sirleaf government sold it to a newly formed outfit named Liberian Forest Products, set up by a syndicate of British investors, including Daniel Betts, who had been gold prospecting in Liberia. But after the new Sirleaf administration found 'gross irregularities and non-compliance with the law' in the original negotiations, Liberian Forest Products was bought out by

Nardina Resources, which became Equatorial Biofuels, which in turn became Equatorial Palm Oil. The terms were renegotiated and no one from the original syndicate is now involved.

EPO briefly ran out of cash after the credit crunch. But in September 2010, an Indian industrialist named Chinnakannan Sivasankaran, who made a billion dollars pioneering cheap PCs and mobile phones at home in the 1980s and 1990s, came calling. He bought a big stake and injected fresh cash. His Siva Group 'is investing worldwide in the palm oil industry', EPO chairman Frayne, an Australian geologist, told me a few weeks before my trip, when we met in his modest second-floor office behind Fortnum & Mason in Piccadilly, London. 'Siva can access banks in a way we could not.' Other backers since 'accessed' include J. P. Morgan and Blackrock. The Siva cash means Bayliss can plant up to 10,000 hectares of new trees each year from now on.

But there is a lot to do to get the existing plantation back into production. The fire in Getty's palm-oil boiler at Palm Bay went out on 21 April 1990. As the civil war lurched on, rebels came and went, looting and wrecking, stripping Getty's buildings and eating Rockefeller's cattle. When I visited, the rusting boiler still contained the last ash, and the old Getty manager's house stood roofless and gutted.

Yet much of the workforce stayed, harvesting and processing the palm oil on their own, boiling it up in small vats, skimming the oil off the top and going to town to find buyers. 'They didn't know it would be 20 years before the plantation revived. But they waited. The loyalty that comes with that is humbling,' said Bayliss. 'When we paid the first wages to women at the nursery recently, some of them said they hadn't seen cash in their own hands for 20 years.'

Bayliss planned on repaying that loyalty. The concessions deal requires that the company sets up schools and clinics. When he opened a clinic in an old shack in 2008, it was the first health-care facility at Palm Bay for 19 years. The resident doctor, in a reassuring white coat and a stethoscope, told me he had seen 900 patients in the previous month, dispensing a few basic drugs; providing contraception, inoculations, dressings, and treatment for common diseases like malaria and diarrhoea; and delivering babies. In practice the clinic was open to all-comers, not just employees, he said.

Kids crowded round as we toured the primary school, a rough construction of breeze blocks with a tin roof. They showed off the pineapples, plantains and cassava in their class garden. They were proud that the new benches were made by local carpenters. The nine teachers ran morning and afternoon sessions, each with 230 pupils. Bayliss promised that soon all children of employees could go there.

This was work in progress. Taxis wouldn't come to Palm Bay yet, because the road was so bad. But Cellcom was erecting a phone tower. Bayliss's staff had started a couple of football teams, and there was basketball and volleyball. 'It's part of growing a community. Stability of communities is essential,' said Bayliss. I was struck by the contrast between Bayliss's professional benevolence and the missionary cluelessness of Calvin Burgess's Dominion on the Yala swamp in Kenya.

Things were happening fast on site, too. As we talked, a local truck owner turned up to move some rusting bits of the old mill. But Bayliss told him to leave an old German tank from the Second World War that had somehow got parked in the main yard. Meanwhile, Malaysian contractors were installing a new mill. The $3 million-worth of kit had been shipped to Monrovia via Dubai, then brought on dozens of trucks, bouncing 40-foot containers along the pot-holed roads and finally up a dirt track to the plantation.

The mill, standing about four storeys high, was set to process five tonnes of the plum-sized fruit an hour, enough to produce one tonne of oil. Soon, it would handle 15 tonnes an hour. Processing requires sterilizing the fruit with steam and squashing it in a screw press to extract the oil. Bayliss said the oil would all be sold in West Africa, where there is a big market for locally produced staple products containing palm oil, such as soap and shampoo and biscuits. Process leftovers would become either fuel for the boiler or mulch for the fields.

The new stainless-steel mill was state-of-the-art and highly automated. But elsewhere, a surprising amount of work was being done by hand. The effluent settling ponds had been dug with shovels. And in the nursery – run by Ian Horton, a weather-beaten old Southern Rhodesian who left when it became Zimbabwe – acres of seedlings were being laboriously watered by dozens of women with buckets. The seedlings stay there for 12 months before being planted out.

Bayliss wanted the plantation to be a catalyst for a wider revival of the local economy. The concession included new land around the old Getty plantation that would be set aside for tenant farmers, from whom he would buy palm oil. 'But I don't want them only growing oil palm. Prices are good now, but they are volatile. So they need to grow other crops.' As Frayne had told me in London: 'We can make good returns, but there is a right way to do it.'

The 'right way' is certainly to involve smallholders as out-growers. Politically, that is a big test of the success of the project, because it can spread wealth and break down the enclave syndrome so long inflicted on Liberia by Firestone. But there are risks. Oil-palm fruit rots quickly. It needs to be turned into oil within 24 hours at the most, said Bayliss. That limits the potential for outgrowers to deliver fruit to his mill. It also raises the stakes in other ways. He told me he feared hundreds of farmers turning up at his gate loaded down with rotting bunches of fruit. 'We are about to become the only palm-oil processing plant in the country. We don't want trucks coming from all over the place, especially if we have to send them back. We could easily become public enemy number one – by trying to do good.'

A lot of native Liberians I met at Palm Bay were delighted the plantation was back in business. While watching workers wielding sharp knives on the end of long sticks to rip creepers out of the old oil palms, I met John Fon. He was 65, wore a broad and infectious smile and had spent many years out of the country during the troubles. 'I was in London. I worked for Cadbury's in Shepherd's Bush. They bought cocoa from here. After that, I worked in Nigeria. But I have come back.' He had a new wife, and he showed me his lovingly tended garden in the shade of the plantation, full of cocoa plants. But like many an old man, he didn't think much of the younger generation. 'The mentality of the children here is not good, because they've been used to guns and not working. They think life should be easy.'

While some of the older workers are keen to resume plantation life, others want their independence and to keep land that the government has given to the new plantation owners. They are regarded as squatters. 'The government told us that they would remove them, but we don't want confrontation,' said Bayliss. He hoped to persuade the majority either to leave or to join his workforce. But he admitted that he would act eventually against any remnant that remained. Whether dealing with the 'squatters' is compatible with his ideals of creating community harmony remains to be seen.

Bayliss's approach, while pragmatic, is not slash-and-burn profiteering. It seemed to me he had a better chance of success than a couple of Asian giants setting up shop elsewhere in Liberia. Both are taking over existing oil-palm plantations, and converting rubber plantations. Indonesia's Golden Agri, part of the Sinar Mas group, has almost a quarter-million hectares in the far southeast of the country. And Malaysia's Sime Darby, reputedly the world's largest palm-oil company, has almost as much. If all three foreign projects proceed as planned, a total of 629,000 hectares of Liberia could be under oil palm before long, more than 6 per cent of the country.

But Sime Darby in particular hit trouble in 2011, with locals refusing to give up land and complaining that the company was engaged in illegal clearing. Alfred Brownell, the activist lawyer, had become involved. In October 2011, an appeal to the industry watchdog, the Roundtable on Sustainable Palm Oil, brought a promise that the company would 'cease their operations immediately' in 25,000 hectares claimed by the villagers and 'open bilateral discussions'. Result.

Before I left Palm Bay, and after walking round the nursery, I asked an idle question about where the seedlings came from. Horton said they had come from the Democratic Republic of Congo (formerly Zaire). Where in the DRC, I wondered. 'From the old Unilever place,' he said. Wow. This was straight out of Joseph Conrad's *Heart of Darkness*. The seedlings, it turned out, had been germinated at a research station at Yaligimba in the far north of that vast country. Then they were taken on a barge for more than a thousand kilometres down the River Congo to Kinshasa, before being flown east to Nairobi in Kenya and then west to Monrovia. Yaligimba had been established almost exactly a hundred years before as part of a huge oil-palm plantation set up by William and James Lever, from Warrington in England, the forerunners of Unilever.

Oil palm is a native plant of Africa. It grows wild in the jungles. The precious oil from its fruit turns up in flasks in Egyptian tombs. It went with slaves to the Americas and was sold to Europe in the nineteenth century for candle-making and as an engine lubricant. The Lever brothers needed huge amounts of palm oil to make their world-beating Sunlight soap, one of the world's first global consumer brands. Initially they bought it from smallholders in British colonies in West Africa, particularly the Niger delta, which was a source of palm oil long before petroleum took over there. But, when the brothers proposed setting up their own plantations, the colonial authorities baulked, not wanting to upset their generally good relations with West African farmers.

So the brothers headed for the Congo, much of which had already been divided up into vast logging concessions by King Leopold II of Belgium. He ran the entire Congo region as his personal fiefdom. It was one of the darkest eras of colonialism, with elephants slaughtered for their ivory, forests of wild rubber trees ransacked, and the forest people brutalized. With international opprobrium at the king's private enterprise growing, the Belgian government nationalized the operation in 1908. And three years later, the Lever brothers signed an agreement with the colonial authorities that gave them exclusive rights to grow oil palm in the Congolese forests around five trading posts.

The brothers' concessions covered a staggering 6.8 million hectares, more than twice the size of Belgium, though in practice the main activity was around a trading post called Lusanga, which they renamed Leverville. Lever Brothers merged with Dutch rival Margarine Unie to form Unilever in 1930. With an ever widening range of products being made using palm oil, the new company held on to Leverville. The Belgian Congo was for some decades the oil-palm capital of the world. But after the Congo's independence in 1960 – and particularly after its takeover in 1965 by Mobutu Sese Seko, whose tyranny was second only in its ferocity to that of Leopold – most foreign enterprises were nationalized and their assets looted.

The country – renamed Zaire during Mobutu's time – rapidly descended into chaos. Factories, railways and truck fleets were sold for scrap, and many plantations were abandoned. The only survivors were those owned by Unilever and a well-connected American family: James, Elwyn, Daniel and David Blattner. At Leverville, which reverted to its pre-colonial name of Lusanga, investment in machinery all but ceased, though harvesting and the nursery continued. Yaligimba lived on.

The big palm-oil boom began in the 1960s, as technological breakthroughs made it easier to use the oil in food products. But this happened just as African production collapsed. Between 1962 and 1990, as international trade increased 17-fold, planting shifted to Asia. By some estimates, one in every three products on super-market shelves today contains the magic oil. And it makes a valuable feedstock for biodiesel, too. Global production is approaching 50 million tonnes of oil a year, and requires some 14 million hectares of land – an area the size of England.

By the end of the twentieth century, more than 85 per cent of the world's palm oil was grown in two Asian countries: Malaysia and Indonesia – most of it on land cleared of rainforest for the purpose. But the industry's defenders say that, actually, palm oil is an environmental saviour. They say we will always need vegetable oils and the oil yield of the palm is double that of soya, and three times that of jatropha. So, growing anything else would be worse, insisted Darrel Webber, secretary general of the Roundtable on Sustainable Palm Oil, when we met in London between sessions at his 2011 annual meeting.

He also argued that palm oil is a tropical crop with huge potential to lift some of the world's poorest people, and economies, out of poverty. 'Palm oil is one of the few crops that allows small-holders to come out of poverty. I know rich palm-oil smallholders driving Mercedes.' Palm oil earns Indonesia $12 billion in foreign exchange annually, while employing some 14 million people, including 3 million smallholders. And maintaining that workforce for the 25-year life of a typical plantation requires investment in housing, roads, schools and other infrastructure.

But land is running out in Malaysia and Indonesia. Most of the rainforests are gone. The CEO of Sime Darby, Ahmad Zubir Murshid, said in the Malaysian capital Kuala Lumpur in 2009: 'It is increasingly difficult to acquire plantation land in Asia, and thus it is imperative that new frontiers be sought to meet increasing demand.' Frayne, in his Piccadilly office, has done the numbers too. He uses them in his pitches to potential City investors for EPO. 'At a current yield of about five tonnes of oil per hectare, the world will need another 4 million hectares of land in six years.' That's an area the size of Denmark. By 2020, it will need 6 million hectares. Even if yields rise, the potential land grab is still huge.

So now oil palm is returning to its native Africa. Frayne says only Africa has the land that these plantations need. Bayliss boasts that at Palm Bay, he is developing 80,000 hectares of palm-oil production 'all within 40 kilometres of a deep sea port'. There are, he says, 'no new sites like that in Southeast Asia'.

Everyone wants a slice of the African oil-palm action. Sime Darby and Golden Agri are in Liberia. Singapore-based Wilmar and Olam are in Côte d'Ivoire. By 2016, Olam also plans to start planting on a 150,000-hectare concession in Gabon, where some of the first oil-palm plantations were established by Catholic missionaries in the 1870s. Wilmar also has 10,000 hectares in Uganda.

In December 2010, the government of Congo-Brazzaville announced that it had given a Malaysian company, Atama Plantation, 180,000 hectares. It called Atama 'one of the world's leaders in the production of palm oil'. That is not clear. Atama did not turn up on any lists of oil-palm companies I could access, did not respond to emails, and its website was 'under construction'. However, the two executives named by Congolese ministers as having signed the deal in Brazzaville, Chua Seng Yong and Robert Tan, are the joint managing directors of IGB Corporation, Malaysia's largest owner of commercial properties. Atama is based at IGB's Mid

Valley City complex in Kuala Lumpur. Another director is Reuban Ratnasingam, boss of a long-standing logging and shipping company in Congo-Brazzaville named Asia Congo Industries.

Zhongxing Telecommunications Equipment, a Chinese state enterprise based in Shenzhen, is branching out into agribusiness – albeit not quite on the scale often claimed. In 2009, its Africa manager Zhang Peng was widely reported as claiming to have a million hectares of abandoned plantations in the DRC to grow oil palm, with 3 million hectares on offer. The real figures are actually only a tenth as much, and the company plans to grow maize and soya as well as oil palm. In late 2011, ZTE was harvesting a 250-hectare farm near Kinshasa, but most of the rest of the promised land had not yet been allocated by the DRC government. Meanwhile, in July 2011, a Chinese delegation showed up in Cotonou, the economic capital of Benin, promising to invest a billion dollars in oil palm, in return for land.

European companies are also keen. The French Bolloré Group – which, as we shall see later, is a huge economic presence in central Africa – has 40,000 hectares of oil palm in Cameroon and more in São Tomé. Its compatriot SIFCA is in Côte d'Ivoire. Italy's oil giant ENI has 70,000 hectares in Congo-Brazzaville and more in Angola. Fellow Italian combine Fri-El Green has been awarded 40,000 hectares of old state-owned plantations in Congo-Brazzaville, with more in Nigeria. Unilever, Belgium's SITA and Norway's NORPALM are all growing oil palm in Ghana. SITA has another 10,000 hectares in Nigeria. No fewer than seven European companies have large concessions in Tanzania. And New York-based Herakles Farms has a 99-year lease on 60,000 hectares of degraded forest adjacent to Cameroon's Korup National Park.

But perhaps the oil-palm flame burns brightest in Liberia's West African neighbour, Sierra Leone. Already engaged there are Portugal's Quifel group; UK-based Sierra Leone Agriculture, which has a lease to rehabilitate old oil palms on 31,000 hectares near Matru on the coast; America's Gold Tree Holdings, which is doing likewise close to the Liberian border; and Luxembourg-based SOCFIN, which has 30,000 hectares to go with its plantations in Nigeria, Cameroon and Côte d'Ivoire.

Sierra Leone is not content, however. Like Liberia, it is in a rush to create an economic boom in the wake of a brutal civil war. In late 2011, Patrick Caulker, CEO of Sierra Leone's Investment and Export Promotion Agency, was offering three large sites. He promised to supply landgrabbers with workers at 25 cents an hour, which he boasted is less than half the rate in Indonesia, a seventh that in Malaysia and a tenth that in Brazil. Land leases cost as little as $5 per hectare per year, he said. Water was free, and taxes virtually non-existent. There were 'no restrictions of foreign exchange; no limits on expat employees; full repatriation of profits, dividends and royalties and 100 per cent foreign ownership permitted'. Competitors in the 'race to the bottom' to play host for palm oil will find Sierra Leone already there.

The huge areas of forest land in the DRC, along with its good soils and year-round rains, make it another potential honey pot, as it was in the days of the Lever brothers. Elwyn Blattner, the New Jersey inheritor of the Blattner Group's land assets, is as friendly with the country's new rulers as he was with Mobutu, and still operates a rubber plantation and several thousand hectares of oil palm across the country. But in 2009, after 98 years of operation, Unilever finally sold out. The business had shrunk. Only 15,000 hectares along the Congo River continued to grow oil palm. The Yaligimba mill shut down in 2008, though the seed nursery at Yaligimba's research station was still going strong, supplying among others EPO in Liberia.

Unilever sold to Feronia Inc, a would-be grabber of African

land, registered in the Cayman Islands. It was set up in 2008 by Ravi Sood, a Toronto venture capitalist, and James Siggs, a British farmer who, like Bayliss at Equatorial Palm Oil, previously worked for New Britain Palm Oil in Papua New Guinea. The company wants to revive 'large-scale plantations in Africa that have fallen into disrepair' and to save the continent from 'sustenance farming by families using traditional methods [that] has led to chronic food shortages ... We select the best lands and utilize the most modern technology and practices in the industry to run highly efficient farming operations, thereby maximizing margins and generating profits.'

Besides growing oil palm, Feronia is getting into arable farming. It promises to help transform the DRC in particular, by turning 20,000 hectares of 'prime lands' into 'a combination of Brazilian and US style large-scale agricultural systems for the greatest efficiency and economies of scale'. I wonder how compatible this is with the observation from Siggs, which I quoted in my introduction, that 'exclusively industrial-scale farming displaces and alienates peoples, creates few jobs and causes social disruption'.

We shall see. But, judging by its output of press releases to date, profits and corporate structure come first at Feronia. Since the Unilever purchase, the company has been involved in a bewildering range of financial and share transactions involving its initial owner, a Canadian investment company called TriNorth Capital, and GTM Capital, an Atlanta-based 'private investment company' representing several hedge funds.

The torch of Western land-grabbing in central Africa has been handed on from the most powerful of the old colonial resource exploiters to a new breed of financial whizz-kids. What it means for Africans is far from clear. I went back to Europe to find out more about those new investors. I went to London, the world's biggest financial centre for land-grabbing.

8

LONDON, ENGLAND
Pinstripes and pitchforks

Redhead Susan Payne is the pin-up of the City of London's pin-striped landgrabbers. They hang on her every word. Her investment fund, Emergent Asset Management, has over five years accumulated one of the largest land banks in southern Africa. But it is her stardust, and that of her former employers at Goldman Sachs, that sets her business apart. She seems set to turn the arcane, bespoke business of buying land in foreign parts into something we can all join in with – just like Goldman Sachs did with commodities.

Payne is a regular at investors' conferences. Her style is a business suit in a smart hotel, not wellies in an African field. She runs Emergent with fellow J. P. Morgan veteran David Murrin. While CEO Payne is a lawyer from Vancouver, chief investment officer Murrin's past is more exotic. Before getting into finance, he was a geologist for oil companies. He did seismic surveys in the jungles of Papua New Guinea where, according to his company biography, he 'worked with local tribes in the Sepik Basin, and started to formulate his theories on collective emotional behavioural patterns'.

Those theories, the pair claim, underpin their investment strategies. Some will think that the world of Goldman Sachs and its weird financial derivatives is probably stranger than anything laid on by the tribes of Papua New Guinea. At any rate, Payne and Murrin are helping bring the glamour and ruthlessness of commodities speculation to the normally more sober world of buying and selling farmland.

Payne is a persuasive speaker. I have heard her several times. Her pitch is that making money in African land today is easy. The continent's GDP has been growing by 5 per cent a year for a decade now. It was barely hit by the credit crisis. And it is urbanizing faster than Asia, meaning lots more supermarket shelves to fill. Payne can play fast and loose with the stats. She told one African Investment Summit in London that 'Africa will have the largest workforce in the world by 2040.' Well, up to a point, Susan. Africa is a continent. If you compare it with individual countries, then it sure will. But if you compare it with another continent, like Asia, it won't.

But her bottom line is that the continent has land in abundance: '60 per cent of the world's uncultivated land' is there. Much of it has access to plentiful water supplies. Making big profits requires little more than adding fertilizer. And land prices right now are so low that, according to one of her most-quoted lines, 'We could be moronic and not grow anything, and we think we will [still] make money over the next decade.'

Like all good speculators, she has mastered the skill of buying cheap while talking up the price of what she is investing in. The company predicted in 2010 that in South Africa 'land values will increase by 300 per cent in the next five years'. And it wants to raise 3 billion euros, so its African Agricultural Land Fund can cash in.

AgriLand's money comes mostly from institutional clients, such as pension funds and university endowments, who are attracted by its promise of 25 per cent returns. Or that's the story. But rumours are rife. A competitor for those funds told me: 'Susan Payne had one big investor. We think it was a big US university endowment, maybe Harvard. But they pulled back and so she has been looking for money again.' I cannot confirm that story, but I came across many such critics. They grumble that Payne's crowd are all talk. And Emergent does seem to be everywhere and nowhere. AgriLand is registered in Luxembourg, while its management is in London. Its land-buying is done through EmVest, a Pretoria-based joint venture with Grainvest, a subsidiary of the Russell Stone Group, a South African company that combines agricultural investment with selling financial services. It banks in Mauritius, a tax haven.

The fund's publicity promises that it is 'breaking new ground in Africa' and bringing development. 'Local smallholders benefit because we hire and train them in new methods of farming,' Payne says. 'Some will want to transfer those methods to their own plots.' Well, maybe in theory. But most of its activity is more prosaic than the PR. Its partners in Pretoria 'have a lot of people of Afrikaner descent, people who were brought up on the land, very capable farmers, very tough,' Murrin told Reuters.

Most of its current holdings are large established commercial farms in South Africa and its neighbours: a loss-making tea, fruit and vegetable company in Zimbabwe called Ariston Holdings; banana and other plantations on the Kalonga Estate near Victoria Falls in Zambia; a 50-year lease on land at Matuba in the Limpopo valley in southern Mozambique. The company variously describes this last holding as 1,000, 1,500 or 2,000 hectares. But at any rate the land came with rights to unlimited irrigation water from the nearby river, and proximity to a railway line that borders the farm. This is hardly 'groundbreaking'. But equally it doesn't pose the threat to subsistence African farmers that the company's critics claim.

Emergent's pitch to potential investors is spiced up with claimed insight into the great geopolitical forces shaping the world. Murrin in particular warns of a future war between the West and China, triggered by the latter's ever rising demand for commodities, particularly in Africa. While that apocalyptic vision might suggest a threat to Emergent's African assets, Murrin figures that in the run-up to war there will be a lot of profit as commodity scarcity causes prices to soar. He embraces other threats, too. 'Climate change means some places in Africa will be drier and others will be wetter. We'll be looking to take advantage of that,' he says.

Murrin also claims to keep ahead of the game by exploiting the Elliott Wave theory of long-term cycles in public mood, alternating between optimism and pessimism. This idea took root when he was in Papua New Guinea, and he discusses it at length in a book called *Breaking the Code of History*. He says: 'There is a tradition that history is about the detail, but I have always believed instead that it is determined on a vast scale, by a specific set of dynamics. Moreover, its apparent randomness is only an illusion: once the sequence of events that we call "history" is shown to be governed by certain behavioural algorithms, we can then discern, with clarity, the degree to which our lives are bound up in numerous interrelationships.' Phew.

Payne's presentations, meanwhile, often include a scary graph showing something called the Kondratiev Cycle, after Nikolai Kondratiev, the Russian economist who invented it. I'm not clear how the Elliott Wave and the Kondratiev Cycle relate, if at all. But her graph shows US commodity prices since 1800 rising and falling in a long cycle with spikes roughly every 50 years. Some have claimed that the supposed cycle is created by technological innovations. Others suggest credit cycles or demographics. Payne proposes a link to conflicts. Her graph captions the spikes as linked to the Napoleonic wars in Europe, the American Civil War, the First World War and the Vietnam War. 'Commodity prices and wars interact,' she says. I wasn't sure whether the price spikes caused the conflicts or vice versa. But at any rate her view was that 'we are on an up-cycle of commodity prices, and we see resource conflicts around 2020'.

These stories of waves and cycles determining history sound flaky. And the company is inclined to oversell its insight. Its website boasts that Murrin and Payne peered into their geopolitical crystal balls to get ahead of the game by spotting 'in late 2007 . . . food security as the next energy security'. The phrase has a ring to it, but this wasn't so much unique insight as fanning the flames of growing panic. In July 2007, the seers at the BBC were already writing head-lines about 'food prices on the rise and rise' and relaying 'doomsday predictions of the price of staple foods'. But a cynic would suggest this is how the masters of the universe operate. No profound insight, just riding the waves and cycles.

Leaving aside the mumbo-jumbo, the thinking of the investors behind today's epidemic of land-grabbing is clear. With world population still soaring, land and water in short supply, and a billion middle-class people in the poor world demanding Western-style meat diets, they see food security as the next big global concern. And growing more food requires more farmland. 'I'm con-vinced farmland is going to be one of the best investments of our time,' says hedge fund guru George Soros. 'Farmland is gold with a cash flow,' agrees Jeffrey Conrad, president of the Boston-based Hancock Agricultural Investment Group. Reuters calls it 'a bankers' hay ride'.

Investors admit that, after the abstractions of financial derivatives, there is something reassuring about land. An investment fund manager in London, Edward Ho, told Reuters that part of the attraction of his new $625-million Altima One World Agricultural Development Fund was that 'you can go to the farm and touch the soil'.

Whether touching the soil turns you on or not, Africa is the place to go. The management gurus at McKinsey trumpet how African agricultural growth has been more than twice that of its economies in general – around 12 per cent per annum in recent years. Governments have got their financial houses in order and 'energized' markets by privatizing state farms and marketing bodies, lowering taxes and improving infrastructure. The potential for further growth remains huge, since Africa has a quarter of the world's arable land, but only 10 per cent of its arable output. Africa could, McKinsey declares, 'meet the world's burgeoning demand for food'. Helping it deliver is a potential gold mine.

If Soros is a bit of an arriviste, and McKinsey's flip charts too clever by half, how about taking the advice of Lord Rothschild? The scion of the great European banking family owns a chunk of the Chiltern Hills so big the locals call it Rothschildshire. He has 15,000 bottles of claret (Château Mouton Rothschild, anyone?) in the cellar of his largest property, Waddesdon Manor. The man is so trusted by the world's richest men that when Russian oligarch Mikhail Khodorkovsky was arrested by Vladimir Putin's police in 2003, he handed Rothschild the voting rights to shares worth $13 billion in his Yukos Corporation for safe keeping.

So when Rothschild said in 2009 'right now is an excellent point of entry for taking a long-term position in agriculture,' he was likely to be believed. Especially as he was practising what he preached. At the age of 72, Rothschild had just added to his portfolio of chairmanships by assuming the top seat at Agrifirma, a Jersey-based company set up by 1970s City whizz-kid Jim Slater, with 42,000 hectares of prime farmland in Brazil's western Bahia (see Chapter Ten).

Nicola Horlick, a prominent City of London investor fêted as a 'superwoman' by the British media, is following Rothschild on the plane to Brazil. She is spending hundreds of millions on farmland in western Bahia through her Mayfair-based Bramdean Asset Management. Her high-powered investors have included the Hampshire and Merseyside county pension funds and Iranian playboy and 'bad boy' property magnate, Vincent Tchenguiz.

London landgrabbers are generally an exotic lot. Other bad (and golden) boys tied up in the land rush include Anthony 'Chocfinger' Ward, whose Armajaro Holdings spectacularly cornered the world's cocoa futures, allowing him to pocket $40 million in two months as prices soared; Guy Hands, ex-Goldman Sachs bond trader and chairman of Terra Firma; litigious Dan Gold and his QVT Financial hedge fund; and Zambia-born former England Test cricketer and spin bowler Phil Edmonds, of whom more later. The *Wall Street Journal* found 45 private equity groups wanting to spend over $2 billion in African agriculture in 2010, with London their biggest centre of operations. Or rather London and the cloud of tax havens that the last vestiges of the British Empire have bequeathed to the world: the Cayman Islands, British Virgin Islands, Isle of Man and Channel Islands.

I continued my tour of London's land investors in a mews side-street behind the rugby stadium in Twickenham, where I met the 'Togo boys'. A group of smart city slickers with nice cars and stubbly chins got lucky with the West African government of tiny Togo. Togo is a generally peaceful country with what looks like elective dynastic rule. When Gnassingbé Eyadema, the victor in a 1960s military coup, died in 2005 after 38 years in the job, his subjects were controversially declared to have elected his son to replace him.

The Eyadema clan subsequently gave Philip Peters and Lawrie Smith a 99-year lease on 2,700 hectares of farmland near the town of Agbélouvé, an hour's drive north of the capital, Lomé. Peters and Smith are the founders of an ethical investment vehicle called Greenleaf Global. They have an arrangement with a Russian agronomist – Vladimir Matichenkov, from the Russian Academy of Science, no less – who has mapped their Togo farm in detail and is bringing in jatropha seeds. The plan is to turn jatropha fruit into oil to make biodiesel for Europe's cars. With booming demand and jatropha oil prices high, the profits on their investment could be good.

Or rather *your* investment. The Togo boys are not punting for big City investors. They want you to buy a lease. Put down £6,000 and the local villagers will plant 5,000 saplings on your two-hectare plot. In a couple of years they will start harvesting the fruit and put it through a screw press. Greenleaf will sell the resulting oil. If things go well, and the promised yields of 10 tonnes per hectare are achieved, you can watch your money grow. Profits should be 12 per cent a year, says Peters. 'Investment bankers are coming in personally to buy plots,' he said. But by late 2011 only 1,200 hectares had been sold – less than half the available land. So it may be a while before they take up their option on another 12,000 hectares nearby.

The guys from Greenleaf insist that it's all up-side for the locals. 'They can't believe their luck that we are there. Nothing was growing there before. The land has never been worked.' Greenleaf is sponsoring six orphaned kids at a local school and promises, if the company is still around, to employ them when they grow up. But there are fewer jobs on offer than promised. The Greenleaf website was still saying 600 in late 2011, when there were only half as many at work, and Peters said the maximum would be 400, because of mechanization.

West Africa is popular with other British 'boutique' investment firms that allow you to scratch a personal profit from a patch of African soil. In 2011, GreenWorld BVI, which is incorporated in the British Virgin Islands tax haven, was offering online gamblers a hectare of 'high quality farmland' to grow rice in Sierra Leone for £1,950. The investment was 'specifically designed to be both profitable as well as socially responsible ... allowing you to invest like a major institutional investor, but at a fraction of the initial cost'. Meanwhile

Agri Capital, based in Alderley Edge, Cheshire, was offering what appeared to be the same land at the same price, with the promise that 'our aim is to harvest your profit.'

Or how about Sierra Leone's immediate neighbour, Guinea? Mark Fitzpatrick Keegan, who owns a large sheep farm in northern England, has been making money for several years by converting Argentine ranches into soya farms. His unlikely-sounding corporate vehicle was a Las Vegas-registered company called Kryptic Entertainment. Now he is taking on Africa, and Kryptic has morphed into Farm Lands of Guinea, operating through a subsidiary registered in – you guessed it – the British Virgin Islands.

Farm Lands of Guinea has an initial lease on 9,000 hectares of 'underutilized' farmland along one of the main roads through the landlocked nation. The lease was granted on 'extremely generous' terms by the government of Guinea, which has a 10 per cent stake in the operation. The company also has an option on a further 98,000 hectares and is surveying what it says is another 1.5 million hectares of underutilized land in order to 'prepare it for third party development under 99-year leases'. Much of Guinea is, it seems, up for sale.

Keegan is certainly thinking big, and he has an eclectic band of fellow board members and investors. His chairman is General Sir Redmond Watt, who was until 2008 the commander of British Land Forces. He presided at the funeral of the Queen Mother. The company's accountant is the chairman of a Guinea gold mining company. Its main investment partner is a secretive, Hong Kong-based investment company called Desmond Holdings, operating through a UK company, AIM Investments, whose acting chairman when the deal was done was Desmond director Mark Pajak. The farm plan has been drawn up by board member and agricultural consultant Nigel Woodhouse, who runs an organic trout farm in Cumbria and is a trustee of the UK Soil Association.

All this may be of interest to people in the villages of N'Dema and Konindou in Guinea, where this constellation of talent was expected to begin planting the first 300 hectares of maize and soya in 2012. Woodhouse told me he visited the villages, attending two one-hour meetings at which the chiefs and others consented to hand over the land to government officials. The land was outside the villages and 'without any human population'. Agreement among the villagers was 'positively universal. Money, in the form of a token, was given to the chief, and amounted to what I thought was the equivalent of three pounds,' he said. It doesn't sound a lot.

Hedge funds and anonymous investment houses and asset managers have driven much of the Western-funded land-grabbing to date. But even bigger than the hedge funds are the pension funds, with their trillions of dollars of assets. Industry analysts say their move into commodities index funds, which did so much to destabilize food commodity markets, is now being extended to farmland.

The giant pension fund for California's public employees has put about $50 million into Black Earth Farming, which has some 320,000 hectares of Russian grain fields (see Chapter Nine), and a string of big Far Eastern oil-palm plantation owners, including Sime Darby, Olam and Wilmar. The Teachers Insurance and Annuity Association of America (TIAA-CREF) has $2 billion of farmland in Brazil, central and eastern Europe and Australia as well as the US, and is buying more. The Swedish National Pension Fund has half a billion dollars invested in farms in Brazil, Australia and the US, and its AP3 pension fund is deep into the rich black earths of Russia.

Oh, and the Danes are giving their pension money to Gary Vaughan-Smith.

After I had visited too many money people without a clue about African farming, and very little interest – people who just felt the smallholders should be swept away and replaced by modern 'efficient' agribusiness funded by them – it was a relief to meet Vaughan-Smith, who seemed to know about both pension funds and Africa.

We met at his office close to Stanfords, the legendary map store in Covent Garden. I had been in search of maps to some obscure parts of West Africa. He said he had got into trouble in the past over his long-running enthusiasm for investing in Africa. He put some of Gartmore Investments' money there once. 'It didn't do well, and I got the blame.' But he had a touch of Schadenfreude that day. Hours before, Gartmore had crashed after some other ill-advised investments.

He was still backing his Africa hunch in his new berth as founding partner of SilverStreet Capital, where he was building a $500 million fund to buy farmland there. 'African farmland looks fantastic right now,' he said. 'Investors these days want to go into real assets, not derivatives.' Through the credit crunch, SilverStreet struggled to raise cash. But Vaughan-Smith struck gold with $200 million from a Danish investment company called PKA that handles pension funds, and the US government's development finance body, the Overseas Private Investment Corporation. 'I find it really exciting to be able to bring this sort of investment capital to Africa,' he said. He was on a plane to New York that afternoon to harvest some more cash.

Vaughan-Smith, a Zimbabwean actuary by training, is small, dapper and bearded. But next to him sat Tim Denton, a big, craggy Zimbabwean farmer who had seen a bit more sun on his neck. Denton had spent seven years on a big coffee farm at Mpongwe in Zambia, when it was owned by the British government's Commonwealth Development Corporation. Then he worked for a George Soros-backed tea and coffee grower called African Plantations, before it merged with tea giant Rift Valley Holdings, which is owned by a Norwegian shipping family. Now he is building a team of Zimbabwean farmers to grow the 'big four' farm commodities – wheat, rice, maize and soya – for SilverStreet. 'We plan five 10,000-hectare farms in five countries: Zambia, Malawi, Tanzania, Mozambique and South Africa.'

I liked these guys. They were serious about Africa and Africans. Denton had no time for landgrabbers who wanted to write peasant farmers out of their script for the continent. He had smallholders at the heart of his plans. One of his first farms, in Tete province in Mozambique, will be devoted entirely to buying their produce. And each of the five farms will have a training centre for smallholders, he promised. He intends the centres to be run by a Harare-based charity called Foundations for Farming. Formerly called Farming God's Way, it was set up by a born-again Christian and pioneer of environmentally friendly zero-tillage farming named Brian Oldreive. It sounded odd, but Oldreive, who was once a Zimbabwean Test cricketer, is reputedly the best in the business.

Denton was optimistic about the potential to improve the yields of smallholder farmers in Africa. 'It's not rocket science. It's just about doing things at the right time. About getting farmers to prepare fields, drill holes, have seeds and fertilizer ready when the rains come, rather than trying to do it all in a rush. That way it's easy to get from one tonne a hectare to three tonnes.' But yields were no good without assured markets. Why produce more if the only result is collapsing prices? So Denton sees central farms as important too, providing secure markets for the produce of surrounding smallholders. 'There is so much we can do to have a positive social impact,' said Vaughan-Smith as I left.

We shall see. I believe he meant it. The trouble is that when the promises and ideals of the farm managers fail to match the imperatives of the investors and their bottom lines, it is quite clear who wins. The promises and ideals go out of the window. Denton will ultimately take his instructions from the Danes and the Americans now.

The rules for almost every company receiving investment capital require that the interests of the investors come first. Many companies investing in developing countries will subscribe to ethical aspirations, such as the Equator principles on social and environmental issues. Their banks and financiers may sign on to these as well. But the rules are couched in general terms. When push comes to shove, it is the bottom line that counts. That's capitalism.

Some people believe foreign landgrabbers can be tamed by national laws. Don't believe it. Many domestic laws governing international land transactions are trumped by international investment agreements (IIAs). A report published in 2011 by Johannesburg-based Standard Bank, a major funder of land grabs, made clear to me how important these agreements are. Written by the bank's director for agricultural banking, Jacques Taylor, and its boss of sustainability, Karin Ireton, the report describes the legal landscape with brutal frankness.

'IIAs are designed to protect investors, with few of the agreements including any investor obligation, or expressing and recognizing the rights of states to regulate in the public interest,' Taylor and Ireton said. But if investors have few obligations, host countries have many. 'Foreign investment creates minimum international standards to which host countries must comply . . . host governments generally accept that they will provide the means for these investors to operate – for example, by providing them with the ability to draw water for agricultural purposes.' This right, they said, 'may become a legitimate expectation of the foreign investor and therefore a legal entitlement under international law . . . even if it conflicts with existing or future needs in local communities for potable water, small-scale farming, small industries or subsistence use'.

Ouch. I found I was rereading every sentence several times to make sure I had not misunderstood. But no. Even if the locals are starving or parched with thirst, in law the rights of the foreign investor come first. When governments sell or lease land to foreigners, the risks that they run 'include cash-strapped local people losing not only their homes but also their source of food and future income as buyers secure the full right to crops and land'. If, say, a drought meant the investor didn't get all the water stipulated in his contract, an international arbitration would probably conclude that this was 'an expropriation of the right to operate the business' by the host country. At the least, heavy compensation would be due.

Oh, and anyone who thinks governments would be justified in banning food exports by foreign investors during a famine could be in for a second think. 'It is commonplace in investor agreements to provide investors with the capacity to operate their investment in accordance with their own needs,' the report says. 'In the case of agricultural land investments, the right to export all or almost all of the production is presumed to be a part of most contracts.' Export bans 'may be in breach of international investment law, if they impact the rights granted to foreign investors'. International law, it seems, is a landgrabbers' charter.

If foreign investors have little to fear from national laws, they have a great deal to fear from their own unfamiliarity with Africa, and its land and people. Older British readers may need only three words to remind them of some painful British imperial history on this score. The groundnut scheme. Peanuts, to you and me. The hubristic landgrabber of half a century ago was a man called Frank Samuel, from the global fats transnational Unilever. In 1946, he proposed to the British government a grand plan to grow groundnuts in Tanzania, then known as the British protectorate of Tanganyika.

He wanted the nuts to help supply a booming market in vegetable oils, including for Unilever's margarine. He hoped the scheme could compete with French plans to grow groundnuts in the Sahel, then mostly called French West Africa.

Local colonial officials in Dar es Salaam were enthusiastic. They believed that the bush in much of the centre of the country was 'empty' because the locals were lousy farmers. They feared food shortages and an exodus to the cities. What was needed, they believed, was Western agricultural know-how. Back in Whitehall, gazing at maps of Africa mostly coloured red for British imperial dominion, they at one stage discussed creating a vast groundnut plantation extending from Kenya to Rhodesia.

But first they earmarked 60,000 hectares of central Tanganyika – an area that the Victorian explorer Henry Morton Stanley had summed up as 'an interminable jungle of thorn bushes'. They recruited 100,000 local soldiers, most of them recently demobbed following the end of the Second World War, to become farm labourers. They built a settlement for them, Kongwa. The company created for the enterprise, the Overseas Food Corporation, was put in the charge of Leslie Plummer, a part-time English farmer, political activist and executive of the top newspaper of the day, Lord Beaverbrook's *Daily Express*. With the media on their side, what could go wrong? The answer was quite a lot.

First they had to clear the land. Plummer bought surplus US army tractors from the Philippines. After being shipped across the world to Dar es Salaam, they had to be dragged up a dirt track to Kongwa after heavy rains washed away the railway line. Once on site, even the biggest tractors could not remove the local baobab trees. The drivers wrecked most of the equipment in the attempt. The demoralized workforce was attacked by elephants and killer bees, rhinos and scorpions. Water had to be shipped in. And still there were no groundnuts in the ground.

The headlines back home that had at first trumpeted the scheme turned nasty. With the project becoming a laughing stock at home, Plummer resigned. The government sent in a major-general to sort things out. Eventually the Overseas Food Corporation planted some nuts. Rains germinated the crop. But then drought baked the soil as hard as concrete, so digging up the nuts proved near impossible. They cut the planned area for cultivation to 20,000 hectares. But after two more years, the major-general had gone home on sick leave, only 2,000 tonnes of nuts had been harvested, and the soils were compacted and ruined.

Five years after the brainwave, amid rising derision at home, the government abandoned the project. Kongwa declined. The school shut in 1958, but reopened soon after as a training base for South African freedom fighters from the ANC. Back home, the groundnut scheme became a standing joke, a metaphor for bone-headed British management everywhere. Ministers instilled fear in their civil servants by threatening to send them off 'to the groundnuts scheme'. They teach the farrago in US universities to this day. It should be a warning to all landgrabbers. And to Africa as well. The fields round Kongwa are still useless except to the thorn trees that gradually returned. The Brits, for the record, have still not apologized for what they did.

PART THREE

ACROSS THE GLOBE

The land rush is global. In the former Soviet Union, old state farms are up for grabs. In Brazil, new money is turning tribal grasslands into high-tech prairies, growing soya to sell to China. Meanwhile, Brazilian ranchers move into the searing heat of the Paraguayan Chaco, and trigger new land wars across the rest of South America. Down south, the magical empty lands of Patagonia are disappearing into the back pockets of the world's super-rich, from Ted Turner to the Benettons. Across the Pacific, the old cattle families of the Australian outback are selling up to foreign land barons. Even the Kidmans are down-sizing.

9

UKRAINE

Lebensraum

Richard Spinks was a footloose Englishman who left school at 16, joined the Royal Air Force for a while, and then spent a decade bouncing around Europe, selling advertising and buying fish at docksides from Gdansk to Archangel, before marrying a Ukrainian woman. Then, in 2005 – on a hunch, and with no knowledge of farming – he sold his fish-processing firm in Poland, moved to Ukraine and started buying up former state land. He wanted to cash in on the coming biofuels boom by growing rapeseed to turn into biodiesel.

He began knocking on doors in the villages of western Ukraine, offering to lease fields from poor peasant farmers. Often sleeping in a tent as he criss-crossed the country, he leased land at $35 a hectare per year, using cash from a couple of friends. He had ambitions to create his own land empire in the former Soviet republic. He set up a company called Landkom International, with headquarters in the village of Bilyi Kamin, east of the historic city of Lviv. Business was brisk. He brought in outside investors. Within a couple of years, he had more than 100,000 hectares of prime fertile land. He floated the company on the London stock exchange, with a prospectus promising to build the land bank to 300,000 hectares. He was, for a while, Ukraine's third largest farmer.

But Spinks had over-extended himself. He had bought far more land than he could farm. His investors moved in, ousted Spinks, cut the land bank by 40 per cent and speeded up planting. By 2011, the new CEO, a Ukrainian tractor salesman named Vitaliy Skotsyk, was cultivating 48,000 hectares, most of it with rapeseed. Spinks's camping-holiday buying sprees were long gone. That's how start-up companies often go: the visionary ousted by the money men. But the money men themselves got into trouble too, later in the year, when rain wrecked the rape harvest and the company's share price collapsed. At the end of the year, the company's management was recommended selling out to Swedish investment company Alpcot Agro.

Rain or not, Ukraine is potentially the bread basket of Europe. It is the continent's biggest producer of barley and among its top wheat growers. Two-thirds of its 600,000 square kilometres are rich humus soils, known as black earth. But thanks to political turmoil and the dead hand of bureaucracy those soils have never fulfilled their potential. In the 1930s, Ukraine became the victim of the disastrous collectivization policies of Stalin. Then in 1941, Hitler invaded as part of a march east in search of what he called Lebensraum, space in which to grow food for his country's ever-expanding population. Hitler was repulsed in 1945, but sclerotic Soviet hegemony was restored. The socialist prairies of Ukraine failed to deliver Stalin's dream of a grain bonanza like the capitalist American Midwest.

After the collapse of the Soviet Union in 1991, the collectives and state farms were gradually broken up and their fields handed over to poor peasants. But the peasants lacked access to capital, and that continues till today. Typical is the fate of the former Dniester Collective Farm. When the farm was broken up in 2001, the few hundred poor and ageing inhabitants of the tiny hamlet of Stinka, southeast of Lviv on the banks of the River Dniester, took over their allotted 750 hectares. They had no money to maintain the land, let alone invest.

So, like hundreds of other communities, they grew what they needed and let the rest of the land run to seed. The country's 50,000 small farms have allowed an estimated 200,000 square kilometres, a third of the country, to go uncultivated in recent years. Yields on the rest are less than half those on poorer soils in the European Union. With the second-largest land area in Europe, Ukraine's grain output is still considerable. But the continent's agricultural giant continues to sleep.

Enter the landgrabbers. A few local corporations with access to capital are buying land from communities like Stinka. Mriya Agro, based in the western provincial town of Ternopil, has expanded from 50 hectares in 1992 to 220,000 hectares, thanks to loans from the World Bank. Agroton of Lugansk, set up in 1992 by a medical doctor, Yuriy Zhuravlov, to raise bees, now has over 150,000 hectares in the east of the country and is Ukraine's biggest grower of sunflowers.

But more recently, foreigners have come calling. They spent some $8 billion on land leases from 2008 to 2010. There were entrepreneurs like Spinks. But also hedge funds and investment banks like Morgan Stanley, all eager to harvest profits by bringing Western expertise and capital to the rich black soils. Grain yields could be doubled to match those in the EU, they say. Exports could triple. And with land prices still not much more than 15 per cent of the typical price in the European Union, the potential profits are huge.

Charles Beigbeder, a controversial French financier and online wheeler-dealer, has 50,000 hectares, through his latest firm, AgroGeneration. He aims to double that holding by gobbling up failing Ukrainian farms. Serbian sugar tycoon Miodrag Kostic has 40,000 hectares around Kiev. The Maharishi organic farm movement runs 50,000 hectares on behalf of Viktor Pinchuk, a Ukrainian billionaire steel magnate, media mogul and organic enthusiast, who boasts of friendships with Bill Clinton and Elton John. Colonel Gaddafi did a deal with the former Ukraine president Yulia Tymoshenko's government to lease 100,000 hectares to grow wheat for Tripoli in return for oil and defence equipment, though that was on hold in mid-2011 because of the fall of the Gaddafi regime. Brokers from the United Arab Emirates, including the president's brother, had been on a tour of the black soils. China's Ex-Im Bank talked in late 2011 of investing $10 billion in Ukrainian agriculture, but it was unclear what role land grabs might play.

The Ukraine government bans outright sale of farmland to foreigners, but rumours have been rife about officials secretly sanctioning black market sales of former state farms. An investigation by journalist Mark Rachkevych in the *Kyiv Post* in 2010 quoted a leading lawyer for the Ukrainian Agrarian Federation, which promotes foreign investment, saying that leading politicians 'are not ready for a transparent system [of land ownership]. Many are big landowners,' he said. And if deals became public 'they'd have to explain how they obtained some land in huge amounts'.

Ukraine is highly prized for its soils, but it was only one corner of Moscow-controlled Eastern Europe. Other foreign landgrabbers are spreading their nets more widely across the old Communist bloc in search of bargains. Trigon Agri, owned by a consortium of rich Danes and Finns, is growing wheat and sunflowers on 170,000 hectares of black-earth farms from Kirovograd in central Ukraine to Samara close to the Caspian Sea in Russia, and from Estonia on the Baltic to Stavropol in the Russian Caucasus. It is aiming for 300,000 hectares by 2015. The giant American grain trader Cargill is buying land in Bulgaria. Danish bacon entrepreneur Erik Jantzen has tens of thousands of hectares in the Czech Republic, Slovakia and Romania, where about a tenth of farmland is already in foreign hands.

Some projects have come unstuck. An Irish company, Greenfield Project Management, hatched a scheme to grow sugar beet in Belarus, on abandoned fields in the exclusion zone downwind of Ukraine's stricken Chernobyl nuclear reactor. The idea was that, while the land was unfit for growing food, it could grow biofuels. The company claimed the distillation process that turned the crop into ethanol would leave the radioactive strontium and caesium behind in the residues in the bottom of the distillery. The fuel would be free of radiation, and the residues could go to a radioactive waste dump. But the claim was unproven and the plan collapsed when the Belarus government withdrew support.

The biggest three former-Soviet states are Ukraine, Russia and Kazakhstan. Between them, they 'could produce half of the world's grain export needs, including 60 per cent of the world's wheat needs', says Gilles Mettetal, director of agribusiness at the European Bank for Reconstruction and Development, which is dedicated to promoting Western investment in the former Soviet Union.

Unlike Ukraine, Kazakhstan has kept many of its large state farms intact, privatized but not broken up. They are run as businesses, usually by their former managers. Kazakhstan has the world's two largest private arable farming operations. Nurlan Tleubayev, head of the country's grain-growers' union, has 800,000 hectares, and a Russian, Vasily Rozinov, has 600,000 hectares, split between Kazakhstan and Russia. But others see the potential. China signed a deal with Kazakhstan's president, Nursultan Nazarbayev, a leader left over from the Soviet era, to take a million hectares for growing soya and rapeseed. Gulf and Saudi organizations have also done deals. Both Switzerland's GAIA World Agri Fund and the British hedge fund Dexion Capital's global farming fund, set up by former Goldman Sachs trader Robin Bowie, have been talking to leaders in the world's ninth largest country.

But Russia is still the biggest player in this part of the world. Vladimir Putin's agriculture minister Aleksey Gordeyev claimed in 2008: 'Russia is often perceived round the world as a major military power. But perhaps above and beyond anything else, Russia is a major agrarian power.' Most years it is the third biggest wheat exporter, behind the US and Canada. When measured per hectare, its yields may be mediocre. But Russia has 7 per cent of all the world's arable land.

There are two sides to Russian farming. Household plots occupy just 6 per cent of the country's farmland but produce half of its total agricultural products, including half its livestock and milk, 90 per cent of its potatoes and 80 per cent of its vegetables. But former state farms that have stayed in business produce the bulk of the grain exports. And by some estimates, there are millions of hectares of abandoned former state and collective farms awaiting rehabilitation. Russian oligarchs, gorged on profits from oil and mining, now see these farms as a new source of easy profit. In particular, they are taking over the black-earth zones bordering Ukraine.

Among the pioneers is Michel Orlov. He comes from the 'White Russian' nobility who went into exile after the revolution a century ago. Before then, his grandparents owned a string of huge estates. Born in Switzerland, he returned to Russia after the fall of the Soviet Union in 1991, and became director of the Moscow office of the Carlyle Group, a US-based global investment firm second in wealth only to Goldman Sachs. 'I am a modern businessman. The trick here is not to harvest crops but to harvest money,' he told the *Financial Times*. Under Putin, he started to buy up state collective farms on his own. In 2005, he created Black Earth Farming, with the help of funding from the super-rich Lundin Group, a creation of Adolf Lundin.

Lundin, who died in 2006, was a Swedish legend. He was an oil engineer turned mining maverick, who had a reputation for going where others wouldn't. In the 1970s, he discovered off Qatar what is still the world's largest natural gas reserve – singlehandedly making that tiny emirate among the world's richest nations. In the 1980s, he gained control of some of the world's largest copper and cobalt mines in Mobutu's Zaire. In the 1990s, he bought into Russian oil and gas during the wild days of Boris Yeltsin's presidency, when vast state assets could seemingly be obtained for a song. Then he started buying into Russian black earth. Lundin's family owns a quarter of Black Earth Farming which, through its Russian subsidiary Agroinvest, has some 320,000 hectares of prime farmland. Black Earth Farming, run by English agriculturalist Richard Warburton, describes its business goal as the acquisition of 'cheap, neglected but fertile land in the fertile Black Earth region in southwest Russia'.

The Swedish connection has grown. Would-be purchaser of Landkom, Alpcot Agro, has control of 170,000 Russian hectares, most of them in Voronezh and Kursk in southwest Russia. It is financed by the Swedish AP3 pension fund. Meanwhile in the Russian Far East, South Korea's desire to improve its food security has seen Hyundai Heavy Industries take 50,000 hectares of former state farms near Vladivostok. The US's Minnesota-based grain and food producer CHS Inc., the creation of a series of mergers between farmers' cooperatives, has bought Agromarket Trade, Russia's second-largest grain exporter, and its 100,000 hectares of farmland around Stavropol in the Caucasus. And the fast-growing RAV Agro-Pro, controlled by the secretive Israeli real estate tycoon and grain trader Roni Yitzhaki, had 160,000 hectares in the black earth region till its sale to the PPF Group, the Czech Republic's largest investment company, in July 2011.

Everyone, it seems, wants a stake in the black earth, their piece of Lebensraum. But if there is one place even more desired by the world's grain merchants, it is the Brazilian *cerrado*. That's where I went next.

10
WESTERN BAHIA, BRAZIL
Soylandia

It was hard to believe, as I sipped a glass of wine and tucked into a steak in front of the pool, while a light plane landed behind me on the farm airstrip – but a quarter of a century ago, all the land around me had been Brazilian badlands. A wild west, where men on horses staged gun battles on empty grassland they could buy for the price of a packet of cigarettes.

Times change. I was joined for lunch at Campo Aberto by a

dapper British financier in a blazer and panama hat. He used to be something big in Rolls-Royce, and he had just flown in with his wife to consider investing in the farm – part of a 42,000-hectare agricultural empire called Agrifirma, assembled by Lord Rothschild, the head of the world-famous banking family, and the once-notorious 1970s corporate raider Jim Slater. The incorrigible pair, both past their 75th birthdays, were betting their profits from a successful speculation in gold and uranium on Brazilian agriculture.

We were in the heart of the *cerrado*, the most biologically rich savannah grassland in the world, in what was once the outback of Brazil. But the lawless days are disappearing, and with them the bio-diversity. For this land is turning into one of the most unremitting commercialized monocultures on Earth. It is the first place in the tropics to successfully recreate on a large scale the high-tech, high-input, high-investment farming system pioneered in the American prairies. In recent years, the place has out-invested the prairies, with its endless fields of GM maize, soya, cotton and coffee. Even more than the black earths of Eastern Europe, the financiers say, this is the future of farming.

The *cerrado* was an enormous patchwork of tall, waving grass-land dotted with dry woods. It occupied an area approaching a quarter of Brazil – 2 million square kilometres of the high plains on the Atlantic side of the Amazon basin. It teemed with unusual mammals, including armadillos, anteaters, tapirs and maned wolves. There were thousands of endemic plants, uniquely adapted to drought and fire. These ecological riches were harvested, but rarely destroyed, by bands of Indians.

It took a long time for Europeans to penetrate Brazil's empty heart. The soils of the *cerrado* were deep, well drained and under-lain by abundant reserves of water. But they were too acid to grow most crops. So the land was either left alone or given over to extensive ranches, with the existing grasses nibbled at by cattle.

Even after the 1960s, when Brazil built its shiny modernist capital Brasilia in the middle of the *cerrado*, the farm invasion was slow. But in the last 30 years, all that has changed. More than 60 per cent of the *cerrado* – an area the size of Britain, France and Germany combined – has disappeared under the plough. The ecological consequences are huge.

Brazil is justly proud of how much it has reduced deforestation in the Amazon. Rates of forest loss fell by 70 per cent between 2004 and 2010. Companies that process products made at the expense of the Amazon are ostracized. The world's largest producer of beef, JBS-Fribol, has agreed to stop buying cattle from ranches associated with illegal deforestation in the Amazon. The country's biggest bank, Banco dá Brasil, has been sued by state prosecutors in Pará for making loans that broke conservation laws. But the saving of the Amazon has been accomplished at a high price – the invasion of a new ecological frontier of almost equal importance.

As the country's ploughs have moved south and east, the *cerrado* has suffered. In recent years its grasses and woodlands have been disappearing twice as fast as the Amazon rainforest. But so far the outrage has been minimal. Investor literature in London and New York and Chicago notes with anticipation that Brazil still has more uncultivated land than the European Union has cultivated land. It declares that, since the Amazon is no longer the target, uncultivated land can be ploughed up at no ecological cost. Half of it is in the *cerrado*.

What transformed the *cerrado* from badlands to agricultural bonanza? Science. In the 1970s, Brazilian government researchers worked out how to farm the *cerrado* soils. The solution was to apply industrial quantities of lime to neutralize the acid – typically five tonnes per hectare. By the early 1980s, the soils were being transformed. Pioneers began arriving. At first, they were often bandits. But eventually the government quelled the land wars and, with cheap credit and other inducements, persuaded farmers to move in.

Most were from the far south of the country, and of German, Italian or Japanese descent. They were attracted by cheap land. For every hectare they sold in the south, these 'gauchos' could buy 10 to 40 hectares in the *cerrado*. The Brazilian scientists encouraged them to plant soya, a crop native to Korea and Japan that they had successfully bred for the tropics. But with time the smaller farms have been amalgamated or bought out by big farmers.

'I was brought up in Mato Grosso,' says Valmir Ortega, *cerrado* director for the environment group Conservation International, which is working to protect the region's ravaged grasslands. 'I can remember as a child seeing the first soya. Before that, the land was cattle range. At first there were a lot of small farmers, but now those colonizers are being forced out. It's the big guys now.'

Other people have been forced out, too, as the big farmers have consolidated their rule in the *cerrado*. The indigenous inhabitants of the region – the Tupi, Botocudos, Cariris and Xavante – were gradually corralled into a handful of small reserves that today, as University of Iowa anthropologist Laura Graham puts it, 'seem like islands in a sea of soy'. Cut off from their hunting grounds, they are at the mercy of gangmasters from the big farms. They are the forgotten people of Brazil. Most Brazilians only know the name Cariris as a brand of flip flops.

For many years, Mato Grosso was the front-line state for the invasion of the *cerrado*. Soya production there increased fivefold between 1985 and 1995. Two cousins became the world's largest soya growers. Blairo Maggi, head of the Amaggi Group, and Erai Maggi Scheffer at the Grupo Bom Futuro, now farm about half a million hectares between them. Their blitzkrieg was part-funded by the International Finance Corporation, the private lending arm of the World Bank, and a $230-million loan from European banks, including the Dutch Rabobank and HSBC.

Blairo Maggi became governor of Mato Grosso from 2003 to 2010, and is now its senator in Brasilia. The clearing of forests and grasslands in the state reached a peak after he became governor. With backing from commodities giants like Cargill and Bunge, he pushed through a plan to pave 1,600 kilometres of highway from his state to the Amazon river port of Santarém, where Cargill built a soy handling dock. Soya farms spread all along the road. The Maggi family benefited hugely. Conflict of interest? Maggi replied from the governor's office: 'It's no secret that I want to build roads and expand agricultural production. The people voted for that, so I don't see the problem.' And he famously told the *New York Times*: 'To me, a 40-per-cent increase in deforestation doesn't mean anything at all, and I don't feel the slightest guilt over what we are doing here. We're talking about an area larger than Europe that has barely been touched, so there is nothing at all to get worried about.' Some say he has gone green of late. The Amaggi group is in the forefront of the new Round Table on Responsible Soy. But it is too late for Mato Grosso.

The Maggi soya revolution has made Mato Grosso the biggest magnet in Brazil for foreign investors. A fifth of the state is now foreign-owned. But what happened there is now happening across the rest of the *cerrado*. There has been nothing like it in the world in the past 20 years. Brazilian agribusiness is the world's largest market for agricultural machinery, and most of the equipment is destined for the *cerrado*. The *cerrado* produces 70 per cent of Brazil's crops. Much of the maize grown there is consumed in Brazil, and the sugar cane often goes to fill the tanks of the country's ethanol-fuelled vehicles. But the soya, cotton, coffee and other crops largely go for export. Thanks to the *cerrado*, Brazil is the world's largest exporter of soya, beef, chicken, sugar, ethanol, tobacco and orange juice. They call it Soylandia now.

But don't be misled. Brazilians don't eat the produce from the rape of the *cerrado*. According to Conservation International's environmental policy director, Paulo Gustavo Prado, 'some 60 per cent of Brazil's basic foodstuffs still come from *campesinos* farming fewer than 20 hectares. Big farms are for export.' And that raises important questions when many see the industrializing of the *cerrado* as a model for transforming Africa's huge expanses of unploughed and unfenced savannah grasslands. If it is, then the model won't feed starving Africans. The contrasts between rich and poor in the *cerrado* and across Brazil are extreme, and seem to grow as the agricultural economy booms. The disparities that could arise in Africa could be a whole lot worse.

The Mato Grosso is lost. So I spent a week visiting giant industrial farms along the new agribusiness highway through western Bahia in northeast Brazil. The distances are huge, and so are the farms. The scenery is less than bucolic. You don't see many trees. What you do see is a constant stream of signboards beside fields, advertising the latest strains of agrochemicals being sprayed or seeds being planted: Bayer's soya, Syngenta's maize or Du Pont's Pioneer Hi-Bred cotton.

Agrifirma's Campo Aberto farm is the largest of three farms owned across the *cerrado* by Rothschild and his partners. To find it, I drove for three hours from Barreiras, the bustling agribusiness capital of western Bahia, and then a further 40 kilometres down a rutted track shared by a host of other farmers. I was greeted by the company operations manager, Rodrigo Rodrigues, an engaging and confident technocrat in his 30s, who is in charge of the place. I hadn't imagined the septuagenarian financiers did much farming themselves.

Rodrigues is from a well-to-do farming family. His father, Roberto, was a sugar cane producer in São Paulo state. He pioneered growing sugar to make ethanol for biofuels, and then became the first minister of agriculture under President Lula da Silva in 2003.

Rodrigo lives in São Paulo and runs his own farms in three states, as well as supervising the British investment. One of the four Cessnas sitting on the airstrip behind the hacienda was his. I discovered that Rodrigo once owned Campo Aberto himself. He had bought it from Milton Da Silva, the wealthy landowning father of the Formula One champion Ayrton Senna, reorganized it and sold it to the British high-rollers in 2008. For a tidy profit, I imagine.

'Farming is a factory without a roof,' Rodrigues said proudly as we headed out after lunch to view the fields. He grows soya, maize and cotton, in strict rotation. That's normal here. But he prides himself on fine-tuning the system, constantly testing different combinations of seeds, chemicals and planting regimes. He had the data at his fingertips: the pH of any patch of soil, rainfall for every day the crops had been in the ground, what chemicals had been added, and their impact on the chemical composition of the soil.

Like most farmers on the *cerrado*, he was growing GM crops, like maize and soya. He was proud of his yields. His 10.5 tonnes of maize per hectare was close to American standards. 'When I graduated from college in 1997 we thought five tonnes was good,' he said. But he was more concerned about his bottom line. 'Last year we lost money, so we are trying to keep the same yield now with fewer inputs and using less machinery. My aim is to economize, not maximize.'

Was he a landgrabber? He didn't see things that way. After all, whatever the cowboys got up to in the past, stealing land from the Indians and ploughing up the wildlife, he had simply bought the farm from Da Silva and sold it to British investors. Yes, he agreed, there were indigenous communities living near the farm. Yes, they were its former inhabitants. But he had commissioned an anthropologist to tell him their needs. He held a Christmas party for their children, even if he was frustrated that some of them 'stole the presents'. He offered them the chance to grow food for the company canteen, though 'they didn't respond.'

He hired them to work on the farm too, 'when we can; when they are qualified'. But the jobs were limited. Agrifirma's high-tech farms have only 180 staff to run 42,000 hectares. That is fewer than one employee for every 200 hectares. He said he had given the local communities help in getting formal title to land they currently occupied. How much land was that? Some 500 hectares – for 300 people. That ought to be, as he said, 'enough to grow their own food'. But it was a tiny fraction of the size of the farm and of what they must have had before. He aspired, he said, to deliver 'the 3 Ps: people, profit and the planet'. I am pleased he thinks about people and the planet, but profits come first. Rothschild and Slater, I am sure, would have it no other way.

Across the table at lunch, Rodrigues's new would-be British investor had been sizing up the margins. I also sat next to a European lottery entrepreneur, spending his winnings from other people's bets by taking a flutter on another farm down the road. He said he had been introduced to the area by Rothschild. Driving back down the track to the main road, I passed a farm bought in 2007 by George Soros's Adecoagro enterprise. Adecoagro is registered in Luxembourg but has farms in Brazil, Argentina and Uruguay. It claims to be 'one of the leading companies in the production of food and renewable energy in South America'. It raised $300 million in early 2011 to buy more land and build a sugar-processing plant. The Qatar Investment Authority took a share.

Next, I retraced my steps to Barreiras, the engine room of the current assault on the *cerrado*. I wanted to discuss the ecological importance of the region with a local biology professor, Fernando Lutz. We sat in a bare lecture room on the new campus of the University of Bahia. The globalization of the *cerrado* is a tragedy for nature, he said. The world has shown its enthusiasm for saving the

Amazon, but it has ignored the fate of the *cerrado*. It contains a third of all Brazilian biodiversity, including some 10,000 plant species, more than 4,000 of them found nowhere else.

Or at least it used to. For the high plateaus of the *cerrado*, which are the most biodiverse, have proved the most tempting for farmers. The best is already gone.

Lutz planned a three-year expedition to explore, metre by metre, a 75-kilometre cross-section of the district of Formosa do Rio Preto, just north of Barreiras, to find out what it still contained. But he had better be quick, said Flavio Marques, an environmental adviser to the Bahia state prosecutor, whom I met across town later that afternoon. Marques was sitting in front of a giant floor-to-wall satellite image of western Bahia. Green slivers of natural *cerrado* vegetation followed some river valleys. But elsewhere, and particularly in the plateau close to the border with neighbouring Tocantins, including Formosa do Rio Preto, the colouring was almost universally pink. Pink denoted crops.

The fastest loss of *cerrado* today is in Formosa do Rio Preto, he said. More than 200,000 hectares disappeared to agriculture in that district alone between 2002 and 2008. I didn't need telling why. As we spoke, trucks from all over the district were lining up nearby to empty its latest harvest into Cargill's soya-collecting silos.

Marques told me he was in charge of imposing in western Bahia the minimum environmental standards required by Brazil's long-standing forest code. The code said that developers in the *cerrado* should leave 20 per cent of the land intact as 'legal reserves'. But he was in despair. Three years before, he had sent out a letter asking all farmers of more than 5,000 hectares to show him details of their legal reserves. So far, he told me, only a tenth of them had bothered to reply. 'The majority of them don't have legal reserves, but they think they can get away with it,' he said. They are probably right. 'The state of Bahia often offers amnesties. The private landowners have traditionally done whatever they want here.'

Brazilian farmers freely admit they have never followed the law. Indeed during a high-profile campaign against the code in 2011, that admission became part of their case for changing it. 'What is important is that 90 per cent of Brazil's farmers [should] no longer be considered illegal,' the Brazilian Confederation of Agriculture and Livestock said. 'If all rural producers are unable to comply, the problem cannot lie with them.' And they won the argument. In May 2011, the Brazilian Chamber of Deputies voted overwhelmingly to approve a drastically watered-down code. It sent the new code to President Dilma Rousseff for approval. She had supported the old code, and seemed uncertain how to respond. In the hiatus, Brazilian farmers continued to ignore it.

If the code goes, said Lutz, 'the consequences for the *cerrado* will be very bad.' But then he surprised me. For there was another, more troubling side to the code, he said. If landowners kept reserves at all, they were often the places where they dumped traditional communities and sited encampments for their farm workers. They were often the only place that these marginalized people had left to grow crops to feed their families. He conceded that 'strict policing of the environmental laws would, in practice, damage the lives of the poorest – the occupiers of the legal reserves'.

It was a familiar story that I heard in country after country: the poor being squeezed between commercial farmers and the demands of conservationists. But sometimes 'squeezed' isn't the right word. It was far worse than that, said Marques. He mentioned the troubling case of a huge 295,000-hectare farm, the Condomínio Cachoeira do Estrondo, on the soya front line in Formosa do Rio Preto. The farm was, he said, the biggest landholding in Bahia and, until recently, far from official oversight on the border with Tocantins.

The land occupied by the farm used to be the home of three traditional communities, with hundreds of members. 'They owned the whole area.' Some were indigenous people, and some were residents of *quilombos*, the homes of the descendants of escaped African slaves. Then, in the 1970s, the area was bought by a businessman and real-estate owner from Rio de Janeiro called Ronald Levinsohn, who later became notorious over the collapse of a savings bank he owned. He established Condomínio Cachoeira do Estrondo, which is not so much a farm as a small state. Levinsohn 'gradually eased the former residents out, until they were housed in a few fragments of forest reserve', said Marques. Then, Levinsohn divided the giant property into more than 30 individual farm operations – condominiums, as he called them – for sale.

In recent years, as law enforcement has begun to encroach on the 'condominiums', lurid stories have surfaced about the way the farmers who run each condominium have treated employees and the people who live within and around their borders. In 2009, local newspapers reported near-slave conditions. There were, they said, 'watchtowers with armed guards at the entrance to the extensive farm'. The original inhabitants were confined to river banks, suffering violence and intimidation.

Government agencies investigated and charged gangmasters on several of the farms with running what amounted to slave camps. The gangmasters picked up women and youths as young as 16 on the street in nearby towns and from settlements near the farms. They took them to the farms, set them to work weeding the fields and accommodated them in makeshift canvas shacks without mattresses, water or sanitary facilities. Allegedly, they were held in debt bondage. They were prevented from leaving until it was time to pay their wages, from which were deducted the cost of the overpriced food and toiletries they were given at the camp. Meanwhile the federal environment agency IBAMA estimated that the farm operators between them had felled 77,000 hectares of forest between 2004 and 2006.

Levinsohn hit back. He claims to have been the first business-man to 'believe in the *cerrado*', which he had 'reclaimed from squatters and outlaws'. He compares his investment in the *cerrado* to Deng Xiaoping's work in transforming China after Mao. He is being pursued by a campaign of 'media persecution', he says.

The night after hearing these stories, I watched a DVD of *Grapes of Wrath*, the tale of sharecroppers caught up in the dust bowl that engulfed the American prairies in the 1930s, and how they were expelled to make way for big landowners who wanted to cultivate the land with one worker and a caterpillar bulldozer. At one point Tom Joad, played by Henry Fonda, rails at the injustice of a system where there is 'one guy with a million acres, and a hundred thousand farmers starving'. Times don't change much.

Two hours down the road from Barreiras is Luis Eduardo Magalhães (LEM), an even newer agricultural boomtown. According to legend, in the early 1990s the town was just a gas station run by a poacher of the giant flightless rhea birds, who live amid the grasslands. What is certain is that it has grown in a decade from nothing to a town with a population of 60,000, centred on Brazil's largest soya-processing plant, owned by commodities giant Bunge, and a John Deere dealership that sells tens of millions of dollars' worth of harvesters each year. Now Cargill is here, too. And Massey Ferguson and Mitsubishi, Syngenta seeds and Dow Agrosciences. On one side of the highway, dirt tracks lead down from truck stops to stinking barrios full of booze joints and brothels. On the other side are the paved roads, starred hotels and gated estates. In the middle is a giant bus station, from where you can go almost anywhere in this vast country.

The administrative district around LEM covers 400,000 hectares. But it has only had an environment secretary for a year. Fernanda Aguiar, who has the job, is a smart young lawyer who previously made a living representing farmers in environmental cases. She told me she had a staff of just five. 'When this town got started, they just wanted people to come and get rich quick. There were no services or planning. Things were done without any respect for the law.' A decade on, she says, 'nobody feels they belong here because nobody was born here. People have no idea about taking care of their town, let alone the *cerrado*.'

All across Aguiar's domain, the land is dominated today by big farms, locally called *fazendas*. Some have names straight out of the TV mythology of the American West, like Fazenda Chaparral and Fazenda Bonanza. Others betray the curiously cosmopolitan origins of their proprietors, like Fazenda Oriental (proprietor: Mr Ming Quang), Fazenda New Holland, Fazenda Hoshino and Fazenda Warpol, a giant spread with cotton fields that went on for miles.

The gun-toting pioneers who cleared this land have mostly gone, selling out to a new generation of well-heeled entrepreneurs and agribusiness corporations. But fortunes have been made by those who stayed. Men like Levinsohn in Formosa do Rio Preto and his buddy Walter Horita, a Japanese-Brazilian who staked his claim back in 1984, right after bandits had murdered a neighbour. Today, Horita and his two brothers grow cotton on most of their 45,000 hectares.

South of LEM, on the road to Brasilia, I pulled up at the São Sebastião Farm. A red crop-spraying plane buzzed around as Anildo Kurek, a Brazilian of Dutch extraction, told me how he began here in 1989, at the age of 35. 'Then it was still all natural *cerrado*,' he said. He bought his first thousand hectares with bags of soya – the preferred currency in those days – paid to 'one of the earliest pioneers, who had cleared the land of bush – and people too, I expect'. Kurek came with his father-in-law and brother-in-law. 'It was an adventure. There were no roads, no water and it was hard to get fertilizer. There was no law. Well, no law enforcement anyway. No government agencies.'

Times have changed, he said. The three of them bought 20 neighbouring farms, one at a time, and created a single operation covering 23,000 hectares, which Kurek now runs with 130 full-time employees. 'We have to follow the rules now, well mostly,' he said, as we stood in one of his maize fields. Dwarfed by his crop, he was still slightly puckish, still slightly surprised at his luck in life, at the huge amount of land he controlled, and the giant harvesting equipment at his disposal.

São Sebastião felt more like a traditional farm than anything else I visited in the *cerrado*. Walking to lunch on the veranda of Kurek's hacienda, we passed chickens, a vegetable plot, a playground swing, a native tree called a *goyaba*, and a guard dog lazing in the shade. A cockerel crowed as the soya trucks headed out of the gate, destined for Bunge or Cargill.

But Kurek's neighbours were mostly from a different generation. Next door were the 22,000 hectares run by American-owned Iowa Farms, which had recently been renamed Grupo Iowa to make it sound more Brazilian. Then there were the Argentines over at Los Brobos. Would he stay? 'I live in Brasilia at the weekend now. It's a four-hour drive. And my family has gone back to the south. I've had offers for my land but I've turned them down,' he said. 'So far.' He was disappointed that none of the next generation of the family was interested in taking over. And the number of Brazilian farmers around there who might be keen to buy him out was diminishing. So who might buy when the time came? Would it be the British lords and asset strippers at Agrifirma? Or how about SLC Agricola, Brazil's largest agricultural enterprise? It already has 11 farms in the *cerrado*, covering a total of 230,000 hectares. They include the nearby Panorama Farm, which was my next stop.

SLC does smooth corporate-formula farming. Some call it the McDonaldization of agriculture – adapting the local environment to fit a standard business plan. Each of its farms runs the same cotton–soya–maize rotation, scheduled by head office a year ahead, and personally approved by its chairman and patriarch of 40 years, Eduardo Silva Logemann. Each farm is also built to a standard design, with the same recycling bins and floodlit soccer fields and internet-enabled club for employees. Panorama's manager, Marcelo Pegrow, said the farm was one of the company's newest, amalgamating three old farms that had covered 27,000 hectares. The company planned to buy or rent more neighbouring farms if the chance arose. It certainly had the cash. Since floating shares on the Brazilian stock exchange, it had doubled its turnover in four years.

The Brazilian agricultural boom just keeps on going. And the *cerrado* keeps on disappearing. The main impediment to further expansion right now, several farmers told me, was transport. Getting the crops to market is still a slow and expensive business. Rodrigues reckoned that half the cost of his soya at the coastal port of Ilheus, more than a thousand kilometres to the east, came from trucking bills. But a new 1,500-kilometre railway is being built into western Bahia, reaching Barreiras by the end of 2012 and LEM soon after. That would provide another boost to agribusiness.

So can anything hold back the tide? I had travelled with the Brasilia staff of Conservation International. They have a strategy for engaging with farmers, trying to create a coalition of those willing to comply with existing conservation laws, to protect 'legal reserves', and to establish conservation corridors across the *cerrado*. Curiously, CI's corporate partner and link to the farmers was one of the biggest beneficiaries of the agribusiness bonanza, Monsanto.

Is the strategy working? I certainly met farmers who now talk the talk – but only, they made clear, if conservation and profit can go together. And some of the effects of CI's interventions have been perverse. When I asked Kurek how his newfound respect for environmental law was going, he told me an unexpected story. CI's help with mastering the minutiae of conservation bureaucracy meant he now had an environment licence that allowed him to clear another 4,000 hectares of wild grass and bush on his land. 'We were waiting for the environmental licence before going ahead with the clearance, and CI helped us get it,' he said. Not, perhaps, what they had in mind.

But Kurek was keen to show how wildlife could thrive on his farm. 'We see maned wolves here sometimes in the maize fields,' he told me as we drove around. 'And rhea. They like the soya beans.' Right on cue, one of the large emu-like birds shot out of a soya field and ran down the track ahead of our SUV. We chased it for a mile before the exhausted bird found an exit back into the field. Nature is surviving here, but only just.

The truth is that the global market is winning every round in the fight for the *cerrado*. The soya market is booming, in particular because it is an ideal feed for the growing herds of livestock in Asia needed to satisfy soaring demand for meat and dairy products. China in particular relies on Brazilian soya. But Asian countries are no longer happy simply to buy the produce from the *cerrado*. Like their Arab counterparts, they no longer trust the markets to meet their needs, and want to control the supply chain.

Tough new Brazilian rules on land ownership by foreigners may cramp their style a little. But there are ways round the problem. In early 2011, the giant Japanese trading house Mitsui bought control of the Swiss-based grain broker Multigrain. Mitsui said the purpose was 'to ensure stable supplies of grains from Brazil for the Asian market [at a time of escalating] global competition for crop land'. Multigrain had purchase contracts, but it also had some 100,000 hectares of farmland in the *cerrado* that would help Mitsui meet its target of securing access to 10 per cent of Brazil's total soya exports. Weeks later, the Korea Agro-Fisheries Trade Corporation, which has been charged by the South Korean government with helping secure the country's grain supplies, was in Bahia talking to Cooproeste, a state farm producers' cooperative, about a joint venture. And the Chinese were not far behind.

At Barreiras airport, I was waiting for the commuter flight back to Brasilia, known to locals as the 'agribusiness express'. Suddenly, a small chartered plane landed and a delegation of more than 20 Chinese piled out. They explained that they were from the Chongqing Grain Group. They had crossed the world with $2.4 billion to spend on setting up a plant in the city to process 1.5 billion tonnes of soya beans a year. Once in operation, it would displace Bunge's LEM operation as Brazil's largest soya-processing plant, and could handle half the state's current soya harvest. Local officials were there to meet them. It looked like a done deal.

The Portuguese word *cerrado* literally translates as 'closed' or 'inaccessible'. But now that the *cerrado* is open and accessible, it looks doomed.

11

CHACO, PARAGUAY

Chaco apocalíptico

Our six-seater Cessna took off at dawn from Asunción, the capital of Paraguay. Stretching north and west for a thousand kilometres was a plain as flat as a tabletop, covered in dense thorn forest, some of it only ever penetrated by local indigenous tribes. The Paraguayan Chaco is the last great wilderness in South America. If you have never heard of it, you won't be alone. Despite occupying almost two-thirds of the country, it is *terra incognita* even to most

Paraguayans. I had come across the border from Brazil to see where Brazilian ranchers are going, now that expansion in the Amazon is frowned on and they are being priced out of the *cerrado* by the soya boom.

The Chaco thorn forests have many of the odd creatures that live in the neighbouring *cerrado*, like giant anteaters, tapirs and maned wolves. But they have some more of their own, including no fewer than eight species of armadillo, and the Chacoan peccary, a prehistoric pig-like creature that was known only by fossilized skeletons till someone stumbled on a live animal out there in 1975. The plant life beneath us as we flew on was equally mysterious. Besides the ubiquitous thickets of squat bushes with vicious thorns, there were giant cacti and bottle-shaped trees, whose trunks hold moisture like a camel's hump.

The Chaco is more ancient and bizarre than the Amazon. Toby Pennington of Edinburgh's Royal Botanic Garden calls it a 'museum of diversity, a refuge over millions of years for species adapted to its unique environment'. It is one of the few places on the planet where the region between the tropical and temperate zones is occupied not by desert, but by thick vegetation. And it has, perhaps as a result, some of the most extreme weather on earth, combining torrid 50-degree summers with below-freezing winters, and searing droughts with extensive floods.

All this has made the biology different, and human invasion perilous. Until now. For the Chaco is changing fast. The thorns and the climatic extremes are losing their power to protect it from the modern world. The landgrabbers have made it even here.

I spent nine hours flying low over the Chaco with conservationists from Guyra Paraguay, an NGO that is recording the escalating destruction, and Britain's World Land Trust, which is funding the purchase of land to protect it. The need is urgent. A few minutes into the flight, we began seeing huge straight-edged lumps taken out of the forest, revealing bare earth. There were bulldozers at work below, and the smouldering remains of fires. In places there were new pastures, often seeded with alien, fast-growing grass imported from the African savannah. We could see scattered cattle grazing.

As we flew on, the farms grew bigger. Ninety minutes out, there was a single spread covering 50,000 hectares, rather larger than the Isle of Wight. It was laid out in 500 rectangles of cleared land separated by thin strips of trees, so it looked like a giant's paved pathway across the forest. Soon after came another 10,000-hectare gash in the forest, all cleared in the previous year. I was reminded of what Pennington had told me before I left for Paraguay. 'Without knowing it, we could be losing a flora that is not just incredibly evolutionarily distinct, but of vital importance. The Chaco is a forgotten forest that we know next to nothing about. At a time when we fear climate change, it seems especially crazy to be losing species that are obviously incredibly well adapted to extreme climate.'

The Chaco forest once extended north to Bolivia and Brazil, meeting the *cerrado* in southern Mato Grosso, and south deep into Argentina. It covered 1.3 million square kilometres, five times the size of Britain. But it was gradually eaten away by farmers. Most of what survived into the twenty-first century was its thickest, hottest, most distinctive and most forbidding heart – in Paraguay, where it covers two-thirds of the country but contains just 3 per cent of its population. Now that heartland too is under threat. Not in the main from locals, who still hate the place, but from foreign landgrabbers.

Since 2003, Brazilian cattle ranchers have been crossing the border into Paraguay in ever larger numbers. Called Brasiguayos by the Paraguayans, many are German speakers from the south of Brazil. At home, they are selling their ranches for thousands of dollars a hectare to agribusinesses that want to plant them with soya, cotton and maize. In the Paraguayan Chaco, they can still buy land for less than $300 a hectare.

As a result, the Chaco is changing fast. Paraguay's largest national park, the once-remote 760,000 hectares of the Defensores del Chaco, home to uncontacted bands of Ayoreo Indians, is now entirely ringed by a road from which new ranches sprout. Since the 1990s, deforestation rates across the Paraguayan Chaco have risen from virtually zero to more than a thousand hectares a day, or a soccer pitch every 90 seconds. More than a fifth of the Chaco administrative department of Alto Paraguay has been turned into giant ranches.

From above, you see the big landscape changes, as the mass application of land-clearing equipment makes bizarre excavations of the natural forest. You would not know that anyone lived there before the ranchers arrived. But they did, and do. And for them, it is the details that count. 'On the white men's maps, no one has ever mentioned the Ayoreo,' says Mateo Sobode Chiquenoi, president of the Union of the Native Ayoreo of Paraguay. 'But we can locate our territories on a map. We cannot show a land title, but there are still signs of our presence from the past and from today, which prove that it is our territory. There are our huts, our paths, our crops planted in the forest, and the holes carved in the trees from where we harvested honey. These are our property documents.'

We landed at a grass airstrip on a Brazilian ranch not far from the new road to the national park. The road was busy with cattle trucks, and there wasn't a thorn tree for miles. Mosquitoes buzzed in the noonday sun. But their targets these days were humans and cattle, rather than wildlife. I asked who owned the ranch. It turned out that is a question visitors are not supposed to ask. Many of the new landowners here are anonymous. A loophole in Paraguayan land law means ownership doesn't have to be declared. That loophole allows the big boys to escape rules intended to prohibit large landholdings. It also means estimates that 90 per cent of the new ranches in the Paraguayan Chaco are owned by foreigners cannot be verified. But my impression was that much of the northernmost 200 kilometres of Paraguay is now, in all but name, part of Brazil.

The Paraguayan Chaco has a brutal and bizarre history. The country's generals fought a war here against Bolivia in the 1930s, after Bolivia had invaded in search of oil. By the time the combatants went home, more exhausted than defeated, almost one in 30 Paraguayans had died defending a land where none of them lived. The preposterous conflict was satirized in Hergé's Tintin adventure *The Broken Ear*. Even today, there is only one road through the Chaco. Constructed in the 1960s, the Trans-Chaco Highway runs straight as a die for 900 kilometres from Asunción to the Bolivian border. It is paved now for three-quarters of the way. As far as Mariscal Estigarribia, where in the 1980s the US military constructed an airstrip 3.5 kilometres long – enough for the biggest military transport plane to land.

Our Cessna touched down at one end of the runway, feeling very small to me. While we refuelled, I could see the strip might be handy for an assault on the stroppy leaders of Bolivia. But I can report that the rumours of a permanent US military garrison at Mariscal Estigarribia are false, unless they are camped out in the bush with the Indians. The only evidence of life of any kind was an aircraft filling station smaller than the average roadside petrol station, and a guy in fatigues who arrived out of nowhere on a motorbike to check our ID. (In another blow for conspiracy theorists, persistent stories that George W. Bush bought a giant piece of land hereabouts also seem to be untrue. A former US ambassador, Timothy Towell, did buy the 70,000-hectare Fortín Patria ranch in the far northeastern Chaco. Some of the Bush family visited it. But locals say the ranch was then purchased by a Washington environmentalist, who got bored and sold it to a Paraguayan newspaper magnate.)

One group of outsiders did set up here in the Chaco, however, long before the Brazilian ranchers rode in. Back down the Trans-Chaco Highway from Mariscal Estigarribia are three isolated colonies occupied by German-speaking Mennonites. The Christian Anabaptist sect came to the Chaco more than 80 years ago, from scattered homes in Ukraine, Russia, Canada and later Mexico. At the invitation of the Paraguayan president, they took over 56,000 hectares of the most remote part of the Chaco, an area their own chroniclers described as a 'green hell'.

The Mennonites had been on the move for centuries, because they would not give their loyalty to any nation. They shunned military service and even refused to send their children to public schools. They became international nomads. But that independent spirit proved no problem in the Chaco, where the Paraguayan state was effectively non-existent anyway. In effect, the Mennonites set up a state within a state. It wasn't easy. In the early years, they suffered typhoid epidemics, droughts, plagues of grasshoppers, and invasions of soldiers demanding provisions en route to fighting Bolivia. But they persevered, setting up schools and hospitals and factories. And buying more land.

Their main town, Filadelfia, appears like a mirage in the thorn bush. Though it has only 10,000 people, it is still the biggest place for 400 kilometres. It is, by its own lights, a success. After decades of poverty and deprivation, the fierce Mennonite devotion to taming the Chaco has brought dividends. The main streets, such as Avenida Hindenberg, are wide enough to turn an ox cart, but this is Land Cruiser territory now. Filadelfia is one of the most prosperous towns in Paraguay, full of air conditioners and four-by-fours. The big-box store still has a wide range of farm implements, but they are being pushed aside by garden furniture and barbecues. The agricultural college boasts a Conservatorio de Música on the side.

Filadelfia's museum celebrates both the Mennonites' past and the wildlife that they are continuing to destroy. I spent an hour exploring one room full of stuffed armadillos and boa constrictors; skunks and red-bellied toads; a giant anteater and a two-metre caiman; a maned wolf as big as the jaguar and a greater rhea as tall as a man; a bizarre range of rodents and a rare Chacoan peccary. Another room displayed mementoes from the Mennonites' former lives, including Russian fur overcoats, delicate Chinese porcelain and a German trombone. There was a picture of a tree trunk that someone had hollowed out to make a child's coffin during the typhoid epidemic of 1927. Poignant group shots of migrants on their way to the Chaco in 1930 showed children with downturned mouths, women looking wry and sad, and strong-jawed men with scared eyes.

Filadelfia's Mennonite farms and factories now attract other Paraguayans and indigenous Indians to provide labour. But the pecking order on the streets seems pretty clear. When the factory hooter at the dairy sounds at 7am, the white-skinned Mennonites drive their Mercedes out of their compounds on the north side of town, Spanish-speaking Paraguayans buzz about on motorbikes, and the indigenous people walk from their barrios.

It would be churlish to deny that the Mennonites have earned a place in the Chaco. They were the first outsiders to figure out how to raise cattle here. They now graze and till an estimated two million hectares. They produce two-thirds of Paraguay's milk and much of its meat. They export to Bolivia, and even have a Tetra Pak plant. In the eyes of most Paraguayans, they have ceased to be bizarre aliens in an even more bizarre wasteland. They have become the pioneers of a new wave of commercialized cattle ranching, joined by many fellow German-speaking ranchers from Brazil to create a new front line of Latin American agriculture in one of the continent's most forbidding environments.

But equally we cannot forget that the land taken over by the Mennonites was never empty. A picture in the Filadelfia museum, dated 1931, shows a meeting of Mennonites and unnamed natives in the Chaco. The natives are near-naked and carrying spears and bows and arrows. The Mennonites wear panama hats, white shirts, bow ties and even a tuxedo. In these encounters, the Mennonites presumed they were in charge. But while some of them said the Indians should be 'located in remote protectorates where the savages could live unmolested in their original ignorance of the whites', others thought that they should be educated and forced into a sedentary life. As the Mennonites themselves took ever more land and needed labourers, the latter view won out. Through the mid-twentieth century, most of the indigenous people were lured from their land by missionaries, and bundled by gangmasters into shanty settlements, work camps and worse.

Today, several thousand Ayoreo, along with other tribal groups such as the Enxet and Sanapaná, live in roadside camps dotted among the Mennonite villages. Of the 18 Ayoreo settlements in Paraguay, thirteen are in the Mennonite zone, mostly created by the evangelist New Tribes Mission at Campo Loro, north of Filadelfia. Last time I checked its website, the New Tribes Mission had 72 conspicuously pale-faced and mostly American missionaries in the country. Most of the Ayoreo in their charge work on the Mennonite farms.

Some isolated groups of Indians remain in the bush. Of the 2,000 or so Ayoreo in the Paraguayan Chaco, some 100–200 are wandering hunter-gather families who remain uncontacted, a term that in reality usually just means they live apart from people other than their own kind. But, often lacking immunity to common diseases, they are immensely vulnerable to almost any contact with white people. And the outside world is closing in. Our Cessna flew over a giant ranch covering some 78,000 hectares, owned by a Brazilian company called Yaguareté Porã. Local NGOs, backed by Survival International, accuse the company of invading and clearing forest claimed by a branch of the Ayoreo known as the Totobiegosode, or 'people of the peccaries'. An uncontacted band there reportedly hunts wild pigs and tortoises, and grows beans and melons on small plots within earshot of the company's bulldozers.

In 2010, when the company's invasion gained international publicity, executives acknowledged the presence of the Ayoreo. They did not deny converting thousands of hectares of their forests into cattle pastures. But they said they were going to leave a third of the land as a nature reserve in which the Ayoreo would be free to hunt and fish. As I write, the dispute remains unresolved. But meanwhile, immediately to the south of the Yaguareté Porã ranch, another Brazilian company, called River Plate, had by April 2011 bulldozed almost 4,000 hectares of a newly purchased 22,000-hectare tract of forest. This land is also claimed by the Totobiegosode. Paraguayan officials said they regarded River Plate's felling as illegal, since the company did not have a licence.

According to a study by the Union of the Native Ayoreo of Paraguay, other uncontacted groups of Ayoreo live on other land recently occupied by Brazilian ranching companies. Those companies include Ganadera Umbu, which has a licence to deforest 24,000 hectares, and Los Molinos, which is at work on the northern boundary of the Defensores del Chaco national park. The leader of a group of Totobiegosode that emerged from the bush in 2004 said: 'When we were in the forest things were good. But we could not stay because the whites have cut everything. The whites are violent. They just want land. We are afraid of them because they are very aggressive.' Savages.

Some tribal groups are fighting back against the grabbers of their land. They are taking their cases to the Inter-American Court of Human Rights, based in Costa Rica. The court has handed down a series of judgments against the Paraguayan government, and there are signs that ministers in Asunción are taking notice. In 2010, following a 19-year legal battle and five years after a final ruling by the court, the government bought a 10,000-hectare ranch from a private owner to house 65 dispossessed Enxet families. And 66 Sanapaná families, who have won a ruling from the same court, hope they may now get the 11,000 hectares they claim. The government's 2011 budget also included money to buy 98,000 hectares for the Totobiegosode clan of the Ayoreo.

It is progress. But the 50 different clans of the Ayoreo, including the Totobiegosode, between them claim the majority of the Chaco – tens of thousands of square kilometres, stretching north from the Mennonite colonies into Bolivia, and east to the River Paraguay. Many outsiders will say that such small numbers of people have no right to such large areas of land in our crowded, modern world. But why should a handful of Brazilian ranchers have the land, whereas a handful of native families cannot? Who is really being greedy?

Some parts of the Chaco forests are, for now, being preserved. As we flew north towards the Bolivian border, the ranches suddenly gave way to a big patch of forest stretching towards the horizon. It measured roughly 90 kilometres by 40 kilometres. 'That's the Moonies' land,' shouted Oscar Rodas, habitats coordinator for Guyra Paraguay, sitting beside me in the Cessna. Sun Myung Moon's South Korea-based Holy Spirit Association for the Unification of World Christianity has over the past two decades amassed 800,000 hectares of forest, both here and across the River Paraguay in Brazil's Pantanal swamp.

Groups of mostly Japanese and Korean Moonies are setting up small communities amid the thorns and mosquitoes. One is at the tiny river port of Puerto Leda, where they have also constructed a

VIP mansion reserved for visits by the Reverend Moon himself. They grow crops, largely for their own consumption. They maintain their borders and defend their property with large dogs. As ever in this part of the world, there are bizarre theories about the Moonies being engaged in drug-running and right-wing conspiracies. Moon calls his Latin American domain 'the best place to practise heavenly life on Earth'. But what that practice involves remains unclear. Maybe not even the reverend has figured that out.

Soon, we spotted an old railway snaking through the Moonies' forest. This land was, until 2000, owned by descendants of a swash-buckling Spanish-born Argentine called Carlos Casado. He bought more than five million hectares back in 1886. A lot of Paraguay was up for sale then. The country had contrived to go to war against Brazil, Argentina and Uruguay all at once. A staggering 90 per cent of its adult males are said to have perished. After finally admitting defeat, the bankrupt government sold millions of hectares of public land to foreign investors to pay off its debts.

For a century, Casado stripped his forest of an endemic Chaco tree with extremely hard wood. It is known locally as *quebracho*, meaning axe-breaker. The wood contains lots of tannin, which is used for tanning leather. The 150-kilometre narrow-gauge railway moved logs out of the forest to the tannin factory in the estate town, Puerto Casado. The accessible *quebracho* trees on the estate are gone now, and the railway is abandoned. But the 6,000 residents of Puerto Casado were furious when they discovered in 2000 that the Moonies had taken over their town. The Paraguayan Senate ordered that the town be returned to the residents. But that decision was overturned by the Supreme Court. In 2009, the Moonies handed back some land, but the battle continues.

At least the Moonies' purchase has protected the forest from further clearance by ranchers. And there is good news too upstream at the 4,400-hectare Cardozo estate, 40 kilometres west of the sleepy river port of Bahia Negra. Much of the estate remains intact *quebracho* forest, but the owner agreed to sell up to conservationists from Guyra Paraguay and the World Land Trust. We flew low as the Trust's Roger Wilson checked the tree cover. It was, he said, 'due diligence' before the purchase went ahead in June 2011. The signing was a relief for him. A previous purchase at nearby Puerto Ramos had failed when they were outbid, at the last moment, by a land company called Scimitar Oryx, headed by a former senior agriculture official in the Uruguayan government and a young British investor called Stephan Winkler. (The company also has land in Nigeria, Zimbabwe and Vietnam.) Part of the cost of the Cardozo estate is being paid by Swire, a British shipping company that also owns the airline Cathay Pacific, in return for voluntary carbon offsets.

Can conservation be reconciled with the demands of indigenous groups? If sensibly managed, it should be. After all, the tribes of the Chaco have a long history of protecting their environment. They are the only people who truly know how to live there. Before buying the Cardozo estate, Wilson reached an agreement with the 1,500 or so Ishir fishing people, who live along the west bank of the River Paraguay. They still use spears to fish, and bows and arrows to hunt. Guyra Paraguay and the Ishir will manage the forest jointly for 20 years, after which the Ishir will assume full title, on the understanding that the forest is maintained.

Sadly, however, not everyone conserving the forest wants to make friends with the former custodians. The Ishir are in a bitter dispute with the Moonies, whose territory includes Ishir sacred burial grounds near Puerto Leda. Cándido Martínez, an Ishir community leader from Bahia Negra, told me: 'Those cemeteries are our most precious land. We are not even allowed to visit them.' So much, you might say, for the Moonies' view of 'heavenly life on Earth'.

But the Ishir are resourceful. They want to live in the real world, not a mythical past. And they make friends. More than a century ago, a Czech cactus-collector and ethnographer called Alberto Vojtech Fric visited their community on the banks of the River Paraguay. His romance with a young Ishir woman called Lora-y, or Black Duck, produced a child. That child, Martínez said proudly, was his grandmother. She only died in 2010, at the age of 104. After Fric returned home, he stood up at a conference in Vienna in 1908 to denounce German settlers in Brazil and Paraguay, exposing how they hired killers to eradicate the Indians, then enslaved their children and grabbed their land. Fric went back to Paraguay, taking medicine for a disease then decimating the tribe. The Ishir still remember him and maintain links with the Czechs. Now they have persuaded some British greens to buy back forest for them. They are survivors, I would say.

Back in Asunción, it still seemed to me that the odds were heavily stacked against both the Chaco and its traditional custodians. The commercial pressures to clear the thorn forests are intense. Paraguay is determined to compete with Brazil, Argentina and Uruguay in the booming market for agricultural commodities. The country has trebled its beef exports in the past decade. The cattle herd in the Chaco has risen to almost four million. And achieving that has taken a lot of land. Ranchers currently clear almost three hectares of the Chaco to sustain one cow. And stocking rates are falling as they clear more remote, drought-prone and waterlogged land. While paying lip service to protecting the Chaco and its indigenous inhabitants, the Paraguayan government continues to approve almost all proposals to clear the forest and extend the ranches.

Not everyone, even within government, approves of this. When I met the chief environmental prosecutor from the attorney general's office, José Luis Casaccia, he was angry. Ministers neither knew nor cared what happened in the Chaco, he said. He was just back in Asunción from a boat trip up the River Paraguay, which sounded like the plot of the film *Apocalypse Now*. 'There is a complete lack of government there,' he said. 'The ranchers on their huge estates make their own laws. They pay hunters $200 for a dead jaguar or puma, because they want to protect their cattle. It's all illegal. The animals are protected. But the Chaco is a no-man's-land. Anything goes.'

Casaccia was briefly minister for the environment himself. But he said the current president, Fernando Lugo, removed him soon after taking office in 2008. Casaccia's crime had been to suspend licences to clear forests in the Chaco. Casaccia said his successor 'is very weak and is doing nothing for environment protection. Right now 95 per cent of the deforestation of the Chaco is legal, because the minister has issued so many licences for ranchers to clear the land.' I asked what fate he thought awaited the Chaco. '*Apocalíptico*', he replied. 'On current trends, everything that is not protected will all be gone by 2025.' Was this a victory for the landgrabbers? Only in the short term, he said. 'They are wrecking the Chaco. It will be reduced to desert, with all the species in it lost.' Such a scenario would doom its indigenous inhabitants, too.

12

LATIN AMERICA
The new conquistadors

The British private beef combine, the Vestey Group, held out for a decade against demands from Venezuela's president Hugo Chávez that it should give up its 200,000 hectares of ranchland in the northwest of his country. Squatters came and went during that time, but the fourth generation of British corned-beef kings to raise cattle in South America stayed put. Until 2010, when the Caracas courts ruled that their hundred-year-old estates were not being fully utilized. The owners of the Fray Bentos brand finally consented to the nationalization of their local subsidiary Agroflora – or 'La compañía inglesa' as Chávez called it in weekly radio harangues against the old imperialists. The Vesteys gave up their four surviving ranches, 130,000 cattle and 5,000 buffalo to peasant farmers as part of Chávez's 'Bolivarian revolution', which has distributed more than two million hectares of large estates to landless peasants since his election in 1999. About time, too. But it was a rare victory for fairer land shares in Latin America.

The misuse and misallocation of land has been a huge issue across the continent ever since the arrival of the conquistadors half a millennium ago. The disputes intensified in the twentieth century, when the entire region became known as Uncle Sam's back yard. American fruit companies, following in the footsteps of Europeans like the Vestey family, virtually took over whole states in Central America. They created and sustained servile and corrupt governments that became known as banana republics. These days the demand is more for crack cocaine than soft fruit, but the relationship persists and the history of centuries of land-grabbing continues to loom large.

United Fruit was the creation of a boy from Brooklyn. At the age of 23, Minor Keith was working for his uncle's Tropical Trading Company, building a railroad in the Central American state of Costa Rica. It was the 1870s. The idea was to get the country's main export crop, coffee, to the Atlantic coast for export to Europe. But the jungle, the mountains and the insects made track-laying expensive, difficult and dangerous, with thousands of workers dying from malaria and yellow fever. When his uncle died, Keith took over the project. But, facing bankruptcy, he offered the Costa Rican president a deal. He had noticed how well bananas grew along the track, and how popular they were among his workers. So, he said, 'Give me land to grow more, and I will finish the railroad.' He eventually grabbed 320,000 hectares of the Costa Rican interior, filled his underused trains with bananas, and began shipping the strange new fruit to the US, where unzipping a banana proved an instant hit.

The deal, of course, was a variant on a theme popular among landgrabbers today: land in return for the promise of economic development. But bananas and railroads proved a profitable combination. Keith repeated the trick in neighbouring countries, and cemented his success with an audacious series of land purchases and corporate mergers, including the marriage with Andrew Preston's Boston Fruit and its Caribbean plantations that finally created United Fruit. By the turn of the century, Keith had hundreds of thousands of hectares of banana plantations in Colombia, Cuba, Jamaica, Nicaragua, Panama and the Dominican Republic. Fearing banana saturation in the US, he created a shipping line that gave him access to European markets. And, for an encore in the new century, he moved into Guatemala, taking over the postal service, then the telegraph lines, then the railroad and finally much of the land to grow yet more bananas.

Keith had a rival: another banana empire run out of Honduras by Samuel Zemurray, an emigrant from Russia. Following Keith's land-grabbing motif, Zemurray had persuaded the Honduran government to give him 160,000 hectares, around a quarter of the agricultural land in the tiny country, along with the railroads. Zemurray's domination of his Honduran hosts inspired O. Henry, an American writer resident there, to coin the term 'banana republic' in his 1904 book, *Cabbages and Kings*. Six years later, Zemurray seemed determined to live up to the fictional image. Fearing US bankers wanted to force Honduras to tax his business to pay off national debts, he hired mercenaries to carry out a coup that put his man, Manuel Bonilla, in charge – and secured yet more land for his company.

In 1930, following Keith's death, Zemurray's empire and Keith's United Fruit merged. The years that followed were the glory days of monopoly and profit. But, after the Second World War, rumblings of discontent and demands for land reform grew across Uncle Sam's back yard. In Guatemala, a reformist president called Jacobo Árbenz decided to take on the landed elite, including United Fruit. His reforms began by expropriating 60,000 hectares of unused land that the company held along the Atlantic coast. Zemurray was having none of it. United Fruit lobbied against Árbenz, particularly in the US where it branded him a Communist fifth columnist. The lobbying was so successful that this time the company didn't need to hire mercenaries. Instead, in 1954, in one of the more notorious cold-war episodes, the CIA sponsored a coup to get rid of Árbenz. And, no doubt coincidentally, to stifle land reforms. One of the coup's chief architects was Howard Hunt, later famous for his involvement in both the abortive Bay of Pigs invasion of Cuba in 1961 and the Watergate scandal under Richard Nixon.

There followed four decades of civil war, during which Guatemala nurtured state terror, right-wing death squads, and what amounted to genocide against Mayan indigenous groups. A US-brokered peace finally broke out in 1996. The peace accords promised land reforms. But the entrenched power of the major landowners has ensured that the reforms have never happened. Less than 2 per cent of the population still own 70 per cent of the land – bad even by Latin American standards. The world of Keith and Zemurray persists.

Today, Guatemala's fast-growing population of 16 million, half of it Mayan, is mostly penned on to ever smaller plots of land in the southern highlands, while agribusiness dominates the fertile northern lowlands. Poor farmers are often forced to become seasonal labourers on the plantations, or cross the border into Mexico in the hope of making it to the US. Guatemala is among the world's leading exporters of sugar and coffee – and of course bananas. US companies like Dole, Del Monte and United Fruit (now renamed Chiquita) are still there. Agribusiness and its representatives in parliament continue to rebuff land reforms. But there are new landgrabbers, too. Drug traffickers, made rich by the huge fortunes to be gained from selling their products to North America and Europe, have moved in from Mexico and elsewhere.

The traffickers have bought huge areas of lowland cattle ranches, both as a convenient way of laundering their profits and as a means of hiding the airstrips where cocaine going north and east can be switched from one small plane to another. The US State Department reported in 2010 that 'entire regions of Guatemala are now essentially under the control of drug trafficking organizations, the most visible of which is the Mexican group known as the Zetas.'

Thanks to a toxic mix of corruption and intimidation of officials, they enjoy a 'prevailing environment of impunity'. The land is theirs.

Along the way, drug gangs have trashed an estimated 300,000 hectares of forests. Conservationists trying to protect the giant Maya Biosphere Reserve, the conservation crown jewels in the north of the country, told the *New York Times*: 'There's traffickers, cattle ranchers, loggers, poachers and looters. All the bad guys are lined up to destroy the reserve. You can't imagine the devastation that is happening.'

Too much of Latin America is like this. And it is hard to avoid the conclusion that unfairness in the distribution of land is a central reason for it. Peasant movements demanding reform have rarely gained traction. The big landowners are bolstered by their connections to financiers, industrialists and agribusiness, and they remain in charge. Tin-pot generals and weak and unscrupulous politicians of all hues have not helped. But often, of course, the politicians and generals are big landowners themselves.

What land redistribution there has been is often being rolled back. Peru has seen a revival of mega-farms in its fertile Pacific coastal zone. Investment has surged since the repeal of 1960s land laws that limited land holdings. Today in the coastal provinces, 34 owners hold 225,000 hectares, including a series of sugar complexes that resulted from privatization of state assets. Besides domestic companies, Dallas-based Maple Energy has acquired 13,000 hectares of what it describes as scorpion-infested desert in the Chira River valley – plus exclusive use of the river's water. Maple expected to begin production of irrigated sugar to make ethanol for the US in late 2011. Altima Partners, a British-owned hedge fund, has teamed up with Peru's COMISA Corporation for a similar project on 26,000 hectares in Piura.

Next door in Bolivia, some 200 Brazilians and Argentines have in the past two decades quietly bought around half a million hectares of the giant eastern province of Santa Cruz to grow soya, and as much again for cattle ranching. In theory, the resource nationalism of Bolivia's indigenous llama-herder-turned-president, Evo Morales, should be holding back the capitalist tide. But the province's 2,000-kilometre border with Brazil is impossibly porous. And, as in Paraguay, Brazilian farmers have found that rules limiting any new land holdings to under 5,000 hectares are no impediment to buying out land-rich local elites, says Lee Mackey of the University of California at Los Angeles, who is studying how Brazil is spreading its industrialized agriculture round the tropics. Land titles are often dubious, but with prices a quarter those in Brazil, 'the profitability [for the Brazilians] is so high that in the short term it is worth the risk,' says Miguel Urioste of Fundación Tierra, a Bolivian NGO. Brazilians own a quarter of the country's soya farms, and repatriate most of their profits. The largest covers 46,000 hectares. 'There is a progressive foreign hoarding of the best agricultural land,' Urioste concluded in a report for the UN. Anti-Brazilian sentiment reached a peak in Bolivia in late 2011, when protests against a planned Brazilian-built road through indigenous territories forced Morales to abandon the project.

In the fevered environment of land grabs, there have been reports of isolated indigenous Guarani groups being subjected to forced labour on Bolivian ranches and plantations. It sounds like a reversion to the horrors of the nineteenth-century rubber boom in these parts, when what is now the Brazilian state of Acre was part of Bolivia but in practice run as an independent fiefdom by Brazilian rubber tappers. In the 1880s, a syndicate of US bankers and rubber barons tried to annex the state and turn it into what amounted to a US colony. The plan failed, but in the end Brazil bought Acre for two million pounds.

Back then, landgrabbers in the remote headwaters of the Amazon ran rubber outposts as tyrannous as anything contrived by the agents of Belgium's King Leopold in his Congo Free State in Africa. Perhaps the worst was a Peruvian rubber trader called Julio César Arana who controlled a slice of rainforest the size of Belgium, on the border between Peru and Colombia. He sent thugs through the forest setting fire to crops and raping women, as a way of intimidating the tribes into joining his rubber-tapping work camps. Once there, the men were put into chain gangs where the price of not meeting your latex quota could be death, and the women joined breeding farms to provide the next generation of slaves. By the time the camps were shut down, amid growing international scandal, an estimated 50,000 Indians had died.

In Colombia, a modern combination of cattle ranchers, cocaine barons and paramilitary groups is scarcely less toxic. A peasant army called the Revolutionary Armed Forces of Colombia (FARC), launched back in 1964, took over parts of the country in an effort to wrestle back the land from ranchers and others. Its methods were often vicious. But to defeat them, the government resorted to giving a free hand to the landed elite and some insalubrious friends. Right-wing paramilitary groups set up to fight FARC often turned out also to be drug barons.

Most notorious were the Castaño brothers, Fidel, Vicente and Carlos. They came to rule huge areas of Choco province in north-west Colombia. According to Teo Ballvé of the University of California at Berkeley, the brothers formed a paramilitary force after their rancher father was kidnapped and assassinated by FARC. Initially called the Peasant Self-Defense Forces of Cordoba and Uraba, the 8,000-strong private militia was trained by the Colombian military to conduct a 'dirty war' against FARC in the 1990s. That war involved slaughtering thousands of people suspected of harbouring FARC fighters, and the displacement of millions of others, many of them from the Afro-Colombian community of former slaves who formed the majority in Choco.

For their assistance in fighting communism, the brothers 'received generous logistical and financial support from business-men, wealthy landowners, drug traffickers and members of the army', says Ballvé. They 'bought vast estates during the narco land rush of the early 1980s. The violent momentum of their growing war machine became driven by its own internal metabolism, gain-ing vast amounts of land, businesses and weapons while eliminating political opponents and protecting their most lucrative activity, drug trafficking.'

FARC, which also came to rely on taxing coca farmers in areas under its control, is a diminished force today. But that has left the narco-militias as the big winners. Worse, Ballvé says the gangsters are now being laundered back into legitimate society through the fast-growing and lucrative oil-palm business, which the government sees as the likeliest route of recovery for an economy wrecked by decades of conflict. 'Palm is a perfect way to consolidate their militarized social control over a territory and invest capital accumu-lated from drugs into a profitable business,' says Gustavo Duncan, a security analyst in Bogotá. More than 20,000 hectares of the Afro-Colombian land in Choco's Curbarado river basin have so far been expropriated and 'carpeted with palm oil', says Ballvé.

This rebranding of the drug barons comes with some unlikely assistance. Many of those moving into palm-oil production have in recent years received financial help from USAID's anti-drug trade programme. Its Colombia Plan was intended to wean poor farmers off the cultivation of illegal crops like coca, by introducing them to other cash-generating substitutes. But, almost inevitably, the cash has often ended up in the wrong hands. Ballvé says that one recipient, to the embarrassment of USAID, was Carlos Mario

Jiménez, widely known as Macaco, who has confessed to killing many civilians in his pursuit of FARC and who is, at the time of writing, awaiting trial in Washington DC on narcotics and terrorism charges.

Maybe this is all in a good cause. In many ways Colombia is one of the more civilized countries of Latin America, with good health care and schools in much of the country. Ministers in Bogotá hope Colombia will be the next Brazil. They say four million hectares, much of it recaptured from FARC and its sympathizers, is available for legal crops now. But have they really weaned the drug barons off drugs and into legitimate agriculture? Or are they further institutionalizing the narco-state and the massive illegal land grabs that took place during the dirty war? Elisa Wiener Bravo of the International Land Coalition, which fights for the land rights of the poor, called the new concentration of land ownership in Latin America 'reminiscent of the period of the banana plantations'.

And not just reminiscent. In 2011, Comisión Intereclesial de Justicia y Paz, a Colombian human rights organization, reported that thousands of poor peasants were being recruited to invade Afro-Colombians' land in Choco to grow bananas for sale to a Medellín-based company that sells to Europe and the US. Fancy a banana, anyone?

13

PATAGONIA

The last place on Earth

Doug Tompkins and his wife Kris once sold the world backpacks, outdoor gear and high fashion. North Face and Esprit were his companies; she was CEO of eco-fashion pioneer Patagonia. Then he went on a camping holiday to Patagonia, and decided to buy the place. Well, not all of it, but he now has a chunk of the wild, empty and much mythologized 'cone' of South America that is around 250 times the size of Manhattan. And if the couple get lonely, there are plenty of similarly minded super-rich a short executive flight away. The idiosyncratic Benetton clothing family from Italy owns an even larger estate. The American media mogul Ted Turner has a patch of Patagonia ten times the size of Manhattan. Next door, when he is not supervising his Argentine vineyards, lives the Texan inheritor of a potato-crisps fortune. Then there is the hideaway Brit who made his fortune betting against his own national currency on Black Wednesday in 1992.

Patagonia occupies the emptiest, southernmost part of South America. It is the planet's most surreal backwater, but also a place of transcendent beauty: of endless fjords; of glaciers amid fungi-covered rainforests; and of Tierra del Fuego, the 'land of fire' where Charles Darwin was transfixed by super-intelligent natives. It is a land of tales about human giants, sea monsters and horned burrowing rodents that inspired my favourite travel book, Bruce Chatwin's *In Patagonia*.

There are not many places where a couple can have their own private, erupting volcano. But Doug and Kris Tompkins have one, named Chaitén, which has been spewing ash and gas since 2008. It is a thousand kilometres south of Santiago, at the farthest end of their rainforest-covered Pumalín Park. The 300,000-hectare park, with its own airstrip beside the Renihue fjord, almost divides Chile in two.

South of Pumalín Park, they had the 76,000-hectare Corcovado mountain estate – bought with close friend Peter Buckley, another rich American outdoor-loving clothes entrepreneur who became a green philanthropist – until donating it to the state. They still have an 84,000-hectare spread in the nearby Chacabuco Valley. Surrounded by glaciers, the Chacabuco sheep ranch was first fenced by one of Britain's great imperial landgrabbers. Lucas Bridges was a child of British Anglican missionaries. He grew up with the native tribes of Tierra del Fuego, an upbringing he chronicled in his

1948 book, *Uttermost Part of the Earth*. We discover more of Bridges's footprint in Zimbabwe in Chapter Twenty-three.

The Tompkins couple say that the tens of thousands of sheep on Bridges's ranch have almost turned the area to desert. So they are reducing the flocks, tearing down the fences and returning the land to wilderness. Some Chilean politicians see them as vandals for dismantling the work of the great (albeit also foreign) nation-builder. Doug calls this 'nothing more than a temporary opposition'. Conservation, he says, is 'the most elemental form of patriotism'.

Maybe, but Doug's environmentalism transcends all boundaries. Over the Andean mountains in Argentina, the couple have another series of holdings. They include El Pinalito, a reserve for pumas and other wild cats originally set up by a Briton named Peter Moore; El Rincón, a mountain summit nobody has ever climbed; almost 200,000 hectares of the Ibera swamp in the Argentine Chaco; and 95,000 hectares around Estancia Monte León on the Atlantic coast, home to sea lions and Magellanic penguin rookeries.

The Tompkinses are serious about the environment. Though they made their fortunes selling clothes to those willing to pay top prices for the perfect soft shell jacket, they are now proponents of anti-materialist green philosophy. The Foundation for Deep Ecology is led, funded and housed by them in California. Doug has a strict Malthusian view that there are 'too many of us'. He calls Greenpeace's wetsuited eco-campaigners 'wimps', and spends part of the year helping to crew the *Sea Shepherd*, a ship that regularly rams Japanese whalers in the iceberg-strewn waters of the Southern Ocean. The couple are serious too about protecting Patagonia from all-comers. They have been opposing plans for roads and dams in their area of Chile, to the anger of many locals.

Altogether, they have more than a million hectares of Chilean and Argentine Patagonia, most of it owned through trusts registered back home in Sausalito, California. His is the Conservation Land Trust, and hers is Conservación Patagónica, which receives money from her old company. They dream of seeing their land holdings in both countries eventually form the core of a giant transboundary park stretching from the Pacific fjords of Chile to the Atlantic shores of Argentina. Should I be opposed to such elite jet-setters buying up such a place on such a scale? Is this altruistic conservation or land grab? I wasn't sure.

Buying wilderness is increasingly popular among the green-minded super-rich, in Patagonia and many other places. Most of the big Patagonian purchases happened in the 1990s, after the fierce winds of free-market economics had blasted through the cone of South America. Chile, under General Pinochet, more or less invented Reaganomics. The Argentine government of Carlos Menem oversaw the sale to foreigners of an estimated eight million hectares of homeland. 'Land is very cheap, property rights very stable – and the locals often want to sell,' says George Holmes, a British academic from Leeds University who has followed the gringo trail. 'One reason the Tompkinses and others have been able to buy is because no one else wanted the land.'

And gringos abhor a vacuum. The founder of the cable news network CNN, Ted Turner, has a sizeable back yard at home in the US. He owns a million-hectare land bank in 12 states. He has ranches in Montana and the sandhills of Nebraska – home to 50,000 bison, the biggest herd in the US. And he has 2 per cent of New Mexico, where you can join his $12,000-a-week elk-hunting safaris. But if he ever feels crowded at home, he also has a 55,000-hectare ranch called La Primavera Argentina, with some of South America's most exquisite trout fishing, in Argentine Patagonia's Neuquén province.

Some of these green grabbers try to get along with the locals.

But others seem more divisive. The billionaire brothers Carlo and Luciano Benetton, the ageing founders of Italy's Benetton clothing group, have accumulated 900,000 hectares of sheep farms in Neuquén, Rio Black, Chubut and Santa Cruz. Their interest is at least partly business. The biggest private landholders in Argentina, they have a quarter-million sheep on their land, supplying some 6,000 tonnes of wool a year to the family firm, which is one of the world's biggest buyers of wool. But they live back home in Treviso, Italy.

The Benettons' first and main purchase was the Argentine Southern Land Company. The British-owned ranch operator had been given a ten-ranch empire a century before by the government in Buenos Aires. The land was in settlement of debts incurred by the government to finance an invasion of the previously untamed Argentine Patagonia. The 'conquest of the desert', as they called it, resulted in the final step in the European colonization of South America, taking the lands of indigenous groups.

Locals whom Paul Theroux met in *The Old Patagonian Express* thought the company belonged to 'the Queen of England . . . lots of cattle – very nice'. But, shortly after his journey, in 1982, Argentina nationalized the company, and much of its land was abandoned. A decade later, it was bought by the Benetton brothers, through their Edizione Holdings. This annoyed some members of the largest surviving indigenous group, the Mapuche. Around 100,000 of them still live in Argentine Patagonia, mostly working as labourers on ranches or living in the slums of big cities. But in the 1980s, some began campaigning to reclaim their ancestral lands. In 2001, a group of them took on the Benettons, by occupying a few hundred hectares of Edizione land around the village of Leleque, 60 kilometres north of Esquel. 'We went to the land without harming anyone,' says Atilio Curinanco, one of the returnees. 'We didn't cut a fence, we didn't go at night, and we didn't hide ourselves. We waited for someone to come to let us know if it bothered them . . . and no one showed up.'

Eventually someone from Benetton did show up, and went to court. A judge ordered the eviction of Curinanco and his compatriots. After an intervention by Argentine pacifist and Nobel peace laureate Pérez Esquivel, the Benettons offered alternative land elsewhere in Patagonia. But, with the backing of the provincial government, the Mapuche turned down the offer, saying the land at Leleque had spiritual meaning for them, and contained an important cemetery, while anywhere else would not.

Sadly, the Benettons – who at the time were famed in Europe for their offbeat advertising, associating the brand with human rights and other liberal causes – dug in their heels. They refused to concede. The Mapuche note bitterly that the Benettons had created on their land a tourist museum about the history of the people of Patagonia. It represented them as relics from distant lands and distant times, rather than the rightful owners of the present estate.

It seems that even in the vast wilderness of Patagonia, there is little land that isn't claimed or owned by someone – little that is truly virgin, just awaiting a foreign claimant. For global nomads like the Benettons, Tompkinses and Turner, such blood ties to the land as those claimed by the Mapuche can have little meaning. It seems to me they are drawn to the wild land at the end of the Earth for its sense of otherness, because of its difference from their own homelands.

So it was with Joe Lewis, an ultra-discreet British financier, brought up in the East End of London. He made a killing with fellow landgrabber George Soros on Black Wednesday in 1992. He spent some of the cash on a 14,000-hectare estate that circles Lake Escondido on the Chilean border near Bariloche. He hasn't come up against indigenous claimants. His antagonists might be wearing one of Tompkins's packs on their backs. Under Argentine law, landowners must allow public access to river banks and lake shores, but an Argentine TV investigation accused Lewis of blocking access along a mountain trail across his land to Lake Escondido, causing intense local anger.

But, as one of Britain's 20 richest people, Lewis has other hideaways. He divides his time between Patagonia, Florida, Britain, the Bahamas – where he has a home in one of the world's most exclusive neighbourhoods, a gated enclave known as Lyford Cay – and his 70-metre yacht, the *Aviva*, which sails complete with works by Picasso and Miró. His private investment company, the Tavistock Group, has its fingers in everything from real estate and biotechnology research to brewing and Tottenham Hotspur football club.

Another part-time Patagonian resident is Harvard graduate Warren Adams, who made his fortune by inventing the first social networking site, PlanetAll, and selling it to Amazon for a reported $100 million. He says Amazon boss Jeff Bezos failed to develop it – and the rest is Facebook history. Like the others, Adams pocketed his fortune, went travelling and ended up star-struck by Patagonia. Unlike the others, he is not content to be a custodian of the land. He thinks it should earn its keep.

So in 2007, Adams founded Patagonia Sur, a 'for profit' company that now has 25,000 hectares in six blocks of southern Chile, from the mountain glaciers to the ocean. He is still buying. The company makes money by planting trees for carbon offsetting, and through real estate schemes. He formed an exclusive club in which would-be visitors put down $40,000 for membership, giving them the right to bring their families to one of his eco-lodges, at a bargain-basement $300 a night per person. These upmarket timeshares are going well with upmarket Chileans. Meanwhile his foresters, in collaboration with South American 'sustainable' timber giant Arauco, are planting fast. 'We are a business, not an activist company,' Adams says. He is still seeking new ways of squeezing a profit from Patagonia Sur. He would like to sell water, melted from his own glaciers, to Africa.

Back in Argentina, another giant ranch, Estancia Alicura, has been bought by Ward Lay, son of Herman Lay, who founded the Frito-Lay potato-crisps company and became chairman of PepsiCo after the two companies merged. Ward Lay bought the 75,000-hectare ranch in 1998, from the Benetton family. He converted it from sheep to a hunting and trout-fishing resort. He claims that it has one of the world's largest herds of guanaco, the wild ancestors of domesticated llamas, as well as wild boar from Europe and red stag from New Zealand, corralled within a 7,000-hectare fenced enclosure.

Conventional environment groups have also been purchasing pieces of the end of the world, usually thanks to rich benefactors. Former US treasury secretary Henry Paulson, a nature buff, found himself in charge of 260,000 hectares of forest in Chilean Tierra del Fuego. It happened because a US logging company defaulted on a loan from Goldman Sachs, which Paulson chaired at the time. At a loss about what the masters of the universe could do with a Patagonian hardwood forest, Paulson donated it to the US-based Wildlife Conservation Society in 2004.

Britain's World Land Trust – the low-profile conduit for green donations from the rich and unfamous that we saw at work in Paraguay – has enabled local partners to buy 6,000 hectares of tree-less Argentine steppe on the Atlantic coast. The steppe is rather like the windy wastelands of the nearby Falkland Islands, but with pumas and guanacos, and without the land mines left behind by the Falklands War. But the real spectacle of the Estancia La Esperanza lies just offshore, where killer whales come in search of their favourite food – sea lions.

Patagonia is a truly wild land, in which the myths sometimes turn out to be true. But the biggest and most bizarre monsters here are the wild men from the rich world, determined to stake their claim to the last place on Earth. So far Sun Myung Moon, the South Korean head of the 'Moonies' church, has not ventured this far south. Perhaps his 800,000 hectares of the blistering hot Paraguayan Chaco and fetid swamps of the Brazilian Pantanal are enough to slake his land-grabbing thirst. Or maybe it is just a matter of time before his search for 'the best place to practise heavenly life on Earth' brings him to Patagonia.

The pros and cons of 'green grabs' would occupy me later when I returned to Africa.

14

AUSTRALIA

Under the shade of a coolibah tree

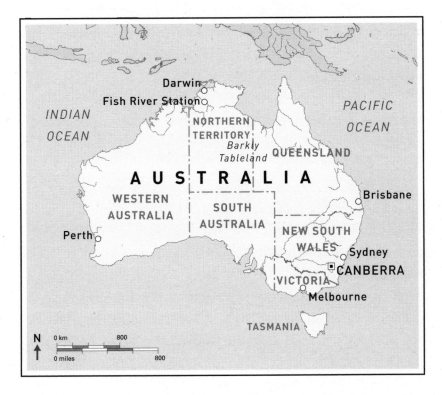

The Aussies are in a tizzy over people buying their land. It's under-standable. A nation built on big sheep and cattle ranches – or stations, as Australians call them – is finding that its pastures are falling into foreign hands. Droughts that settled over Australia in the past decade have left big landowners bankrupt and selling up. With many eager foreign buyers, Australia is beginning to wonder if this fire-sale of its heritage is altogether wise.

The Australian Agricultural Company is Australia's largest and oldest operator of cattle stations, founded by a British Act of Parliament almost 200 years ago. It has nearly seven million hectares – an area roughly the size of Scotland, most of it on the black soils of the giant Barkly Tableland in the sub-tropical Northern Territories. There, its giant stations such as the 1.2 million-hectare Brunette Downs, have 600,000 head of beef cattle. But in 2009, to stay solvent after a long drought, the company's board sold a controlling interest to a partnership of Dubai food- and fats-giant IFFCO and the world's largest plantation operator, Malaysia's privatized state enterprise FELDA.

Next to succumb to foreign investment was the second-largest rancher – but the biggest name in the business. Consolidated Pastures was once the proud property of Australia's legendary buccaneering entrepreneur, Kerry Packer. The polo-playing Packer was an impulsive gambler (he once reportedly won $13 million during a three-day baccarat binge in Las Vegas, but lost a similar amount in London) and a media tycoon (he once bought most of the world's best cricketers to put his World Series Cricket on his TV station, Channel Nine). He was also a winner. When he died in 2005, he was Australia's wealthiest man. Yet five years later, his family's 5.7 million hectares of Northern Territories' grassland disappeared for half a billion Aussie dollars into the back pocket of the British private equity firm Terra Firma, founded and chaired by ex-Goldman Sachs private-equity star Guy Hands.

Hands said his purchase was 'driven by a number of recognized global macroeconomic themes, in particular global population growth, a shift in Asian diet towards higher protein consumption and limited supply of productive land'. Lots of Asians want beef, in other words. But for Australian farmers who once would have followed Kerry anywhere, this takeover looked more like the end of their world. And 2009 wasn't over.

Next, the low-profile British agribusiness company M. P. Evans, chaired by former rubber trader Peter Hadsley-Chaplin, bought a 30,000-hectare cattle ranch in Queensland. Add that to his one-third share in 130-year-old North Australian Pastoral, which owns 13 cattle stations covering almost six million hectares of Queensland and Northern Territories, and Hadsley-Chaplin was, if anything, an even bigger rancher than his compatriot Hands. (M. P. Evans also has 40,000 hectares of oil-palm plantations in Indonesia.)

Iconic Aussie ranching families that have owned much of the country for a century and more seem to be losing heart. The cattle- and sheep-raising Kidmans are still just ahead of AAC as Australia's top rural landowners, with an empire the size of Hungary scattered across the country. The jewel in the Kidman crown is Anna Creek. The world's biggest working cattle station covers 2.4 million hectares of South Australia, an area larger than Belgium, and takes five hours to drive across. Salivating over the distant link to Nicole Kidman, one British newspaper noted that Kidman Holdings was the eighth largest private landowner on the planet. But the empire, founded by 'Cattle King' Sir Sidney Kidman in the nineteenth century, is contracting. In 2011, it sold the 1.2 million-hectare Quinyamble station, near Broken Hill in South Australia, to kangaroo farmers Mutooroo Pastoral.

Then the 160,000-hectare Bullo River cattle station in East Kimberley, made famous in best-selling books by its matriarch Sara Henderson, went up for sale. Likewise the 230,000 hectares of Sterling Buntine's Amburla station near Alice Springs. What then of other big ranching families, such as the sheep-raising MacLachlans at Jumbuck Pastoral? Would there be any work for the country's wannabee jackaroos and jillaroos? This was cultural carnage.

The list of sales must freeze the spirit of outback-loving Aussies from Woomara to Arnhem Land. Brazil's JBS-Fribol, the world's largest producer of beef, now owns 1.5 million head of cattle in feedlots in Queensland, through its purchase of Australia Meat Holdings. Nippon Meat Packers of Japan runs the country's largest feedlot at Whyalla in South Australia. Cargill's subsidiary Black River Asset Management owns another giant feedlot.

It's not just meat businesses that are coming under the auctioneers' hammer. The US's Westchester Group, a vehicle for pension funds, owns 73,000 hectares of Australian cropland. A Canadian company, Agrium, owns the Australian Wheat Board. More Canadians have the Barley Board. Both the Chinese government and Singapore's Wilmar are buying into Queensland sugar. Another Singapore conglomerate, Olam, has 9,000 hectares of orchards, which among other things deliver half Australia's almond harvest. In 2007, at the height of the drought, Olam also bought Queensland Cotton, giving it what it calls a 'dominant position' in another quintessential Aussie industry. Water is key. And that is all some grabbers want. In 2009, Summit Global Management, a San Diego-based investment firm specializing in 'hydrofinance', spent $20 million buying up water licences in the Murray-Darling river basin, where Australia grows 60 per cent of its crops. Many years, the rivers run dry.

In 2011, Qatar's voracious state-owned Hassad Foods bought 8,000 hectares of Victoria, and 12,000 hectares of sheep stud farms and cattle ranches in New South Wales, to go with its 125,000 hectares of sheep grazing in Queensland's Clover Downs. Other state-owned Gulf companies have snaffled 100,000 hectares in Western Australia. Then, most bizarrely, came a South Korean whose previous main claim to fame was to have cornered a third of the world's manufacture of baseball caps. But Baik Sung-hak switched to a cowboy hat and bought 180,000 hectares of cattle, sheep and goat pastures in New South Wales. The new proprietor of newly named Ho Myoung Farm grew up as an orphan during the

Korean War of the 1950s. He learned English from GIs and ate food he pilfered from US military garbage trucks, before getting a job as a janitor in a cap factory and rising to become the owner of the Young An Group, which also makes buses and forklift trucks. Now he's a cow-puncher, too.

And let's not forget the Chinese. In mid-2011, Western Australia's farmers reported that representatives from an unnamed Chinese company were touring their homesteads looking to buy a total of 80,000 hectares of grain fields. The aim was to 'import all their fertilizers and chemicals and export the grain straight out through the ports'. And a Chinese textile producer from Shandong, YuYi Huagong, looked set to outbid Bahrain entrepreneur Ahsan Ali Syed for the Cubbie Station in Queensland, a former ranch turned cotton farm covering 80,000 hectares.

'The truth,' wrote the *Australian* in late 2010, 'is that many farmers are broke after years of drought.' But farms were shutting down because of the reluctance of local banks to keep credit lines open till the rains returned. During the first decade of the twenty-first century some 45 million hectares of Australian land, mostly pastures, ceased production. That's an area almost the size of France. It looked like only foreigners appreciated the value of Aussie land.

Whatever the financial risks and benefits, and whether farms shut down or sold up, the anger against foreign land grabs was growing. 'Australians are in danger of becoming servants and not masters of their own food resources,' said the *Sydney Morning Herald*. A Senate inquiry called for an audit of foreign ownership. The Green Party called for a ban.

There were similar sentiments two hours east in New Zealand, when the Shanghai Pengxin Group, owned by dollar-billionaire Jiang Zhaobai, wanted to buy 16 farms on the North Island owned by the bankrupt Crafar Farms company. It made headlines for weeks. With another big purchase in the wings for the country's biggest milk supplier, Dairy Holdings, which has 14,000 hectares on the South Island, the prime minister was forced to plead for an end to the 'xenophobia against the Chinese'. The sense of siege was not helped by the discovery that German companies had purchased five farms in Southland, at the bottom of South Island, and two more in Canterbury. And it turned out that a Malaysian called Tiong Hiew King, reputedly the world's largest logger, also had some 50,000 hectares of forest, via a Liberia-registered subsidiary. We return to him in Chapter Sixteen.

None of this was quite the end for farming down under, of course. New Zealand's dairy cooperative Fonterra went from strength to strength, grabbing milky assets for itself in China. Cotton planting in Australia picked up in 2011. Ron Greentree in New South Wales, reputedly the world's largest wheat grower with 94,000 hectares under the plough, was hanging in there. As was John Nicoletti with more than 70,000 hectares in Western Australia. And Australia's Macquarie Agricultural Fund continued aggressively to fund foreign land grabs on Australia's account, notably in Brazil. But farmers are gloomy folk. And the bad news left many seeing no future on their land. Where would it end, they asked. Maybe, a few began to suggest, there was another use for the land, beyond stocking it with cows and sheep and the odd kangaroo.

Some state governments and NGOs in Australia have been considering buying some of the unused land for conservation. The pastures stretching across the tropical north of Australia in particular are among the world's last great unfenced savannah grasslands. They are of comparable value, say ecologists, to the *cerrado* in Brazil. And Aborigines, the original owners of every billabong and backwood, have a claim too.

Right on cue, the US Nature Conservancy passed around the hat, got a big donation from the 3M Corporation, and bought 180,000 hectares of savannah grassland beside the Daly River south of Darwin. The land comprised the abandoned Fish River Station cattle ranch. Yet another foreign land grab? It seemed not. The title to the land was promptly passed on to the Australian government's Indigenous Land Corporation, for the use of aboriginal people. Here at least, foreign money was being used to give the land back to its rightful owners.

PART FOUR

CHINA'S BACK YARD

China is southeast Asia's big brother – grabbing its land and stripping its resources. In Sumatra, Chinese billionaires are evicting forest tribes and pulping one of the world's great rainforests – for paper. Shanghai timber merchants are buying the jungles of Papua New Guinea, and grubbing up the rice fields of Laos to plant rubber for tyres on China's cars. But the West is also to blame. Cambodian peasants, not long resettled after the brutal years of Pol Pot, are now losing their land so we can have sugar in our coffee.

15

SUMATRA, INDONESIA

Pulping the jungle

All seemed to be well at first, as we travelled up the Indragiri River, snaking through the Sumatran rainforest. We passed a few fishermen in their boats, and heard the occasional sound of motorbikes. There was a mobile phone tower in the distance. But trees covered the river banks even as we approached Kuala Cenaku, a straggling bankside community of some 7,000 inhabitants. It was only as I clambered off the boat and walked down a long, swaying boardwalk that I realized something was amiss as, beyond the trees, I caught sight of an empty, mangled and burnt land stretching into the distance.

The people here in Riau province in central Sumatra have for centuries depended on the forest around them. They have harvested rattan creepers to make furniture, taken honey from hives deep in the bush, cut timber to construct their homes, and planted rubber trees in clearings on their traditional lands. Things have gradually changed, of course. There is a road now, along which trucks bring soft drinks, biscuits, jars of coffee and other basics of modern life. The villagers sell produce to raise cash to buy these and other twenty-first-century necessities, such as mobile phones and motorbikes.

But the modern world had always impinged as fast or as slowly as the villagers have wanted. Nothing prepared them for the loggers. Mursyid Muhammad Ali, the village head, grabbed my arm as I left the boardwalk. He said that a year before my visit, the loggers just showed up, like invaders from outer space. 'One day, we were just robbed of our communal land.' The outsiders arrived with bulldozers and chainsaws, and claimed some 8,000 hectares of their land. The forest had been given to their company by the government.

There was no argument, no arbitration and no means of redress. The chainsaw gangs began cutting down the forest, for five kilometres south of the river. They burned the scrub. They cut canals into the boggy ground to float the logs out. They shipped the most valuable timber to a plywood company in the neighbouring province. They chipped the rest on site, and sent it off to a pulp mill 70 kilometres to the north, run by a company called Asia Pulp and Paper.

That mill, the residents of Kuala Cenaku swiftly learned, was one of the world's largest producers of pulp to make paper. The mill was gobbling up the forests of Riau as fast as loggers could deliver the wood. Until the late 1980s, Riau was 80 per cent jungle. Today the figure is just 30 per cent. The people of Kuala Cenaku had just become part of a global network of exploitation that ultimately fills desktop printers across the planet with shiny white paper. The juggernaut that supplies that network would leave behind nothing of their rainforest.

Sheltering from the rain in the loggers' abandoned sawmill behind the village, my guide from the environment group WWF checked her laptop for Landsat images. The loggers had cleared 100 square kilometres of jungle around here in the past 18 months. All was silent now, but they had left behind a wasteland of charred wood on drying peat. Mursyid said that, as village head, he had filed a report to the authorities about the invasion, claiming this was a violation of their land rights. 'The district government said that it would issue a warrant for the company to stop. The land should return to the status quo till the dispute was resolved,' he told me. 'But the company ignored that. I have had no response since.' A year on, the land grab was a fait accompli. That's the way things have been done in Indonesia. 'We have no means of living here now,' he said. 'People are leaving to get jobs elsewhere.'

Tied up at the river jetty was a boatful of rubber seedlings. The remaining villagers had bought the seedlings in the nearest town, Rengat. They planned to plant them, as a first step to restoring their forest. 'We want to plant rattan, too,' one villager told me. 'But we have to get our land back first.' Fat chance. The logging company now planned to plant oil palm on their land. And the intact forest beyond the charred lands, which the community said was also theirs, was earmarked for a new logging concession. Its trees too would end up in the mill.

Travelling the backwaters of this rapidly deforesting land, I spotted Syamsir in his longboat, checking his shrimp nets. Fishing the rivers is a major activity here. Or was. He brandished a small plastic bag containing two days' catch. 'The river is polluted after the loggers came,' he shouted. 'I used to catch 10 kilograms a day, now I get less than one kilogram.' We gave him a tow back to the jetty where he would sell the shrimps for 40,000 rupia, or around $4. With that, he had nine children to support.

These are the everyday stories of economic development in Indonesia today. Development built on one of the largest, most systematic and ruthless land-grabbing operations in the world. The island of Sumatra, Indonesia's largest, is twice the size of Britain. It was until recently home to one of the world's largest intact rain-forests. Its inhabitants still claim their customary land rights. But these were made virtually worthless half a century ago. The country's newly installed President Suharto declared the forest lands of his sprawling nation of a thousand islands to be 'state forest'. They were to be deployed in the name of national development, part of the 'new order' initially thrust on him by a group of US-trained Indonesian economists known as the 'Berkeley mafia'. In practice, in his hands, it meant they would be handed out to anyone with the cash and the connections.

What future did that leave for the forest residents?

In this part of Sumatra, their fate has been sealed over-whelmingly by two men, both Chinese Indonesians, who are now among Asia's richest men. Their adopted Indonesian names are Sukanto Tanoto and Eka Tjipta Widjaja. They have been fierce rivals for decades, as they got rich building two of the world's largest pulp mills, and then feeding those mills with timber. The mills are located 40 kilometres apart near Pangkalan Kerinci, in what were once the jungles of Riau.

Until the first bulldozers arrived in 1994, Kerinci was a tiny forest village. Then 4,000 Indonesian labourers cleared 17 square kilometres of forest, constructed a river port, laid 45 kilometres of site railways and erected a billion-dollar pulp mill designed by Tanoto's Finnish consultants. Machinery arrived from Sweden, Japan, Canada, the US, Germany, Taiwan, India and the UK. Soon after, Widjaja took over and expanded his own mill, which now covers 24 square kilometres and employs 10,000 workers. Pangkalan Kerinci became a boomtown of 50,000 people, with a company airport receiving regular flights across the Straits of Malacca from Singapore. This was development of a sort, bringing in labourers from across the island and beyond. But the cowboy economy was a disaster both for the inhabitants of the forests and for the environment. And it would only last as long as the trees.

Together, the two mills represent probably the most concentrated industrial demand for wood in the world. They each consume around 10 million tonnes of timber a year, perhaps a third of it hacked from the natural rainforests of Riau. The rest is harvested from huge stands of acacia and eucalyptus being planted on deforested land. The two mills produce more than four million tonnes of pulp annually from the 20 million tonnes of cut timber. That pulp is turned into paper sold around the world. There is a fair chance their products are in your printer right now.

This is industrial forestry on a grand scale. Nobody can compete. Forests from Vermont to Finland have closed in the past decade as Sumatra's pulp bonanza has taken their markets. And business continues to boom. Industry analysts say Asia will need 100 million cubic metres more pulp by 2020, requiring four million hectares more forest. Both companies say they have plans to expand their mills further. Both companies continue to make pulp from cleared rainforest.

Eka Tjipta Widjaja was born Oei Ek Tjhong. He emigrated from China to Sulawesi in Indonesia with his family at the age of nine. He started in business selling biscuits from a bicycle rickshaw. Later he sold provisions to Indonesian troops across the far-flung Indonesian archipelago. He founded his industrial combine, today called Sinar Mas, in 1962. As it grew, it acquired paper and pulp mills, oil-palm plantations, banks, chemical works and huge land concessions.

Sinar Mas's biggest subsidiary, in charge of Widjaja's pulp and paper business, is Asia Pulp and Paper. APP has logged forests from Yunnan in China to Cambodia to the Indonesian side of the island of New Guinea. But its biggest operation is in the forests around its huge mill in Sumatra. Since the mid-1990s, APP has been responsible for destroying more than a million hectares of Sumatra's rainforests.

Widjaja, named Indonesia's richest man in 2011, is flamboyant, famously wearing a belt buckle that spells out his first name, Eka, in diamonds. He is also a dynastic patriarch. He has more than a dozen wives and at least 40 children, several of whom have taken top jobs inside his growing corporation. APP, like its owner, has a cowboy reputation. It has been convicted of illegal logging in several countries. An American researcher writing in the *Asian Times* concluded in 2004 that 'APP's business model is a tactically aggressive one: it turns huge profits by quickly stripping forests bare, exploiting age-old forests and indigenous peoples, and leaving town before the environmental consequences are felt. By the time communities and governments lodge complaints and lawsuits, APP has divested itself of local interests and assets.'

Well, that is sometimes true. But in Sumatra, buoyed up by strong political connections, APP seems to be in for the long haul. And that looks like bad news for the locals. For where they have objected to the takeover of their land, the company's response has often been ruthless.

Take the activities of one of Sinar Mas's logging subsidiaries, Arara Abadi. It operates in a part of Riau known as Siak, a former sultanate from the days before Suharto. In the late 1990s, Arara Abadi was under intense pressure to keep the new mill supplied with timber. According to the NGO Human Rights Watch, it moved its chainsaws unannounced on to land occupied by indigenous Sakai and Malay families, who practised shifting cultivation as well as tapping local rubber and collecting rattan and forest fruits.

Usually people slink away when the loggers arrive. But the Sakai felt unusually sure of their rights. The Sultan of Siak had acknowledged their traditional claim to the land, and given them formal title in 1940 – a fact acknowledged on post-independence state maps. State officials had ignored this when, in 1996, they handed over 100,000 hectares of forest around the village as a logging concession to Arara Abadi. Since then, the company had been trying to evict the villagers, with the help of local police – who were no doubt grateful that the company had recently built them a new police station in the district capital.

After the company seized lands around the village of Mandiangin, villagers blocked logging roads, trapping equipment. The company responded in force to reclaim the land and equipment. According to Human Rights Watch, 'hundreds of Arara Abadi enforcers armed with clubs attacked three villages with disputes against the company, beating scores of residents, injuring nine seriously, and abducting 63.' The company denies that any force was used.

It was not just their land that the villagers were losing. An elder at one of the villages said afterwards: 'What will happen to us? We will become just thieves and gangsters and prostitutes. Before we used to assist each other. When people made an agreement, we considered it agreed. Now everyone distrusts everyone else, and there is no feeling that law or rights have any meaning.'

The confrontations between Arara Abadi and the Sakai have continued ever since. In December 2008, Amnesty International reported that a decade-long dispute over the village of Suluk Bongkai had culminated in police helicopters dropping fire bombs, while some 500 paramilitaries invaded. Two children reportedly died, and 400 villagers fled to the forest as their homes burned. It said Arara Abadi then bulldozed the village. The National Human Rights Commission concluded later that police had committed human rights abuses, but no one was brought to justice.

However, Arara Abadi's public relations manager Nurul Huda denied that the company had used intimidation or violence against villagers. 'We are not robbing the community's land. We control the land for conversion into pulpwood plantation,' he said, under a 1996 concession from the Ministry of Forestry. The company had sought a legal settlement of the dispute.

APP's assault on the jungles of Riau seems to have been fuelled in part by competition with Widjaja's rival, Sukanto Tanoto. The son of a migrant from Fujian province in China, Tanoto was born Tan Kaung Ho in northern Sumatra. Like Widjaja, he worked his way up from humble beginnings by using powerful politicians as patrons. His talent was spotted by Suharto when he was 26. The connection allowed him to raise cash to build a mill near his birthplace to turn timber into rayon, a textile made from cellulose fibre. His Indorayon Utama mill produced the cheapest pulp in the world, he said at the time. Maybe so. But it also cut corners and attracted huge local opposition over pollution.

After a crackdown on protesters in 1989 had left several dead, Tanoto was forced to shut the plant for five years. But by then he had moved on, eventually relocating his business empire, Raja Garuda Mas International, to Singapore. The basis of its wealth today is Asia Pacific Resources International (APRIL), the pulp giant that built the second giant Riau mill complex. I went to visit.

Around the mill complex, Tanoto has created an almost self-contained empire in the jungle. It has a road network largely independent of the state highways, travelled by vast 44-wheel 'road trains' that are too heavy and dangerous for public roads. They supply 22,000 tonnes of timber a day to the mill. 'The gobbling monster requires feeding,' said my company guide, APRIL's then sustainability director Neil Franklin. And so do customers across the world. The company's flagship brand of office copying paper, PaperOne, is sold in more than 50 countries.

In the past decade and a half, APRIL has chopped down more than 800,000 hectares of forest in Riau. That is almost a tenth of the province. It claims that it has subsequently planted about half of the logged land with acacia, giving it 'the biggest plantation operation in the world'. Local environmentalists question this claim. In any event, like its rival, it remains a major deforester.

From the number of mud-spattered Land Cruisers travelling the logging roads of Riau, it is clear that the destruction is generating wealth. But in this 'wild east', there are more losers than winners. And the companies' attitude to people whose lands they have grabbed is troubling. 'We turn former illegal loggers into committed stakeholders,' says APRIL's company video. But such language is deliberately derogatory, and shows ignorance of the people they are talking about. As the Minority Rights Group notes: 'The term "illegal loggers" is frequently used to obscure community rights claims, and make legitimate grievances . . . appear as criminal activity.'

The idea that APRIL is creating jobs for the locals is also PR gloss. One of the company's field managers told me: 'We never use local labour when we can avoid it. We normally employ people from other islands in Indonesia. They are less likely to cause trouble or engage in sabotage.' More than 70 per cent of APRIL's plantation labourers are migrants. At one camp I visited, 400 Sambas people had just been delivered to the company by gangmasters from across the Straits of Malacca in western Borneo. They were sleeping under plastic on logged land. 'They are natural loggers, very hard working. Thousands come out from a very small area,' one manager said. Why were they living under canvas in the rain, I asked. 'It's their choice. They hate zinc roofs.'

The Indonesian archipelago is one of the world's three great tropical forested regions. Its deforestation began in earnest under Suharto. The world now recognizes that he ran a hugely corrupt crony regime. One of the world's largest and most populous nations was his personal fiefdom, sustained by a rhetoric of nation-building and fighting communism. He rewarded his family, friends and generals with huge concessions in the state forest. If you had the support of the president, and the required muscle to subdue the locals, you could take whatever land you wanted. If you required labour, Suharto could supply it. He revived and expanded an old Dutch colonial strategy known as the Transmigration Programme, that shipped thousands of people out from densely populated islands like Java to distant jungles. But for most of his 32-year rule, from 1967 to 1998, Suharto had the staunch support of the West as a bulwark against communism.

Under Suharto, the customary land rights of the country's rainforest-dwelling majority, known as *adat*, were recognized in Indonesian law. But they were superseded by the nationalization of the forests, and rendered defunct if they conflicted with development projects of national importance, whether logging, mining or plantation agriculture. Landgrabbers ruled in the jungle. As Suharto put it, 'nomadic farming should be terminated'.

One of the most notorious landgrabbers was Mohamad 'Bob' Hasan. Born The Kian Seng, the son of a Chinese tobacco trader who moved to Java, he rose through lucrative smuggling operations and the assistance of patrons in the military to become Suharto's trusted lieutenant for expanding logging. He was there as, between

1967 and 1980, the government forest service allocated more than 500 logging concessions to private investors covering a staggering 53 million hectares, an area twice the size of the UK.

Hasan used his regulatory position, as the spider in the centre of Suharto's web, to accumulate fabulous personal wealth. He became the legally required local partner when the US corporation Georgia Pacific started logging in Indonesia in 1970. When the company departed in 1983 – reportedly unwilling to join Hasan's push for investment in downstream activities like plywood and pulp production – Hasan took over the operation for himself.

During this time, Hasan became the undisputed 'king of plywood', not just for Indonesia but for the planet. His company, the Kalimanis Group, accumulated almost a million hectares of logging concessions, and set about becoming one of the world's leading plywood suppliers. An ambition helped by Hasan's position as chairman of the state-backed plywood association APKINDO, which gave him advantageous rights to export Indonesian plywood.

I remember meeting Hasan in London during a high-level sales promotion in 1990, when he was at the height of his power. By then, he controlled a staggering 70 per cent of the world trade in plywood. He claimed a patriotic purpose. He told environmentalists he would create a 'sustainable' forest industry in Indonesia, based around acacia plantations. I still have the publicity literature from the time. But the plantations only emerged when the forests were all gone. He continued to oversee unprecedented forest destruction.

The wheels nearly came off the deforestation juggernaut after the 1998 Asian financial crisis. This followed huge forest fires in Sumatra and Borneo during the 1997 El Niño drought, which had alerted the world to the parlous state of the Indonesian forests. Both APP and APRIL effectively went bust as global pulp prices collapsed and their activities came under international scrutiny for the first time. They had borrowed huge sums to set up the two Riau mills, and invested heavily in the logging to feed them. APP owed $14 billion. It was the largest corporate debtor in Asia.

But, deemed too big to fail, the two companies were eventually bailed out by the Indonesian government. Where did the bail-out money come from? On IMF advice, ministers in Jakarta auctioned off hundreds more logging concessions. The rate of deforestation across Indonesia doubled after 1998.

While the loggers were too big to fail, the same was no longer true of Suharto. In a post-cold-war world, the bulwark against communism was no longer needed, and he was becoming an embarrassment. He reluctantly resigned in 1998 as Indonesia's financial crisis escalated, the currency collapsed, riots filled the streets of Jakarta and thousands of people lost their lives. Suharto retired to his fortified villa in Jakarta with a family fortune estimated at $15 billion. He died ten years later. With the departure of his mentor, Hasan's star also fell. In 2001, he was convicted of fraud and misusing $250 million of state funds. He spent three years in jail. Fellow foresters report that since his release, he has retired to the country's many golf courses – another legacy of the Suharto era – and 'got religion'.

But thanks to the bail-outs, Widjaja and Tanoto simply carried on. Land proved more durable than patronage. Their main change was to begin copying modern Western business practices. They hired foreign consultants and published 'sustainability action plans'. Both promised that by 2007 they would finally be running their mills entirely from plantation timber. Wrecking the rainforests would be a thing of the past. They started applying for eco-labels for their paper and for certification of their mills by the Forest Stewardship Council.

APRIL began talking to environment groups in Sumatra about protecting the diminishing number of biodiversity hotspots where Sumatra's tigers, elephants and rhinos lived. It collaborated with

WWF on a plan to conserve the besieged Tesso Nilo national park in southern Riau. According to WWF's Michael Stuewe, the idea was to create a 'ring' of acacia plantations around a central protected area. Under company control, the ring would protect the park. But when I visited in 2007, the park was being invaded by migrants looking for land to grow oil palm. Worse, they were arriving down a new road that had been built by APRIL to extract timber from the acacia ring.

I met three young men smoking at the roadside. They said they had come from northern Sumatra, where other 'development' projects had taken their land. 'We have no land in our village now. We want to cultivate land, so we came here.' One of them, 20-year-old Nainggolan, had come with his parents and four brothers. He said that the chief in a nearby small town called Bukit Kusuma had charged them $900 in return for two hectares where they could plant oil palm.

A bit further on, three more men were living in a small hut. They were from the southern tip of Sumatra. They said they had been installed in the hut by the executive of a local oil-palm plantation company, and told to work on 20 hectares of land he had bought as a private venture from the same chief in Bukit Kusuma. Meanwhile, deeper in the park, an entire village had been built, complete with a mosque, we were told.

All this was, of course, against the law. But Bukit Kusuma – a town right on the northern edge of the park with a couple of seedy bars and a lot of muddy four-by-fours – was evidently a local centre of illegality. It had become a magnet for desperate, dispossessed people willing to do anything to make a living, and exploited at every turn by corrupt officials. My WWF guides would not stop there. Five months before, one of them had been beaten up by a gang near Bukit Kusuma. Not long before, two of APRIL's staff had been murdered when they banned trucks carrying logs cut in the park from boarding a company chain ferry.

What could be done? Where was the government? I went to the capital of Riau, Pekanbaru, to see the provincial conservation officer. Mohammad Zanir was in charge of protecting one of the world's great rainforests from destruction by two of the world's most rapacious logging companies and the insalubrious types that their activities attracted. He didn't, to put it mildly, seem up to the task.

I had spent two days with campaigners from WWF who had laptops carrying up-to-date satellite images of the deforestation, and could pinpoint any activity that threatened the forests. But Zanir had no computer, only a pile of dusty files on a shelf and an old-fashioned bottle of ink on his desk. Outside his office, seemingly mocking his impotence, a large stuffed crocodile occupied most of the foyer and two tigers prowled the corridor.

He knew the problem. 'We need more habitat for the Sumatran tigers,' he said. 'But we have two giant pulp companies whose mill capacity is bigger than their plantations, so they are consuming our natural forests. If nothing is done there will be no forest land left outside the parks by 2015.' But he had no solution. After all, official planning maps zoned most of the remaining natural forests for clearance, plantations and other commercial development by the end of the decade. Their destruction was government policy.

And corruption was endemic within parts of the administration that Zanir served. He did not mention it, but the new Riau police chief was, at the time of my visit, conducting a detailed investigation of illegal logging. He had identified for prosecution 14 companies, seven providing logs for APP and seven serving APRIL. But the provincial prosecutor refused to take action – saying the companies had mostly been acting within the terms of their licences – and the police chief was moved on. Two top officials were later convicted of corruption and jailed. They included Asral Rachman, who had, as head of the Riau forestry agency in 2004 and 2005, been in charge of handing out logging licences. But the companies themselves remained untouchable.

There was one wild place left where the environmentalists believed they might stop the juggernaut. It was Riau's hottest biodiversity hotspot, and had so far been saved by its isolation. On the Kampar peninsula, jutting out into the Straits of Malacca, right across from Singapore, was one of Southeast Asia's largest peat swamps. Until 2002, the 4,000-square-kilometre mass of peat, some of it 15 metres thick, was still largely covered by rich rainforest. The place could only be reached by boat. Some 50 Sumatran tigers lived there, along with clouded leopards, elephants, sun bears, tapirs and other rare species.

But in the past decade, having cleared most of the thousands of square kilometres of easily accessible forests nearby, loggers had inched into the swamp – APP from the north and east, and APRIL from the south and west. They are digging networks of canals. I watched trains of APRIL's barges, each carrying 200 tonnes of logs, being pulled along waterways on the western fringes of the swamp. At huge lumber stations, cranes lifted the logs on to trucks for the journey to the mill.

The canals had a second function – to drain the swamp and make it fit for acacia plantations. As we cruised the waterways, APRIL's peat scientist, Jonathan Bathgate, spoke candidly about the ecological catastrophe unfolding as the bog bled to death before us. As water levels fall and the peat begins to dry, the organic matter starts to oxidize and releases carbon dioxide into the air. Millions of tonnes of it. Emissions continue until any peat above the water table is gone. The thick Kampar peat contains anywhere from one to two billion tonnes of carbon – much more in fact than the forest above it. It is probably the biggest single carbon store in Southeast Asia. The Kampar bog has already collapsed in places by more than a metre.

According to a consultants' study commissioned by APRIL, if clearance and draining continue, it could lose a further four metres within 25 years. But despite such advice, APRIL's subsidiaries have continued to clear forest and drain swamps across Kampar through 2010 and into 2011.

That is a tragedy for the world, as well as Sumatra. But let's not forget the people whose land this was before the logging invasions began; the people whose customary laws are being trashed and drained as fast as the swamp forest. They include indigenous Akit hunter-gatherers and the ten thousand or so inhabitants of eight villages around the swamp, who fish, hunt, plant rubber and tend kitchen gardens there. Few are recent migrants. Even APRIL's staff call them 'the founding fathers of Sumatra'. Yet a study by Friends of the Earth in 2009 found that the company's land claims overlap those of at least three of the villages.

No prizes for guessing who wins when that happens. APRIL's timber suppliers have been involved in a series of disputes with the villages. In May 2009, staff from one of the suppliers, Sumatera Sylva Lestari, armed themselves with spiked clubs and attacked people protesting the invasion of their land. Three villagers died in the battle, and dozens were injured. Two months later, the company bulldozed the disputed lands.

Wary of a growing international campaign to protect the Kampar swamp, APRIL has come up with a new ring plan, similar to the one that failed in Tesso Nilo. It has offered to conserve an inner core of the Kampar swamp. But in return it wants to be able to log the rest of the timber on the swamp and plant a ring of acacia round the swamp – a ring that it claims will keep out migrants. 'The government should use us to protect conservation areas in return for being allowed to make productive use of the rest,' according to Jouko Virta, the Finnish president of APRIL's fibre supply at the time of my visit.

But WWF is fed up with the company's promises. 'I don't believe them,' says Stuewe. 'They have failed in Tesso Nilo and they would fail again in Kampar. We worked for years to encourage and support APRIL to become a leader in the pulp and paper industry . . . However the company has failed to make fundamental changes to its practices.' APRIL, for all its rhetoric, remains part of the problem, rather than part of the solution. He thinks the only answer is to shut the roads, close the canals and leave Kampar to 'the founding fathers of Sumatra'.

APRIL's boss Tanoto has tried to rebrand himself and his company as a responsible corporate citizen. But it is a hard sell when you have been responsible for some of the most rapacious rainforest destruction in history, and gained a $3 billion personal fortune in the process. Especially when the conflicts continue and the forests continue to be cleared.

But his rival is the more brazen. In 2010, APP began running promotional campaigns under the slogan 'APP cares'. It commissioned a series of extremely partial 'independent' studies into the company's practices. Most bizarrely, in TV adverts broadcast around the world it claimed to be preventing deforestation by giving jobs to poor Indonesian farmers who would otherwise chop down trees. But the PR failed to convince forest protectors. That year, the Forest Stewardship Council withdrew its certification of APP's paper, and publicly dissociated itself from the company; and one of APP's subsidiaries, Pindo Deli, lost the right to use the European Union Ecolabel for two paper brands, Golden Plus and Lucky Boss. The EU accepted what everyone in Sumatra knew – that much of the pulp in the paper came not from sustainable plantations but from virgin forest.

When I reported this example of greenwash in the *Guardian*, APP's director of sustainability, Aida Greenbury, told me: 'APP is playing a crucial role as a development agency.' Its environmental opponents were guilty of a 'neo-colonial approach' and 'immoral'. Around that time, APP's international PR consultants, the UK's Weber Shandwick, resigned over unspecified 'strategic differences' in how the company portrayed itself.

The Indonesian government is trying to persuade the world that it is doing right by the rainforests and their inhabitants. In May 2011, it announced a ban on new logging and other concessions in primary forests and on peat. Unfortunately, it was only a two-year moratorium, and as Louis Verchot of the Indonesia-based Center for International Forestry Research in Bogor pointed out, 'many companies are sitting on several large concessions that they have not yet developed. This will not put much of a crimp on the industry.' Meanwhile, tests carried out in mid-2011 by a US laboratory on an APRIL paper brand called Lazer IT bought in Australia found that 80 per cent of it was made of pulp from Indonesian rainforest. The lab identified 12 different species of tropical hardwoods.

The truth is that, while talking about sustainability, the companies are still destroying natural forest, and still taking forests from their inhabitants. The local NGO Scale Up calculated in 2010 that more than 340,000 hectares of land in Riau was the subject of disputes between locals and outside corporations, mostly the subsidiaries of APP and APRIL.

The companies' promises to sustain their mills from plantation timber remain unfulfilled. A 1990 promise became a deadline for 2007 and then 2009, before being postponed again – in APP's case to 2015. In 2011, APRIL and APP still had logging rights to an estimated 800,000 hectares of Riau natural forests. And APP had just won permissions for 100,000 hectares more.

Between them, APP and APRIL are on course to turn Sumatra from rainforest into the largest region of tree monoculture on the planet. One of the most complex ecosystems on Earth is being clear-felled and replaced with horizon-to-horizon acacia plantations crossed by canals clogged with timber-laden barges and networks of company roads down which convoys of trucks feed the 'gobbling monsters' that must be sustained.

APP and APRIL are the profit-making hearts of two giant Chinese dynasties that have gone into battle for supremacy in one of the world's biggest and most environmentally destructive industries. While the war between them continues, the forests' remaining tigers and elephants will search in vain for peace amid the whine of chainsaws and the fierce rumble of trucks carrying logs to the mills. Forest inhabitants will still wake up to find their land lost and their homes bulldozed.

16
PAPUA NEW GUINEA
'A truly wild island'

Papua New Guinea is a poisoned paradise. The South Pacific state, one half of the island of New Guinea, is one of the least explored places on Earth. The jungles that still cover around half its surface are home to more than 10,000 autonomous tribes, many living in remote highland valleys, speaking 800 languages. But logging companies are penetrating ever further – up valleys far from the capital Port Moresby, and inland from the mangrove-fringed coasts.

Timber is one of PNG's biggest businesses. According to the Forest Authority, about a quarter of the country, including much of the highlands, is under logging concessions, mostly to Malaysian companies. From PNG's shores, millions of tonnes of logs and crudely sawn timber are shipped out annually, mostly to China where they are made into furniture and other timber products sold around the world. You probably have some at home. Villagers see little return for this harvest.

Around half of the logging is thought to be done by a complex network of companies ultimately owned by the self-made billionaire and septuagenarian Tiong Hiew King, with his family. The Malaysian, an ethnic Chinese, is the founder of a company called Rimbunan Hijau, one of the world's largest timber traders. The billionaire first got rich as the second-biggest logger of the forests of Sarawak, the Malaysian province on the island of Borneo, where he still lives. There are not many trees left in Sarawak today. But he has moved on. Rimbunan Hijau is now the largest logging company in Asia, with operations in the Solomon Islands, the Russian Far East, New Zealand and several countries in central Africa, where it now rivals the European timber combines. But PNG is the jewel in Tiong's corporate crown. His companies remove more than a million tonnes of logs a year from the country.

Besides his hold on PNG's forests and their timber, Tiong also controls one of the country's two major newspapers, and is big in fisheries, shipping, insurance, IT and retailing. Not much happens there without his involvement. The British queen, Elizabeth Windsor, remains the head of state and Queen of PNG. She gave Tiong a knighthood in 2009 'for services to commerce, communities and charitable organizations' in PNG. But perhaps 'Sir Tiong' is the true king-across-the-water here.

Tiong is no longer the chief villain for people concerned about the fate of PNG's rainforests, however. Not since the country succumbed to one of the most outrageous, mysterious and little-known land grabs anywhere in the world. According to the man who did most to track it down, Colin Filer of the Australian National University, in the past decade more than a tenth of the country's land has been secretly handed over to foreign corporations and their shadowy local representatives, through complex leasing arrangements. It is a scam on a huge scale. In two provinces, Western and West Sepik, over a fifth of the land has been signed away. Here's how.

The customary rights of the forest communities to their neighbourhood forests are supposedly enshrined in PNG's statutes. But the country's Land Act also contains provisions that allow those communities to do deals with outsiders to kick-start economic developments, for instance by establishing commercial farms in their territory. This is done by leasing forest land to the government, which in turn can issue 'special agricultural and business leases' to private companies. This arrangement means the government can act as the policeman for the schemes to prevent isolated communities from being defrauded. Initially, it worked well. Several small agricultural projects were set up that benefited communities.

But from 2003, the provisions were hijacked for a series of large logging projects. That was never the idea. Companies justified the logging on the grounds that, after the trees were cut down, there would be farming on the cleared land. Usually oil-palm plantations. But Filer says in most cases the outsiders securing the special leases only ever wanted the timber. The promises of farming and economic development were usually a sham. And when he started talking to communities about the leases, he discovered that many of them had little idea what they were signing up for. And in some cases they hadn't signed up at all.

The island of Lavongai (formerly known as New Hanover) is at the far end of the Bismarck archipelago in PNG's offshore province of New Ireland. It is 60 kilometres long and 30 kilometres wide. The Lonely Planet guidebook calls it 'volcanic, ruggedly beautiful . . . a truly wild island, complete with dense rainforest, mountains, water-falls and rivers'. It has some 20,000 inhabitants, with their own distinctive Melanesian language and culture. On 4 March 2011, they woke up to hear, by mobile phone from friends reading the *Post-Courier* newspaper in Port Moresby, that their island had been leased to a company registered in Singapore, called Palma Hacienda. It was the first they knew of this, says Filer.

The details were complex. Palma Hacienda is an obscure subsidiary of a Malaysian company called Ayamkuat Maju, an import-export company based in Sarawak's logging capital, Miri. Two New Ireland luminaries allegedly set up the deal. One was a former premier of the province called Pedi Anis. He was by then chairman of a logging company called Tutuman Development, which obtained a series of special leases in the name of local landowners. It then sub-let the leases to Palma Hacienda. Tutuman Development, while incorporated in PNG, was largely owned by a Singaporean woman, Regina Lau Yii Kuong.

The other local was Miskus Maraleu, a lawyer whose role in previous logging operations in the province was described by an official inquiry in 1989 as 'disgraceful and reprehensible'. He had 'disregarded the interests of his own people' and 'served the interests of a foreign paymaster' as well as 'personally benefiting financially from the improper role he played'. He was an improbable partner in any legitimate deal, you might say.

When the story broke, Anis claimed he had terminated the leases, but only after Palma Hacienda had cleared 17,000 tonnes of timber. He denied receiving the $600,000 stipulated in his purchase agreement with Palma Hacienda. The one certainty was that the trees were gone; no oil palm had been planted; and no economic 'development', the supposed justification for special leases, had occurred. What was really in question was how the locals had had control of their land taken from beneath them without their consent – and where the money went.

The scale of the special leases scam is huge. So far, they cover more than five million hectares. But regulatory oversight seems to have been non-existent. Far from protecting the interests of the communities, provincial officials seem sometimes to have been conniving to defraud them. Filer found that many of the leases had been handed out to bogus companies with consent from, at best, individuals with a dubious claim to represent the communities. Sometimes, companies and government officials took a trip to a forest clearing to promise the locals that they would bring roads and phone lines and agricultural projects. But the communities, who are nominally shareholders in the projects in their areas, were rarely told what they were handing over in return.

Among the dozens of special leases signed off by provincial officials, three involved more than half a million hectares. In February 2009, an outfit called Tosigiba Investment, which had not been properly incorporated, was somehow given a 99-year lease on 632,000 hectares in Nomad district. The local villagers denied all knowledge of the deal. So did the chairman of Tosigiba Timber, a properly incorporated company that was owned by the villagers. He accused the government secretary of lands of being 'negligent in the extreme' for issuing the lease to this unknown entity, owned by persons also unknown.

At least the Purari Development Association had a formal existence when it was granted a special lease for 650,000 hectares. But the purpose raised eyebrows. It plans to construct a giant 1,800-megawatt hydroelectric plant that would flood much of the valley of the River Purari and send power by undersea cable 500 kilometres across the Coral Sea to Queensland. Some locals in the flood zone said they knew about the project, but others claimed they had 'never been consulted or given permission' for the takeover.

There seemed to be more local support for a scheme from a South Korean company called Changhae Tapioka. It signed up with local communities in Central and New Ireland provinces to set up cassava farms on previously logged land, and to process the crop at five local ethanol plants. The cassava plantations were developed, and the crops grown. But, despite promises to process the crop locally, they were instead shipping chipped cassava to a Korean ethanol factory.

In a detailed analysis of these and other special leases, Filer concluded that most were grubby, devious and opportunistic. A series of shadowy here-today-and-gone-tomorrow companies, several of them involving Malaysian logging entrepreneurs in cahoots with local politicians and government officials, were trashing the forests using laws designed to ensure that local people consented to, and benefited from, development projects. His wrap-up of one typically convoluted saga concluded: 'The logging company has since departed, the Woitape people still lack road access to Port Moresby, while the fate of the [promised] oil palm seedlings and the new telephone lines is unknown.'

Why the plunder? Filer suggests that there has been a scramble among foreign loggers working in PNG to get as many Papuan logs as possible to Chinese manufacturers of timber goods before tougher rules on sourcing of logs come in. One trigger may be new rules on timber sourcing from the European Union. From 2013, the EU will insist on chain-of-custody paperwork on all timber products, showing where the wood came from, and demonstrating its sustainability. That could make Chinese purchase of PNG timber tricky. So everyone wanted to grab the wood, and take their profits, while the going remained good.

The PNG government reacted to the growing concern about the special leases by 'suspending' them in May 2011 and launching an inquiry into their legality. But nobody knew for how long the suspension would last. Just till the dust settled? Few believed ministers were serious about a clean-up. Filer predicts 'an upsurge of rural social unrest and civil disorder' as the scams unravel. As the poison spreads.

17

CAMBODIA

Sweet and sour

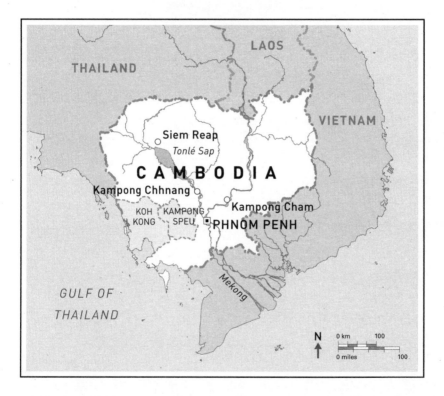

A couple of hours west of the Cambodian capital Phnom Penh, I stopped at random at a meagre roadside shack. I was in sugar land. I knew that one of Cambodia's most powerful politicians, the tycoon senator Ly Yong Phat, had been accumulating land in the area to set up a sugar-cane plantation. The sugar was destined for the European Union, under preferential trade rules designed to help poor nations like Cambodia. In particular, it would end up at the giant Tate &

Lyle sugar plant on the Thames estuary outside London – just downstream from the big banks in Canary Wharf.

But Omlaing commune, in the Cambodian province of Kampong Speu, was a long way from London. Mey Mao and his family lived almost in the open, in a tiny wooden shelter raised on stilts above the frequent floods. They had one bed and an open fire. They had a kettle and pans, but no tap. As the rain fell, the crudely thatched roof dripped. 'We have lived here since 1979,' Mey told me. That was the year Vietnam invaded Cambodia and liberated it from the tyrannous 'year zero' regime of Pol Pot, during which millions died, and most of the rest were forced from their homes into work camps.

Now it looked like this family faced a new 'year zero'. More powerful men were coming to upset their rural backwater. 'The company came and told us the land belonged to them,' said Mey, looking perplexed. But it couldn't be true, he said. He and his family had lived and farmed there for more than 30 years. It was their home. 'The company told us we had to go. That we would be resettled, but they didn't say when and I am worried.' The company was owned by the senator for sugar, Ly Yong Phat.

Mey's land extended for a few tens of metres back from the road. But his livelihood was meagre. 'I have four cows; I grow some cassava and rice, and I have trees with bananas and papaya,' he said. A few chickens also scuttled around. 'Some years it is enough, but not every year. I have six children to feed.' His most valuable possession looked like a battered bicycle. He didn't have a radio or TV. The house had no magazines or books. He knew little of the world beyond his tiny corner of Cambodia. His passivity was distressing.

Five of Mey's children went to school – when he could afford the fees, which were a bit over a dollar a day for them all. One son, maybe 10 years old, seemed to know a little more than his bemused

father. 'We will be resettled on the hillside, up there,' he said, pointing to the distant Pis Mountain. It was beyond Ly Yong Phat's sugar
plantation, which extended ominously down the valley towards
their shack. 'But I've never been there,' interjected the boy's mother.
'It's no good. We won't be able to grow rice there. There is no water,
they say. We don't know what we will do. We don't know what we
will eat. And it will be too far for the children to go to school.'

This is not how modern Cambodia is supposed to be. Back in
the 1970s, Pol Pot's Khmer Rouge abolished all private property
in the cause of creating a Communist agrarian utopia. Its year-zero
policies included destroying most legal documents recording land
ownership. Recently, as part of a reform programme organized with
the assistance of the World Bank, the Cambodian government has
been reinstating formal land titles for the millions of people who lost
their land rights at that time. The declared aim is a property-
owning democracy.

Approaching two million land titles have been handed to
Cambodian peasants so far. But if a big private investor wants some
land, he can apply for an Economic Land Concession. These large
concessions are only supposed to be granted on state land, but in
practice often override the title claims of ordinary farmers. Unlike
Papua New Guinea's special leases, they don't even pretend to have
local consent. All over the country, leading figures like the sugar
senator are muscling in on the land and homes of people like Mey.
Sometimes they are acting as fronts for foreign investors.

There are no official figures, but NGOs reckon that since 2003,
more than two million hectares of Cambodian land – equivalent to
half its arable land – have been handed out in this way to around 150
private companies. This is institutionalized land-grabbing on a huge
scale for such a small and densely populated country. In theory, the
law limits Economic Land Concessions to a maximum of 10,000
hectares. But there is a way round that: the creation of adjoining

concessions under separate names. In Kampong Speu, Ly Yong Phat claimed one 10,000-hectare concession for himself, and another one right next door for his wife, Kim Heang. The two concessions are, so far as I could see, run as a single farm.

There were protests when representatives of the senator's company, Phnom Penh Sugar, first toured Omlaing handing out eviction notices. Mey Mao joined the demonstrations. He said the company offered to give him $200 if he and his family moved. It was not formal compensation, and the offer would be taken away if he did not agree there and then. But Mey had no idea what his land and house by the main road might be worth. In the end, he followed most others and turned the offer down. Now he waited on events. All through Omlaing commune, I found people in a similar situation. Many were bereft, clueless and passive, waiting for their land to be taken. But not all.

I spotted what looked like an oasis of order and productivity amid the muddled patchwork of shacks, trees and rice paddies we had passed. Chhuon Chuon's plot stretched back 500 metres from the road, behind a neat wall. It was full of fruit trees. 'I bought this land from a former Khmer Rouge soldier in 2005,' he told me as we sat in the shade of the orchard. This was not unusual. Remnants of the Khmer Rouge had hung on here for years after they were ousted from Phnom Penh. Chhuon paid about $400 for the plot. 'I cleared it and planted these trees. Now I make enough money to support three families, 17 people.'

This was a proper business. Wholesalers came to his gate to buy his mangoes, papayas and bananas, and the milk from his cows, which grazed among the trees. But unlike many others hereabouts, Chhuon did not feel tied to his land. He was 60 years old, and had seen a lot in this ravaged country. He had been moving around ever since the days of Pol Pot. He had other activities. He was a primary-school teacher. But he wasn't going to give up his plot easily.

Chhuon was fighting his eviction notice. He said records of his purchase of the land had been among many that were mysteriously lost during a local government reorganization. He didn't think this was an accident. 'The company has taken some of my land already,' he said. The compensation it offered for taking the rest was less than one year's income from the fruit on his trees, so he turned it down. Soon after spurning the company's offer, he found himself in court. The charge was encroachment on the company's land. 'I got bail after I got support from an NGO [the human rights group Adhoc]. But I have to appear in court three times a month. I am still waiting for a decision. I am not scared to stand trial. I am a legal landowner.'

He had suggested his own terms to end the dispute, he said with a brief smile. 'I said I'd like $20,000. That would be a fair price, though not as much as I was offered for my land by someone else in 2007.' But the company was not interested. It told the local press that it owned his plot. Simple as that. At the time of writing, the case was still unresolved.

Next, I went to a meeting of other locals fighting the eviction orders. They sat cross-legged on a raised platform, shaded by palm trees. The meeting was friendly, but there was an edge. One woman fiddled with a sharp knife. It marked the first anniversary of a successful demonstration at a provincial court, when some 500 villagers had demanded the release from custody of their local leader. You Tho had been charged with inciting them to protest and to commit arson after a previous demonstration outside the company's offices.

You Tho, a quietly spoken man in his 60s, seemed an unlikely hothead. He was wearing a T-shirt with a picture of the Indian pacifist Mahatma Gandhi on it. He told me that some 300 families in 11 villages in the Omlaing commune were threatened with losing at least some of their land to Ly Yong Phat's sugar plantation, as it expanded down the valley. Their situations varied. In one village, people had been told their houses would be bulldozed. In another, every family had lost rice fields. 'They will have nothing to eat this year,' said women at the meeting. Some just had their pastures fenced off.

The company initially offered alternative land to replace the lost rice fields. But few accepted. 'Usually it was either hill land, where you can't grow rice, or land in other villages that was already owned by the people there,' one man said. There was no offer of compensation for lost pastures, even though raising cattle was good business here. You could get $1,200 for a pair of animals, they said. I asked if they had tried to get work with the company. Some had. But there was only casual work, at $2.50 a day. Most had given up. 'It's hard work, and you have to stay in the sun all day in the fields,' one woman said.

After the government gave him the concession, Ly Yong Phat had come personally to the village, said You Tho. 'He asked me to stop working for the community. He said he would give me a car and five hundred dollars a month if I went to work for him.' Similar offers were made to other local leaders. 'Some have stopped working for their people since,' he said, without malice. 'But I am not going to give up my community. If we stick together we can keep our land.'

The plantation was reaching ever closer to their homes. People were losing their land individually, as the company decided it needed it. Sugar so far covered 5,000 hectares, with 15,000 hectares to go. I went to the main farm gate to ask about progress and discuss the complaints. I was surprised to find that the plantation was guarded by the military, by Battalion 313 of the Royal Cambodian Armed Forces, which is largely composed of former Khmer Rouge soldiers. The government assigned the battalion to Ly Yong Phat's companies as part of a policy it described as encouraging links between the military and private business. In return for receiving security services, Ly Yong Phat provides the battalion with 'charitable support'.

Locals were not impressed with the battalion. 'The soldiers kidnap people and demand ransoms. It's a way of boosting their income,' they told me. At the farm gate, the soldiers were friendly enough to a foreigner. But nobody inside wanted to speak to me.

The casual indifference to people's rights that I encountered in Cambodia seemed at first extraordinary. But soon it began to appear routine. On the way back from the senator's sugar farm, I passed a grand gateway leading to the premises of HLH Agriculture (Cambodia) Co. Ltd. The local offshoot of the Singapore-based Hong Lai Huat Group had in 2009 acquired 10,000 hectares of land that was, technically, within the Aoral Wildlife Sanctuary. The company was growing maize there. Its website said the concession comprised 'vast tracts of uncultivated arable land'. Well, uncultivated yes. But not unused. There was the wildlife, and also the indigenous Suy people who live in the sanctuary. The Suy said their five villages had been encircled by the concession, and the forest where they gathered fruits and other produce had been ploughed up.

It wasn't the Suy people's first encounter with landgrabbers. Back in 2004, a company called New Cosmos Development had arrived in another part of the sanctuary and built what it called an 'eco-tourism' centre, complete with a golf course. The 400 Suy who still live in the reserve claim to be among the last 1,200 of their people left in Cambodia, and hence the world. But, well, golf comes first.

Next day, I took the road southwest towards the coastal tourist resort of Sihanoukville, before making a right turn to Koh Kong province. Koh Kong borders Thailand and is often called the 'wild west' of Cambodia. Remote from Phnom Penh, it has in the past been at the centre of illegal logging, drug cultivation and human trafficking. It is also the provincial base of Ly Yong Phat who, among his many real estate developments here, runs a casino complex at the Thai border, and a Safari World theme park that had been accused in the past of smuggling orang-utans from Indonesia. Some call the senator the 'King of Koh Kong'. He even built a two-kilometre toll bridge linking the province to Thailand, where he owns further land.

Land-grabbing is a daily news story in Koh Kong. Over coffee at the roadside, I read in that day's paper about a huge new tourist development being built on coastal land inside nearby Botum Sakor national park. It covered 30,000 hectares and would house resort buildings, an airstrip and, naturally, golf courses. The developer was the Union Development Group, a state-owned Chinese textile group diversifying into land and tourism.

A thousand families in the company's way had accepted offers of new homes and departed. *Cambodia Daily* had found them. It reported: 'Rows of yellow wooden houses can be seen about 20 kilometres from the coastline, where families now live on parched deforested land, far away from the rows of cashew and coconut trees they once possessed.' The Cambodian League for the Promotion and Defence of Human Rights (LICADHO) said that the 20 families who refused compensation had had their crops and homes burned. The paper quoted a military police commander saying he 'had to protect' the development. 'I do not defend the Chinese, but I do defend Cambodian law.'

The paper reported that further up the road, in the Cardamom Mountains, a former Australian finance minister, Peter Costello, was a partner in promoting a 5,000-hectare banana plantation that conservationists said would block an elephant migration corridor. I turned the page, and Ly Yong Phat was also in the news. In the far north of the country, in Oddar Meanchey province, the senator was reported to be helping set up another enterprise, this time involving linked concessions held by three companies, each headed by Thai nationals who are also senior executives from Thailand's largest sugar producer, Mitr Phol.

I checked Mitr Phol's website. It did not mention the concessions. NGOs said that the village of Bos in the concession had been burned to the ground. People who had lived there since 1998, when it was cleared of land mines left by the Khmer Rouge, had been expelled. They had official documentation of their land title, dated 2003, but were told that their land was now within the new sugar concession.

Back on the road, I was heading for another enterprise of the sugar senator, the Koh Kong sugar refinery. It is Cambodia's first since the French left more than half a century ago. It had been opened by the prime minister, Hun Sen, a year before and occupied an improbably large site that locals said once contained three villages. Most of the land was unused – and the factory was only open for three months a year, during the harvest.

The refinery processes sugar from a 20,000-hectare concession given in 2006 to the ubiquitous Ly Yong Phat and two business partners, the Thai company Khon Kaen Sugar, and Vewong, a Taiwanese company that manufactures sugary soft drinks and instant noodles. The UN Commissioner for Human Rights reported in 2007 that the concession was granted without public consultation, and that to get around the 10,000-hectare limit on the size of concessions, land registration was split between Ly Yong Phat and the boss of Khon Kaen Sugar, Chamroon Chinthammit. In 2011, Ly Yong Phat was reported to have sold his share to the other partners, making the concession entirely foreign-owned.

Before that, in late 2009, Khon Kaen Sugar signed a contract, selling all of its output from Cambodia for five years to Tate & Lyle.

This included the Koh Kong plantations. The first shipment of 10,000 tonnes, valued at some $3 million, left for Europe in June 2010. A month later, Tate & Lyle sold its European sugar business, including its famous brand name and the supply contract with Thailand and Cambodia, to the US company American Sugar Refining.

Just past the Koh Kong refinery, I turned into Srae Ambel, where about 50 people assembled in the village temple, beneath large murals and statues of the Buddha. They sat cross-legged on straw mats made from grass cut from land they could no longer enter. They wanted to tell me about their lost land. Things went slowly. Nobody seemed to want to talk. After a few minutes, I noticed a villager at the back, smoking nervously and taking notes. I discovered later that everyone knew him as the company spy. After he got bored and departed, they loosened up. The stories came thick and fast.

One woman, her hair tied in a tight bun, sat forward urgently: 'Some soldiers came and told me to remove my house, because it was not my land. I said no. I said I would report them to the commune officer. But they just smashed the house down. I built another one, but they burned that. Then they burned our rice and all our belongings. They offered just a hectare in compensation. But it was sacred forest land, which isn't theirs to give. I can't use that land. I'd be scared to.'

Local NGOs calculate that the sugar plantation had consumed some 5,000 hectares of land owned and farmed by local villagers, as well as areas of common pasture. In Srae Ambel alone, 250 families lost land. Most still had enough to grow some rice, but their grazing land had been taken. One gap-toothed old woman said she once had 30 cattle, 'but I only have one left'. A man said: 'I used to have 15 buffalo. If I got sick and needed some money to go to the hospital, I sold a buffalo. But now we have fewer cattle, so we can't do that.

And without the pastures we don't have grass to repair our roofs.'

The pyjama-wearing women didn't know who owned the sugar company. But one man in a blue jacket, a community representative called Konh Song, told them it was Ly Yong Phat. 'He visited two houses here in 2007. He said he would try to find replacement land for the villagers. But the land they offered was not good, so we rejected the offer. We haven't seen him since.' I asked the villagers where they thought the sugar went. Thailand, they suggested. Then someone said: 'That's where it was refined before they built the new factory here. After that it goes to England.' 'So,' I said, 'you lose your land so that I can eat sugar.' The women smiled, but seemed afraid to appear rude by agreeing. Then one of the men, Hun Phan, asked me not to buy the sugar. 'It's corrupt; it's not clean. People are crying here because they have lost their land.'

They said they had legal possession of their land but that the company took it regardless. Economic Land Concessions overrode local land rights. Nor did it matter what they used their land for. One middle-aged man, Teng Kao, had planted 15 hectares with cashew trees along with palms, tamarinds, bamboo and mangoes. 'I had over a thousand trees. I could have got rich and had a car,' he said, putting aside his spectacles to see me more clearly. 'But they destroyed all the trees before I had a chance to make my money.'

Later, one of the village youths drove me on his motorbike through the back roads, past a sleeping guard, on to the farm. We saw two cashew trees in a hedge – all that remained from Teng's orchard. Teng wouldn't come with us. He said he was a local representative of the villagers and that it would anger the company guards if he showed up with foreigners. But maybe he just couldn't face it. He could see what was happening to the village. They used to collect forest products from the mountain nearby, he said, but now the sugar farm was in the way and they could not cross it. The local streams were polluted with farm chemicals and waste from the refinery. The fish were poisoned. 'The children used to drink water from the rivers when they were looking after the buffalo. Now they get sick if they do that.' And there weren't many buffalo these days, anyhow.

It might seem as if it's all over for the people of Srae Ambel and the other victims of the sugar rush. At Srae Ambel, they have done with protesting. When it all started in 2006, they marched in Phnom Penh. They came home and tried to block the company bulldozers. There were arrests. One woman wiped her tears as she remembered: 'We had to sell ten cows because of the cost of going to court.' Some said that, because they got arrested, they got no compensation. In 2007, the UN High Commissioner for Human Rights reported that the sugar concessions in Koh Kong were 'granted without public consultation . . . The clearing of rice fields and orchards belonging to villagers has affected over 400 families . . . and has restricted the availability of grazing land. Some have little or no remaining farm-land. Company security guards have reportedly seized or shot cattle straying into the concession.' The farm had 'expanded activities despite efforts to resolve the dispute'.

Nothing had changed as a result. American Sugar did not reply to questions posed by Cambodian NGOs, or later by me. Five years after the arrival of the senator for sugar, lives in Srae Ambel were disintegrating fast. As I left someone had a parting shot: 'Pol Pot killed us quickly. This is slow. But they are killing us just the same.' Tate & Lyle refer all inquiries to American Sugar.

But the story may not be over. The sugar rush is sustained in Cambodia because of that country's preferential trade arrangement with the European Union, known as the Everything-But-Arms system. Its purpose is to allow the world's poorest countries to export effectively unlimited quantities of certain goods to the EU with zero tariffs. In the case of sugar there are guaranteed minimum prices, too. The European incentives have created a sweet spot for capital, where there is everything to gain and nothing to lose. One result has been widespread land-grabbing.

In May 2011, shortly after my trip, a Swedish member of the European Parliament, Cecilia Wikstrom, followed much the same route as I had. Afterwards, in Phnom Penh, she declared there was widespread evidence of human rights abuses, and that she was not satisfied with the response from the deputy prime minister, Sok An. 'There is no doubt that the villagers have suffered,' she said. 'This is blood sugar.' She called for the Everything-But-Arms terms to be suspended for Cambodian sugar.

At the time of writing, that hasn't happened. But if they were suspended, the bubble would burst. There is every chance the land-grabbing, at least for sugar, would stop here. And some of the concessions might cease business. Some of the villagers might even get their land back.

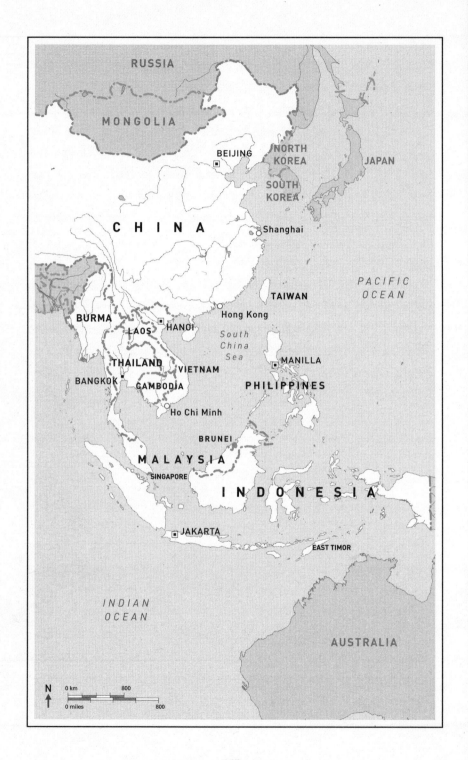

18

SOUTHEAST ASIA
Rubber hits the road to China

In the hills of northern Laos, up near the border with China, the rice paddy is disappearing. For thousands of years, nothing was more important here than to grow a constant supply of rice. But rice is no longer the focus of every meal. Village life is no longer organized around the relentless labour needed to grow it. People ride into town on their motorbikes to buy bread and chickens. So what grows now on the hillside terraces, where rice was once planted on almost every square inch? The answer, in this corner of Laos, is rubber.

The Associated Press's Denis Gray visited the remote village of Chaleunsouk in northern Laos in 2008, and produced a memorable item describing how 'the rice fields that blanketed this remote mountain village for generations' have been replaced by 'neat rows of young rubber trees – the sap destined for China . . . Sixty families in this dirt-poor, mud-caked village of gaunt men and hunched women now are growing rubber, like thousands of others across the rugged mountains.'

There are several large rubber plantations in the hills. But many villagers grow rubber trees on their own land. In any event, the new masters here, whether as plantation owners or buyers, are Chinese rubber companies like Sino-Lao Rubber, Yunnan Rubber and Chia Xuang. In the past decade, they have conducted what Yunnan

University and the International Union for the Conservation of Nature reported to be 'a sudden, rapid and largely uncontrolled' invasion of northern Laos.

Along with other commodity crops such as cotton, rubber has long competed with food for the world's farmland. Early in the twentieth century, Malaya produced three-quarters of the world's rubber, under British control. Today, some 10 million hectares of the planet – an area almost the size of England – is covered in rubber trees. And global demand for rubber latex is rising by 3 per cent a year. As with many commodities these days, China is the demand driver.

China expects to be consuming a third of the world's rubber by 2020, mainly for car tyres. And Laos's Communist state wants to hitch a ride on China's coming car boom to join big producers like Thailand, Indonesia, Malaysia, Vietnam and India. With its long border with China, Laos is ideally placed to become, in effect, China's new rubber-growing province. This, it hopes, will be how the rubber hits the road for the laggardly Lao economy.

So Chinese companies are welcomed as they cross the hills. And Laos was pleased to provide the land for a new road, called the Northern Economic Corridor, constructed through the country's far north between China and Thailand. It will ease export of the rubber from the 140,000 hectares of this small landlocked country that have been converted to growing rubber. It will help Laos meet its target of doubling the amount of converted land by 2020.

Alan Ziegler, a geographer at the University of Singapore, says that a 'rubber juggernaut' is rolling through Southeast Asia. Altogether more than half a million hectares have been converted from peasant paddy and woodland to rubber in Thailand, Vietnam, Cambodia, Burma, Laos and China's Yunnan province. Ziegler compares it to the takeover of Indonesia by oil-palm and timber plantations, many of which also supply China. He fears similarly 'devastating' ecological and social consequences.

Burma is granting Chinese companies giant rubber plantations covering up to 20,000 hectares, riding roughshod over the interests of villagers. It expects to have 400,000 hectares of rubber by 2020. Both Thailand and Vietnam are developing their own rubber plantations, with the Chinese market in mind. They have about a million hectares of latex-producing land. Such is the intensity of demand from their regional big brother that they are invading their poorer neighbours to grab more land to grow more rubber for sale to China.

Among the Vietnamese rubber barons being granted large plantations in southern Laos is Doan Nguyen Duc, a flamboyant figure who claims to have been Vietnam's first private owner of an executive jet. He has grown a small carpentry business into one of Vietnam's largest companies, Hoang Anh Gia Lai. He explained his newfound enthusiasm for agricultural projects to *Forbes Asia* in 2009: 'I think natural resources are limited and I need to take them before they're gone.' He grabbed 10,000 hectares of rubber plantations in Laos in return for building an athletes' village in the capital Vientiane, for the 2009 Southeast Asian Games. Miles Kenney-Lazar at Clark University in Worcester, Maryland, says much of the land given to Doan previously grew rice and vegetables and grazed cattle. Of seven impacted villages, only four knew their land had been handed over when Doan showed up.

Cambodia, meanwhile, plans to multiply its rubber plantations eightfold to 800,000 hectares as early as 2015 to supply China, and recently invited Vietnamese companies to take over 37,000 hectares for the purpose. Doan already has 15,000 hectares there.

Rubber, as we have seen in earlier chapters, has an inglorious history. Not least in Southeast Asia. In the 1930s, French tyre company Michelin ran one of a string of rubber plantations that extended for 300 kilometres along the coast of Vietnam. They were a byword for brutality, and incubated the Communist activism that later threw first the French and then the Americans out of Southeast Asia. More recently, plantations in traditional rubber-growing regions, like former British imperial Malaya, have given up growing rubber in favour of oil palm. Smallholders have often taken up the slack. As much as three-quarters of the world's rubber has come from smallholders in recent years. But in countries like China and Vietnam, estates have retained their control. And as their influence grows, big plantations are making a comeback.

The Chinese are coming. It is a constant refrain. A constant paranoia. In London, Susan Payne's Emergent Asset Management claims to base its investment strategy on the belief that the West will go to war to prevent China from taking over the world's resources. After two decades of double-digit growth, the country of 1.3 billion people is, of course, a fast-growing player on the world stage, demanding an increasing share of the world's resources. But there is much myth-making about Chinese land-grabbing, and how far it might go. So first, how are things in the Middle Kingdom?

With almost a fifth of the world's population, but only a tenth of the world's arable land and much less of the world's water, China is short of some basic resources for growing crops. And it is grow-ing shorter. Urbanization, industrial developments, reservoirs, soil erosion and spreading deserts have cut the amount of cultivated land in China by about 6 per cent in the past decade alone. An estimated 50 million Chinese farmers have lost their land since 1990. Rural protests against domestic land grabs proliferate. Meanwhile, a growing demand for meat and dairy products, which take more land and water to produce, has been stoking up the pressure. China accounts for 30 per cent of global meat consumption. The amazing thing, perhaps, is that for most foodstuffs, China still largely feeds itself. More so, in fact, than almost any other country.

China does need some imports of foodstuffs. It imports a lot of sugar, for instance. And Chinese companies are grabbing land to grow more, partly to make ethanol. Complant International Sugar – which already grows sugar in Benin, Sierra Leone and Madagascar through its Cayman Islands-based subsidiary Hua Lien – in 2011 leased Jamaica's last three sugar estates, covering 30,000 hectares, from the ailing state-owned Sugar Company of Jamaica. A Chinese sugar project in Mali will cover 20,000 hectares (see Chapter Twenty-five); another of similar size is planned in the Philippines.

But China's main need is for soya, which it gets mostly from Latin America, to feed its livestock. China wants to cut out the soya middle men. It clearly does not trust the large American-owned commodity traders like Cargill and Bunge. Leading the way is Beidahuang Land Cultivation Group, a giant state-owned farming business based in the northeast of the country that grows more soya than anyone else in China. In 2011, it secured a deal with the governor of Rio Negro in Argentina to lease some 230,000 hectares. It also tied up a long-term agreement with domestic Argentine land giant Credus, which controls more than a million hectares of farms. Beidahuang said it would also build a new port to export the soya.

China's demand for soya is also taking it to Brazil. And, as I saw during my visit to the *cerrado*, Chongqing Grain Group has sealed a $2.4 billion deal there to set up western Bahia's biggest soya-processing plant and ship 1.5 billion tonnes of soya back to China every year.

While China's demands are large, they are not insatiable. The fruits of its one-child policy are already seeing its population stabilizing, and its headcount could soon be falling. Yes, as the Chinese grow richer, they will demand more stuff – requiring imports of land-dependent commodities like rubber, cotton, timber and biofuels. But the truth may be that China's food consumption explosion has already happened. If Chinese agricultural corporations continue to take over the world, as they may, it will often be to supply other markets. Like you and me.

China is integrating into the global economy. This integration means that, besides large Chinese corporations travelling the world looking to make profits growing food on foreign soils, we may also find more landgrabbers moving into China. It is already happening on a small scale. Take chickens. In 2008, Goldman Sachs, the American private equity bank, spent $300 million buying ten giant poultry farms in China's Hunan and Fujian provinces. Sadly the masters of the universe won't be putting on their wellies. They are outsourcing management. But it is not a one-off. Goldman Sachs, along with Deutsche Bank and others, has also bought into Chinese pig farms. And it has a stake in the Yurun Food Group, the country's second-largest meat processor.

Singapore is developing a high-tech mega-farm, known as the China-Jilin Modern Agricultural Food Zone, near Changchun in the fertile black soils of the far northeast of China. The farm, at 150,000 hectares, is more than twice the size of Singapore. The aim is to grow rice and maize, raise cattle and pigs, and even establish vineyards – to supply both Singapore and China. Meanwhile, New Zealand's dairy giant Fonterra has a number of Chinese farms. It owns 43 per cent of the dairy company responsible for the scandal of milk powder poisoned with melamine that killed six Chinese children and made a quarter-million sick in 2008.

What about Africa? The continent has been the prime focus for Chinese companies searching for metals to sustain their country's fast-growing industrial economy. Beijing promises to build roads, bridges, ports and other infrastructure in return for being allowed to mine Africa. By one assessment there are 1.5 million Chinese in Africa today. Chinese contractors have been digging water canals and pursuing irrigation schemes in Mali. Chinese scientists are manning seed labs in South Africa. Chinese smallholder farmers who have lost their land to domestic land grabs are busy tilling soil from Senegal to Mozambique. But how much farmland are the Chinese grabbing? The answer is much less than sometimes appears.

As we saw in Chapter Seven, reports that the Zhongxing Telecommunications Equipment company has three million hectares of the Democratic Republic of Congo to grow oil palm are out by an order of magnitude. A much discussed scheme in Zimbabwe, in which the state-owned China International Water and Electric Company would get maize in return for building a 100,000-hectare irrigation scheme near Bulawayo, seems stillborn. 'Much of what we hear is misinformation and rumour, about large-scale land grabs and sinister Chinese plots,' says Lila Buckley, a China expert at the International Institute for Environment and Development in London.

There is some activity. But it is not the Chinese way to act in haste. The China State Farms Agribusiness Corporation has been farming in Africa since 1994 and operates seven projects across the continent, including farms in Zambia, Tanzania, South Africa and Guinea Bissau. But according to *China Daily*, in 2010 those farms totalled just 8,600 hectares, mostly comprising a sisal plantation in Tanzania. 'Agricultural investment requires more patience and long-term view than other industries,' said the company's deputy general manager, Xu Jun. 'The fragile political situation is still the biggest challenge for Chinese companies investing in Africa.' Chinese companies also often bring in their own workers, rather than employing locals. That happened on Sino Cam Iko's 10,000 hectares of rice fields in Cameroon, where Chinese managers say locals don't work hard and steal the rice.

Put simply, the Chinese and Africans often don't get on too well, says Buckley, who researched their mutual incomprehension in

Senegal. A Chinese manager told her: 'The biggest problem with agriculture in Senegal is people's mentality. They are very easily satisfied. If they have enough to eat, they won't work any more. There is a lot of arable land that they don't use.' The locals, meanwhile, complained that 'the Chinese want the workers to come and work for eight hours. But we have a different approach. We work for a few hours, then rest by the side of the field, chat with our friends, drink some tea, share our stories.' Such cultural clashes can flare up into something worse. A plan from China's Ex-Im Bank to fund Chinese cattle ranches in Mozambique's Zambezia and Tete provinces was abandoned in 2007 after a public outcry.

East Asians, it has to be said, sometimes have big trouble in Africa. The other major example is the fate of South Korea. The country is one of the world's biggest food importers. It imports almost 90 per cent of its wheat and maize. And it is growing uncomfortable about that. In 2008, Korean food companies suddenly found that key foreign suppliers were banning exports in order to feed their own people. In Seoul, the government established a National Food Strategy to subsidize national corporations willing to annex foreign land to secure key supplies.

There are visceral fears here. Koreans starved to death in large numbers during the Korean War little more than half a century ago. They still do in Communist North Korea. Despite this, modern South Korea has neglected agriculture, concentrating instead on a break-neck industrialization. Its farmers are old and its farms dilapidated. Now it looks with dread at the prospect that, as a major report by the Samsung Economic Research Institute put it in 2011, countries may in the future 'weaponize food' and cut off its breadline.

So, by 2030, South Korea wants to grow a quarter of its food on foreign soil owned or leased by Korean companies. The executives of Daewoo and the other industrial corporations that made South Korea rich are now on a new mission – to scour the world for land to feed their nation.

But not all has gone well. Not everybody welcomes Koreans, even Koreans with money. In 2008, Richard Shin, head of Daewoo Logistics' foreign land purchases, did a deal with the Madagascan president, Marc Ravalomanana, to take over 1.3 million hectares of that country to grow half of South Korea's maize. The proposed land grab represented not much more than 2 per cent of Madagascar, but was the equivalent of a quarter of its current arable land. Daewoo promised in return to build roads and hospitals, and provide thousands of jobs. But the deal collapsed when anger in the African country over the deal unseated the president.

In response to the failure of the deal, Shin said phlegmatically, 'If not this Madagascar project, we will go for another. It's pure business, not colonialism of any form, old or new.' Three years on, the *Korea Times* reported that 73 Korean companies were growing grain on 23,000 hectares in 18 countries. And many more and bigger deals would follow.

Korea has leased 30,000 hectares in the Khalkhgol region in the far east of Mongolia. Hyundai, the world's biggest shipbuilder, bought a two-thirds share in a Russian company farming 50,000 hectares in the Russian Far East near Vladivostock and has its eye on a similar-sized piece of the Brazilian *cerrado*. The Korean International Cooperation Agency said in 2011 that it was shopping for 100,000 hectares of government-designated 'idle land' in the Philippines. Daewoo planned a 20,000-hectare maize farm in Indonesia. The Korean food giant Daesang had hooked up with a Korean expat farmer in Cambodia's Kampong Speu province, Lee Woo-chang, to grow maize on 13,000 hectares for shipping back to South Korea. Like the Chinese, it looks like, for now at least, the Koreans may have better luck in Asia.

PART FIVE

AFRICAN DREAMS

The myth of wild Africa runs deep in Western hearts. We grab its savannahs and forests to protect our vision of nature – expelling its traditional custodians in the process. The Maasai in Tanzania have suffered especially, but green grabs create environmental refugees from the shores of South Africa to the jungles of the Congo. Meanwhile, South Africans are embarked on a 'second great trek' to find new farms across the continent. But in places, land-grabbing by outsiders is going into reverse, as the biofuels bubble bursts, and as the white landowners of Zimbabwe are usurped by war veterans and Mugabe's new oligarchs.

19

MAASAILAND, TANZANIA

The white people's place

Fancy your own private cottage in the Serengeti, with a grandstand view of arguably the most precious wildlife region on Earth, a home of lions, elephants, rhinos, buffalo, cheetahs, and the greatest spectacle of them all, the wildebeest migration? The one I have in mind will cost you $1,875 a night for your own room, or $1,675 if you are prepared to bunk up with a friend. For that you get the sound of wildlife at night and the daytime run of the

136,000-hectare Grumeti game reserve. As the South African eco-safari group that manages the place promises – after mentioning the 'imported chandeliers and hand-crafted furniture', the spa, the lawn croquet and the archery – 'you'll have this wild stretch of Africa all to yourself.'

Everyone agrees that the Serengeti is special. In his 1909 book *African Game Trails*, describing his year-long orgy of hunting through East Africa, former US president Teddy Roosevelt dubbed the Serengeti a 'Pleistocene' landscape, a 'great fragment out of the long-buried past of our race'. But what Roosevelt mentioned only in passing was the human population – the brightly adorned, aristocratic Maasai people – through whose land he rampaged.

Conservationists have often used similar language to Roosevelt. But for me, the most remarkable thing about the Serengeti is not its sense of a land without humans but rather the opposite. For the truth is that this most extraordinary collection of big game has shared this land with native tribes such as the Maasai people and their cattle for hundreds, probably thousands of years. There is a symbiosis entirely at odds with our modern ideas about humans being in inevitable conflict with nature. And because we cannot, or do not want to, see that symbiosis, we have deemed the local herders too dangerous to stay. The long-time custodians of the Serengeti and its wildlife are being systematically expelled from their land.

Bizarre as it may seem, our vision of virgin nature – on the hoof, and red in tooth and claw – has encouraged the takeover of the land by a new breed of super-rich conservationists and safari operators. The Serengeti, these days, is not so much a Pleistocene landscape as the world's biggest zoo, in which the Maasai warriors, with their bright red clothing, elaborate beads and lethal spears, are reduced to decorative walk-on parts.

For an extra $500 per person during your stay, the people at the Grumeti game reserve will let you take a balloon safari across a place where, as they put it, 'the land stretches for ever.' This phrase, by the way, is the Maasai meaning of the word Serengeti. Now, however, it stretches for ever for you, but not for them. While you receive 'seclusion and exclusivity', they and their cattle aren't allowed into the reserve. The concession holders told me they were 'legally bound' to keep 'unscrupulous locals' from bringing cattle on to their traditional lands. But even a travel correspondent for the *Daily Telegraph*, visiting in 2007, felt a pang of unease. With English furniture in the lodge and white South African guides in the Land Rovers, 'the fact that this was Tanzania, with its own culture and ecosystem, seemed almost incidental,' he said.

The Grumeti reserve is roughly the size of Surrey. Overlooking the Grumeti River on the western side of the Serengeti plain, it runs down towards the shores of Lake Victoria. It is a national game reserve under the control of Wall Street hotshot Paul Tudor Jones. A welterweight boxing champion from Memphis, Tennessee, he joined up with his cotton-trading relatives from the Dunavant dynasty, before going into hedge funds. He became a billionaire after successfully predicting Black Monday, the stock market crash in 1987. In 1990, after being convicted of filling in a protected wetland on his Maryland estate, he took up conservation philanthropy. He bought the Grumeti concession in 2002 from the Tanzanian government. In mid-2011, the influential US travel magazine *Travel and Leisure* named his spread the world's best hotel.

Jones is not the only high-roller attracted to the Serengeti plains. The landscape may not be as picturesque as Patagonia, but the big game sure beats llamas. Travel east from Grumeti, to the other side of the Serengeti National Park, and you may stumble on Gulf sheikhs and their friends out to bag a slice of wild Africa. This is a hunting reserve, just for them – thanks to a deal done in 1992 between the then Tanzanian president, Ali Hassan Mwinyi, and Brigadier Mohamed Abdul Rahim Al Ali – 'the brigadier' as he has been widely known locally ever since, though at home in the United Arab Emirates he has since been promoted to major general.

The brigadier's safari company, the Ortello Business Corporation, has exclusive hunting rights to a large area of the 400,000-hectare Loliondo Game Controlled Area. The area is a crossroads for wildlife between the Serengeti National Park to the west, the Ngorongoro conservation area to the south, and the Maasai Mara reserve in Kenya to the north. The brigadier does not own the land, which is traditional Maasai territory and contains several villages. But the Maasai are required to keep out of his way, and the government deploys its elite paramilitary Field Force Unit to ensure they do. The area is so exclusive, so apart from Tanzania, so Arab that if you drive anywhere near it your mobile phone beeps with a text welcoming you to the United Arab Emirates.

The brigadier and his Loliondo land grab were controversial from the start. In 1993, the *New York Times* asked whether, in the light of stories about the brigadier's past Rambo-style hunting excursions on the Serengeti, Tanzania had 'declared open season on its own protected wildlife?' The answer seemed to be yes. Allegations soon surfaced of hunting by the brigadier's guests outside the six-month season, of bush burning to drive the animals towards the hunters, of marksmen going out at night with spotlights to shoot leopards from vehicles using AK-47s, and even of lions being captured and taken from a private airstrip to a zoo in the United Arab Emirates.

The Maasai say their grazing rights have been curtailed to meet the whims of the hunters. The brigadier, who is now a prominent real estate developer in Dubai, has done little to assuage their concerns. Rather the opposite. In July 2009, the Field Force Unit and Ortello's own security staff entered several Maasai villages, evicted the residents and threw their cattle off grazing land. The government's tourism minister, Shamsa Mwangunga, defended the action, saying the Maasai were building houses in the hunting zone and grazing their cattle during the hunting season. But there was a news clampdown. Several European diplomats and journalists were refused permission to visit the area to see for themselves.

The first independent assessment came the following year from James Anaya, a law professor from the University of Arizona and the UN's special rapporteur on human rights and indigenous people. More than 200 homesteads were burned down, he said. Their maize fields and food stores were destroyed. Three thousand people were left without shelter, food or water, and 50,000 cattle without grazing land. Tear gas was used. One woman was raped, some men were chained, and three children had disappeared.

Anaya went on to accuse the Tanzania government of failing to investigate the affair. But he didn't sound too surprised. He said that the evictions followed years of 'ever increasing restrictions of the rights [of the Maasai villagers] to graze and water their livestock within the game control area'. This arose because of 'a larger government policy favouring the interests of private enterprises engaged in conservation tourism and wildlife hunting, principally the Ortello Business Corporation, over the rights of indigenous peoples'. The Tanzanian government did not respond to Anaya's report.

Safari tourism, whether with cameras or automatic weapons, is a huge industry in Tanzania. It is responsible for a quarter of export earnings. Hunting is banned across the border in Kenya, but hunters in Tanzania spend big for the privilege of cruising the Serengeti to bag the 'big five' – elephants, lions, leopards, buffaloes and rhinos.

Jack Brittingham's Tanzania Adventures is state of the art. Brittingham, a Mexican-American, has turned a business making hunting videos into a pan-African safari organization that, he promises in a clear nod to Roosevelt's exploits, will provide Americans with experiences that 'rival even the early years of traditional trophy hunting in Africa'. He has a base camp at the foot of Mount Kitumbeine at the heart of the Serengeti ecosystem, which provides 'a truly unique opportunity to hunt its dense old-growth forest preserve for mountain buffalo and exceptionally large leopard'.

Brittingham's hunting is more traditional than the brigadier's. His marksmen often go on foot in rugged terrain. But they need deep pockets before stepping on to the Serengeti. In 2011, a 14-day buffalo hunt started at $53,000, with an extra $2,000-plus payable for any buffalo actually hit. A 28-day lion hunt cost upwards of $100,000. The trophy fee for an elephant was $22.500, 90 per cent of which went to the Tanzanian government and 10 per cent to the Tembo Foundation, an NGO that fights poaching. (Note: poaching is illegal hunting by poor natives.) Brittingham promises 'to pamper you and your family after a day of hunting'. But those wanting a taste of the real East Africa may feel disappointed. Five of his seven professional hunters are South African whites (*Mzungu*, in Swahili). None is a Maasai.

European colonialists, hunters and conservationists have all found it difficult to believe that the Maasai and their cattle can live in harmony with the wildlife. It runs counter to the mythology of a Pleistocene landscape, to conventional ideas about conservation, and to rather more selfish notions about what an African safari should offer to Western visitors.

In the 1950s, with leaders in Europe talking of granting their African colonies independence, environmentalists warned that Africans could not be trusted with wildlife. Julian Huxley, then head of the United Nations science organization UNESCO and future founder of the environment group WWF, said they would invade the parks and slaughter all the animals in 'a surviving sector of the rich natural world as it was before the rise of modern man'. The Maasai cattle were 'rapidly reducing large stretches of land to dusty semi-desert', he said.

Perhaps the most powerful message came in 1959 in the book and film *Serengeti Shall Not Die*. German conservationist Bernhard Grzimek, with his son Michael, called for the existing Serengeti National Park to be sealed off from human inhabitants. 'A national park must remain a piece of primordial wilderness to be effective. No men, not even native ones, should live inside its borders. The Serengeti cannot support wild animals and domestic cattle at the same time.' The ashes of the two men are buried there. Their views on African ecology were largely mistaken, but their influence lingers on. Bernhard Grzimek was director of the Frankfurt Zoo, which continues to advise on conservation policy in the Serengeti today.

The British wanted to clear the Maasai out of most of the Serengeti, including both the Serengeti National Park and the region round the Ngorongoro crater, a large basin-shaped crater rich in grassland that was the Maasai's best dry-season grazing grounds. And gradually that is happening. Before independence, some 10,000 Maasai and their cattle were expelled from the national park. A decade later, the government of Julius Nyerere removed them from the Ngorongoro crater, which he converted into the country's most popular tourist hub, surrounded by hotels. In 2007, the government proposed halving to 25,000 the Maasai population in the wider area surrounding the crater.

The Maasai are now excluded from two million hectares of the plain. They are routinely blamed for the environmental problems that arise from their being corralled into ever smaller areas, while the safari revenues end up in the hands of travel entrepreneurs, the government parks service and the new network of private, often foreign-owned nature reserves.

The law is little help. In theory, the Village Land Act of 1999 guarantees villagers the freedom to use their traditional pastures. But, as in much of Africa, such vague statements are easily ignored when the overall political landscape is hostile. In his inauguration

255

speech in 2005, President Jakaya Kikwete told parliament that: 'We must abandon altogether nomadic pastoralism.' A few months later, he reiterated: 'I am committed to taking unpopular steps to [stop] pastoralists, in order to protect the environment for the benefit of the nation and future generations.' Close to 40 per cent of Tanzania is now 'protected' in various ways – frequently by excluding the Maasai and other traditional pastoralists. A new draft plan for Loliondo, where the Arab sheikhs roam free, gives only 17 per cent of the land to the Maasai.

The Maasai are not opposed to tourism. Far from it. But they want tourism 'grounded in village rights and not state rights', as Ben Gardner, anthropologist at the University of Washington, puts it. They want to be in charge of their own land, not 'reduced to bead sellers and recipients of philanthropic help from foreigners'. Sadly, the huge profits to be made from tourism, bolstered by shallow environmental rhetoric, mean that they are seldom left alone to achieve that.

Some outsiders continue to believe that, in their philanthropic hands, conservation and community can be reunited. But there is too much history for them to have much chance of success. Take the case of Boston-based Rick Thomson and his partner Judi Wineland. In 2006, their tour company Thomson Safaris (no relation to the British Thomson tour company) bought the 500-hectare Sukenya farm on the Serengeti plain for $1.2 million from the government-owned Tanzania Breweries. The farm is next door to the brigadier's hunting reserve and has filled with gazelle, wildebeest, giraffe and impala – no doubt many of them fleeing the Gulf gunslingers. The couple renamed the farm the Enashiva nature refuge and began inviting tourists.

So far, so good. But it turned out that the brewery had never farmed much of the land, which it had annexed from Maasai pastures in the 1980s. The Maasai had soon gone back to herding their cattle there. So when the American pair showed up two decades later with an ambition to practise 'sustainable and responsible tourism', they met instant opposition. Disputes over grazing rights have proliferated. There have been stand-offs, often involving the police, during which one herder was shot in the jaw. Journalists who have gone to investigate have been arrested. One was declared a 'prohibited immigrant'.

The couple feel aggrieved. 'We have definitely gotten a bad deal,' Wineland told me. 'We are ethical people who have not stolen land or mistreated anyone.' She says they have good relations with a couple of local villages, who are allowed to graze some cattle on the reserve during the dry season. But one clan, the Purko, 'continue to oppose any and all limitations on grazing'. She accuses them of 'spreading lies, inciting fear and co-opting the legitimate cause of Maasai rights' in a campaign against the couple that has made some of their leaders rich. Anthropologists now discuss what went wrong here, as an example of how good intentions are not enough when foreigners take land that others claim.

A similar cultural clash occurred at the Manyara cattle ranch after it was bought up by the Tanzania Land Conservation Trust, a creation of the Washington-based African Wildlife Foundation. The plan was to buy land and manage it in trust for both the locals and wildlife. The Manyara ranch is the Trust's flagship project. It covers 18,000 hectares and sits a little south of the Serengeti plain, between the Tarangire and Lake Manyara national parks, both of which are full of elephants. The Trust wants to conserve the grassland as part of the recreation of the 40-kilometre wildlife corridor between the two parks.

When the government put the ranch up for sale, the local Maasai villages, Esilalei and Oltukai, wrote to the president asking for the land to be returned to them. Instead, the government gave the Conservation Trust a 99-year lease, perhaps attracted by funding offered from USAID 'to conserve . . . a critical wildlife corridor and . . . to benefit partner communities'. The omens looked good. 'The Maasai initially welcomed the ranch as a jointly run conservation area, which they thought they owned,' says Mara Goldman of the University of Colorado, a geographer who has studied the project in detail. It turned out that nobody had got round to telling the villagers that the land was not theirs, and had been bought by the Trust.

Villagers sat on enough steering committees and other bodies to feel involved. But the Trust board was dominated by conservation 'experts' from the African Wildlife Foundation, which formally owns the land, along with others from WWF, the UN Development Programme and the country's National Parks Authority.

To make matters worse, says Goldman, most of the outside experts believed that the local community was causing ecological decline. They held to the conventional view that livestock grazing was fundamentally incompatible with wildlife. The ranch managers began to make decisions without doing more than notifying the Maasai herders. They introduced fines for trespassers, while the wildlife roamed free. Though many of the villagers have jobs on the ranch, says Goldman, 'they resent what they see as an outsider-run conservation area on land taken away from them.'

The cultural drift escalated with the opening in 2010 of an elite private safari camp, which now dominates most of the reserve. The $650-a-night Manyara Ranch Conservancy swiftly applied to build its own airstrip. Such developments are logical steps, no doubt, to ensure long-term funding for outside management of the ecosystem. But what about the residents? Goldman relates how, at the start, the Maasai's proposed name for the conservancy – Ramat, meaning stewardship – was rejected as 'sounding too Arabic . . . during the war on terror'. Now she says, among themselves, the Maasai call it Sunguni, meaning the white people's place.

The Serengeti extends north into Kenya, where land ownership is different from Tanzania, though no less contentious. Most recently, land disputes between tribes boiled over into riots and massacres in 2007. But many of the disputes date back to mass movements of people initiated by the British to create land for themselves.

The district of Laikipia, on the edge of the Rift Valley, is a hotbed of land grabs. A century ago, it was mostly controlled by the Maasai. British colonialists subsequently shipped many of the Maasai out, leaving a majority of Kikuyu, Kenya's biggest tribe. But even though the Kikuyu run the country and form the majority in Laikipia, they don't run the district. It is mostly owned by a motley mixture of old white settler families, and a new high-roller international elite. Independence? Maybe they missed it.

In fact, just 20 people and institutions own three-quarters of Laikipia, an area of almost a million hectares. Many of them are converting old cattle ranches created by white settlers almost a century ago into chic wildlife sanctuaries that have attracted high-spending tourists. Much buying and selling is going on among the elite here. And a colourful lot they are, too.

One of the largest holdings is the 37,000-hectare Ol Pejeta ranch. This land was taken from the Maasai in the 1920s by Lord (Tom) Delamere, the son of one of Kenya's first English aristocratic settlers and a founder of the notorious hard-drinking, loose-living Happy Valley set. Imagine F. Scott Fitzgerald's *The Great Gatsby* reset in Africa. Delamere's family, the Cholmondeleys, who have another huge ranch at Soysambu in the Rift Valley, eventually sold Ol Pejeta to the father-in-law of Christina Onassis, Henri Roussel, who was president of Roussel Uclaf, a huge French pharmaceuticals company. (The Cholmondeleys themselves hit the headlines again in 2005, when the heir to the family estates, another Tom, became the only white inmate in Nairobi's high-security prison after being convicted of shooting dead a poacher on Soysambu.)

The next owner of Ol Pejeta was the Saudi billionaire arms dealer and playboy Adnan Khashoggi, who used it as a hideaway for activities that brought back memories of Happy Valley. But he departed after a dispute over a loan made to him by the buccaneering British entrepreneur Tiny Rowland.

Rowland was born in a First World War refugee camp in India. He initially made his fortune running tobacco farms in Rhodesia. Later, in London, where his London and Rhodesia Mining and Land Company (Lonrho) was based, his feuds were almost as well known as his business activities. He was once famously described by British prime minister Ted Heath as 'the unpleasant and unacceptable face of capitalism'. He took over Ol Pejeta for a while, before selling to conservationists. The ranch is now run as a nature refuge and tourist resort. It is owned by Jon Stryker, the American heir to a fortune made in medical technology, through his Arcus Foundation. Environmental management is done by the British conservation group Fauna and Flora International and the Lewa Conservancy, of which more later.

The 27,000-hectare Ol Jogi ranch is owned by Liouba Stoupakova, the Russian model widow of Alec Wildenstein. Wildenstein was a French billionaire racehorse breeder. He reputedly owned the world's largest private art collection, which he stored in a former nuclear bunker in New York City. Wildenstein's first wife, Jocelyne, whose scandalous New York divorce case against him had the tabloids agog for weeks, said the ranch cost $150,000 a month to run. When he died in 2008, one obituarist said the ranch had become 'a sort of African Versailles, importing giraffe, leopard, lion, white rhino and other big game, some from South Africa'. It had '120 miles of road, 55 artificial lakes, a swimming pool with rocks and waterfalls, a golf course and a racetrack – all maintained by an army of 366 servants'.

The largest estate in Laikipia, Ol Ari Nyiro, is the property of Venetian-born Kuki Gallmann, author of the best-selling book *I Dreamed of Africa*. She has dedicated the 40,000 hectares to her late husband, Paolo, who died in a road accident while bringing home a cradle for their first child. Down the road, the 28,000-hectare Loisaba cattle ranch was bought in 1971 by an Italian count, Carletto Ancilotto. He called it Colcheccio, meaning 'mind your own business'. His heirs have leased it to the Kenya-based Wilderness Guardian Company for $2,800-a-night safari tourism.

An American named George Small inherited the 18,000-hectare Mpala ranch from his brother Sam in 1969. He created the Mpala Wildlife Foundation there, which he bequeathed to biologists at the Smithsonian Institution in Washington DC on his own death in 2002. Other huge foreign-owned properties in Laikipia include the 20,000-hectare Segera ranch, bought by the German wunderkind boss of the Puma sportswear company, Jochen Zeitz, as a 'global ecosphere retreat'; Scotsman Guy Grant's El Karama 6,000-hectare former hunting ranch; Englishman Robert Wells's 20,000-hectare Lolldaiga Hills tourist ranch; and the 20,000-hectare Mugie ranch, property of California vineyard owner Nicky Hahn and his artist wife Gaby.

Several of the big landholdings were originally carved out of the Maasai lands in the 1920s by British soldiers who were given the land by the colonial authorities in recognition of their service in the First World War. Major Gerald Edwards created the Sosian ranch. After he died in 1977, it fell into disrepair in the hands of Munene Kairo, an aide to the current Kenya president, Mwai Kibaki. But it has been spruced up since the late 1990s by the owners of Offbeat Safaris, polo-playing Tristan and Lucinda Voorspuy.

Another beneficiary of the 'soldier settler' scheme was Alec Douglas, who created a 14,000-hectare ranch on the Lewa Downs. Eighty years later, converted into a discreet luxury retreat, it was where Prince William, a frequent visitor, proposed to Kate Middleton. In between times, the ranch has become a beacon of enlightened conservation. Douglas handed it on to his daughter Delia. She and her husband, David Craig, decided in the 1980s to turn 2,000 hectares into a high-security rhino sanctuary, where Kenya's fast declining population of black rhino could be collected and protected from poachers behind an electric fence.

The Lewa Wildlife Conservancy eventually took over the ranch, and later the whole 40,000 hectares of the Lewa Downs, including 6,000 hectares of national forest. The conservancy is the largest employer in the area and has essentially privatized a huge stretch of spectacular landscape and its wildlife. It is patrician, of course. And some of the Craig land is used by the British Army for tropical training. But the Craigs, headed now by their son Ian, have also become pioneers of community conservation. They helped create the Laikipia Wildlife Forum, a democratic association of ranchers, smallholders and native pastoralists dedicated to protecting the land and wildlife for tourism and their own use; and also the Northern Rangelands Trust, which is trying to do the same thing on a larger scale across northern Kenya.

I discovered what these ideas could mean in practice when I went to the Il Ngwesi eco-lodge. It is Maasai-run, part of a collectively owned 'group ranch' on a corner of Laikipia that they have managed to hold against all-comers. And it is the one tourist place in this part of the world that I would thoroughly recommend.

Perched on a cliff top about ten kilometres northwest of Lewa Downs, the eco-lodge has been in business for more than a decade now. My jeep ride from the grass airstrip took me slowly through a tightly packed herd of about a hundred migrating elephants, one of the most breathtaking experiences of my life. Below the lodge there was an animal watering hole visited by buffalo, lions, giraffes, gazelles, warthogs and impala. There were solar panels on the roof, but the 'rooms' were otherwise open to the air. 'Watch out for leopards,' the guard joked as I settled down for the night. I didn't sleep for hours.

Over breakfast, the secretary of the Il Ngwesi group ranch, Morias Kisio, told me how the lodge came about. In the 1970s, European tour operators had set up a camel-trekking operation on the collectively owned 6,600-hectare ranch, but without offering any payment. 'We thought it was their right,' he said. But the Maasai elders met Ian Craig from Lewa Downs, who 'told us we should be paid. So we charged the operators 50 shillings per person per night for everyone who stayed on our land.' That is worth only about 30 pence today. Not much, but it was sufficient to open a bank account, and the community used the money to pay for schooling for their children. 'Then Ian showed us how we could get into business ourselves. He said we could get money to build this lodge. We designed and built it ourselves for under a million shillings. Now we can make two million shillings (£14,000) a year from the lodge. It means we can send students to university.'

There have been conservation compromises. They keep their cattle away from tourist areas now, for instance. And the management is no idyll of social harmony and equality. As geographer Ameyali Ramos Castillo, now at the United Nations University, noted in a fascinating master's thesis on the lodge, it is run by 'the traditional leadership of male elders, and the involvement of the rest of the community has been minimal, at best'. But she concluded that it is nonetheless 'highly sustainable'. They have found a new, and profitable, way of living in their landscape. And exposed as nonsense the belief that the Maasai, their cattle and wildlife are incompatible. 'We still milk our cows,' Morias said with a smile, 'but now, with the tourists, we can milk the elephants, too.'

20
SOUTH AFRICA
Green grab

Anton Rupert, who died in 2006, was a chemical engineer and billionaire. He created the Rembrandt tobacco empire, bought the British Rothmans brand and became an influential member of the secretive Boer organization known as the Broederbond, which had a lot of influence in South Africa during the apartheid era. Less well known, even in South Africa, is that for two decades he also bankrolled the world's premier conservation organization, WWF, during a period when it policed and managed many of the planet's protected areas, engaging in what even insiders regarded as a pernicious form of 'green grab'. For much of that time, his personal nominee was running the organization.

Rupert took up conservation in the 1960s, first protecting traditional Afrikaner architecture and then his country's wildlife. He spread his wings initially thanks to his friend Prince Bernhard of the Netherlands, who had been president of WWF since its creation in 1961. With WWF perennially short of funds, they hit on the idea of creating a $10 million endowment fund called The 1001: A Nature Trust. The Trust, formed in 1970, set out to recruit 1,001 members who would contribute $10,000 each – $10 million in all. Rupert gave the job of finding them to a rising young Belgian executive at Rothmans called Charles de Haes.

'Charles travelled the world using Rothman boardrooms and a Rothman expense account, and with Prince Bernhard's calling card in his pocket,' says Fritz Vollmar, WWF's director-general at the time. Within three years, de Haes had his 1,001 members. The brotherhood, whose membership has always been anonymous, continues. Many of its members are South African or Dutch. Most are business people. New recruits replace members as they die. The perks include exclusive receptions with European royalty and excursions to top wildlife sites. As author Elspeth Huxley put it in her biography of WWF founder Sir Peter Scott, 'gold-plated shoulders could rub together, generally in the presence of a prince of the blood.' I met a bunch of them once, living it up on the shores of the Banc d'Arguin, a breathtaking bird sanctuary in Mauritania virtually never visited by outsiders.

In 1975, with the Trust established as the paymaster for most of WWF International's staff, Rupert and Bernhard installed de Haes as director-general of the organization, a job he held for 18 years. It only emerged later that, for much of his tenure, and at the height of global anger about apartheid, de Haes remained on the payroll of Rupert rather than WWF itself.

In effect, Rupert had taken over. His Trust funded WWF's growth into the world's premier conservation organization. By the early 1980s, it could boast that it was involved in the planning and management of 260 parks and reserves on five continents covering more than 1.5 million square kilometres – 1 per cent of the planet's land surface. Many of them were in Africa, where host governments would have been appalled, in the era of apartheid, to know that they were collaborating with such a figure.

Rupert's influence was evident in what Hans Hussy, a Swiss lawyer and one of WWF's five founders in 1961, described to me as WWF's 'extremely conservative and traditional' approach to conservation. Some of the organization's other founders shared a similarly conservative outlook, which critics describe as 'fortress conservation'. They included its two royal founders, Bernhard and Britain's Prince Philip. But by the 1970s it was Rupert who held the purse strings and called the shots.

With his man in charge, people were expelled from parks (unless they were paying tourists, of course) and poachers were hunted down, sometimes literally. During the Rupert years, some of the continent's most unsavoury characters joined the 1001 Club. They included President Idi Amin of Uganda and President Mobutu Sese Seko of Zaire. Their countries were responsible for some of the more outrageous expulsions as traditional lands of tribal groups and others were grabbed for conservation.

From 1982, Zaire and Uganda were a focus of intense WWF activity to defend primates in general and mountain gorillas in particular. To that end, the Batwa 'pygmies' of central Africa lost most of their hunting lands to national parks. They were replaced by tourists paying to see mountain gorillas. In southwest Uganda, the Batwa were banished from the 3,370 hectares of the Mgahinga

Gorilla National Park and the 33,000 hectares of the Bwindi Impenetrable National Park.

Today, almost two decades after WWF helped create these parks, 'these communities continue to live in wretched conditions . . . as squatters on land purchased for them by charitable organizations . . . and face extreme marginalization and discrimination,' according to a recent report by the Rights and Resources Initiative. They watch from squalid roadside camps as tourists drive by wielding $30-a-day permits to visit gorillas in land that was once theirs.

A later internal history of WWF, called *Treading Lightly*, admitted that 'too often in Africa in the 1970s and 1980s, WWF helped organize the expulsion of tribal groups from their land on the pretext of preserving wildlife. The result . . . was often to alienate the very people who had successfully shared the land with big game for centuries.'

At the time, WWF appeared to be operating as a paramilitary force in Africa. It paid for helicopter gunships that shot down poachers in Kenya. And, in an exercise known as Operation Lock, WWF staff were involved in a Bernhard-funded scheme to hire the British mercenary David Stirling to hunt down ivory poachers and traffickers in Namibia and Mozambique. Mercenaries, who had close ties to South African defence forces, became involved in smuggling themselves.

Few of the organization's outside supporters knew that the funding and the strategy for these activities often came from the Rupert connection. But there was internal unease. As Luc Hoffmann, a founding vice-president whose family owned the Hoffmann-La Roche chemicals empire, told me in the 1990s: 'We paid too little attention to policy activities. They can achieve much more than buying land.' Eventually the unease turned to revolt. Hussy, who headed the Swiss chapter, was one of its leaders.

De Haes was removed in 1993 after a quiet internal coup. A

new generation of activists was determined to end WWF's reputation as a green landgrabber. 'We don't want to be an organization with billions of dollars to spend buying up the world,' Claude Martin, de Haes's successor, told me at the time. 'There is no point in creating protected areas if they fail to recognize the requirements of the people who live in or around them. That can only lead to conflict and reduce the chances of success.' Environmentalism, Martin warned in 1995, was 'beginning to look just as narrow and selfish as the imperialists of old'. On his watch, quintessential imperialist figureheads like Kes Smith, an English zoologist, and her Zimbabwean game-warden husband Fraser – who were said to have effectively ruled half a million hectares of the Congolese Garamba park on behalf of its northern white rhinos for 14 years – were withdrawn. 'The idea is now that the Congolese run things in Garamba and elsewhere,' WWF's Africa head told me in 1998.

The new generation also had new ideas about ecology, especially in Africa. They did not see the need for the rigorous separation of humans and wildlife accepted as axiomatic by their predecessors. In fact, they acknowledged that many of the African habitats regarded by their predecessors as Pleistocene landscapes were in fact a product of the interaction of humans, their livestock and wildlife.

Holly Dublin was chief conservation adviser for the WWF in Nairobi in the 1990s, and author of a study of the changing ecology of Kenya's Maasai Mara national reserve, part of the Serengeti ecosystem. 'It was not until the 1980s,' says Dublin, 'that we began to see that the natural ecology of African savannahs was much more dynamic, involving massive changes in the space of a decade or two, switching between woodland and grassland.' That natural system involved wild animals, cattle and occasional interventions from bush fires. 'Pastoralists have herded their cattle in harmony with wildlife for thousands of years.' Of course that did not mean there were no human pressures. But it did mean that the

Maasai, and the many other traditional users of Africa's grasslands, were not the enemy – they were the landscape's experts and the likely source of solutions to its environmental problems.

Rupert was undeterred by this revisionist thinking. In the late 1990s, with his man deposed at WWF, he started another elite conservation club to protect his vision of wild Africa. This time the 'Club 21' had an entry fee of a million dollars. Most of the first group of 21 sponsors were corporations, including De Beers, DaimlerChrysler and Cartier, large philanthropic bodies like the Rothschild Foundation, and several organizations chaired by Rupert or his eldest son, Johann. Individuals stumping up included the Dutch industrialist and conservationist Paul van Vlissingen and, later, Sir Richard Branson and Ted Turner.

Club 21's purpose was to fund a new body, the Peace Parks Foundation, founded by Rupert and Prince Bernhard. This was something of a rehabilitation for Prince Bernhard, who had been forced to resign from WWF in 1976 after he was revealed to have taken a million-dollar bribe from the plane manufacturer Lockheed to influence the Dutch government. The Foundation was set up 'to facilitate the establishment of trans-frontier conservation areas, also called peace parks', and was based in the Afrikaner heartland city of Stellenbosch, where Rupert lived until his death in 2006, after which his son Johann took over the reins. Its founding board was made up almost entirely of South African friends of Rupert and Dutch friends of Bernhard, several of them also members of Club 21. Its first director was John Hanks, a veteran of WWF in Africa, who had taken responsibility for Operation Lock when it was exposed in 1991.

This foundation has initiated plans for cross-border parks involving every southern African country as far north as Tanzania, and has treaties creating them that involve South Africa,

Mozambique, Botswana, Namibia and Zimbabwe. One journalist hailed it as 'an ecological Cape to Cairo dream'. Its main accomplishment on the ground so far is the Great Limpopo Transfrontier Park, essentially a cross-border extension of the Kruger Park in South Africa into Mozambique and Zimbabwe. It covers 3.5 million hectares. The parks authorities say that they are trying, in Hanks's words, to 'right the wrongs of the past', including those from the apartheid era. Back in South Africa, the people of Makuleke, who were expelled from Kruger Park when it was expanded in 1969, have now had their land rights reinstated – but they agreed not to reoccupy their land inside the park. And the new thinking hasn't prevented them from 'resettling' some 7,000 people in the Mozambique portion.

Rupert and Bernhard are now dead. So too is their friend and fellow green grabber, the Dutch industrialist Paul van Vlissingen. Aside from his place on the founding board of the Peace Parks Foundation and membership of Club 21, Vlissingen was, on his own account, the largest private operator of African national parks. He put $18 million of his own money into kick-starting his African Parks Foundation, which he began in 2000. His foundation was dedicated to taking over ailing national parks and putting them on a sound management and commercial footing. Its seven parks today are in Malawi, Zambia, Chad, both Congos and Rwanda and cover some 3.3 million hectares. They include the Garamba park in the Democratic Republic of Congo, an ironic privatization given WWF's determination a decade ago to give control of Garamba back to its national government.

I met Vlissingen in 2005 at his castle near Utrecht. It was a few months before he died. He was not a fortress conservationist. But he found that some of the governments he worked with were. In 2004, he began negotiations with the Ethiopian government to take over running its Nechisar National Park, close to the border with Kenya.

The Ethiopians wanted to create a Kenyan-style wildlife park to service a Kenyan-style tourist industry. They insisted that, to achieve the ultimate safari experience for Western visitors, they needed to throw the traditional inhabitants out of the park. They wanted wildlife without people. The park would be surrounded by an electric fence to keep the locals from even passing through on their way to the nearest town, already a day's walk away.

Vlissingen refused to carry out expulsions. So in February 2005, in the weeks before he took over the park, the Ethiopian military escorted some 5,000 people from the Kore tribe from their thatched huts and dumped them on distant land owned by other rural communities. No compensation, no nothing. The government said they were squatters. Another group, the Guji tribe and their 20,000 cattle, were also targeted. Their huts were burned. The park fence went up. Then Vlissingen's park managers took charge.

Vlissingen told me: 'We said that we could work with people in the park, as we do in Zambia, but [the Ethiopian government] said no. We didn't want to be involved in the resettlement, so I put a clause in the contract that said we wouldn't take over the park until the resettlement was completed.' In the event, after Vlissingen's death, one of the Guji groups returned to the park. The Foundation negotiated a deal with them for sharing the park, as Vlissingen had originally envisaged. But the government refused to sanction the deal. And in 2007 the Foundation pulled out.

It is hardly surprising that conservation and human rights often come into conflict. More than a billion people live in the world's top 25 biodiversity 'hotspots'. Usually, the people living in those hotspots are the poorest and most vulnerable, who have been squeezed to the margins of society – to the remote places where nature survives because human infrastructure is little developed. Often too, they are indigenous people. About half of the parks and other areas protected for nature in the past 40 years overlap the traditional territories of indigenous people. In Latin America, the figure is 86 per cent. In the cause of conservation, many have been thrown off their land.

Marcus Colchester, director of the UK-based Forest Peoples Programme, says: 'Conservation has immeasurably worsened the lives of indigenous peoples throughout Africa.' He reckons that forest dwellers and indigenous people have altogether lost around a million square kilometres across the continent – more than four times the area of the UK – as a result of green grabs. Kai Schmidt-Soltau, a Swiss social scientist at the International Network on Displacement and Resettlement in Tucson, Arizona, put the number of 'conservation refugees' created around the world in recent decades at 'upwards of 120,000'.

Such calculations are controversial. They greatly anger conservation groups who mostly flat-out deny involvement in expulsions. Schmidt-Soltau says that 14,000 people were expelled from 13 parks created in Gabon in 2002. The parks are now helping the country advertise itself as a green tourist destination. But the New York-based Wildlife Conservation Society (WCS) and WWF, which both supported the creation of the parks, say the park boundaries were deliberately set to avoid inhabited areas. Bryan Curran at WCS said categorically in 2009: 'Not a single individual has been physically removed from any of the protected areas created in central Africa over the past decade.' He accused Schmidt-Soltau and a 'small but highly productive body of researchers' of publishing and repeating lies by claiming the expulsions continue.

Partly, this is a dispute about definitions. Many of those evicted from parks and other protected areas are regarded by their governments and conservationists as squatters, because whatever their traditional rights, they have no formal title to the land. That was the case with the Kore and Guji in Ethiopia's Nechisar park.

And Christine MacDonald reported in *Green Inc*, her inside account of working for Conservation International, that that organization actively encouraged the Liberian government to evict people living in the Sapo National Park after the civil war there, because they were 'squatters'.

Evicted squatters would not count as refugees. And note Curran's phrase about people not being 'physically removed'. That would not include people who were persuaded with inducements to leave their land, or who left because park rules meant they could no longer hunt or harvest the fruits of the forest. Many international refugee agencies would include all these people as environmental refugees. They would also include people who did not move at all, but had part of their traditional environment-based livelihoods taken from them.

Thus in Gabon's Lope National Park, WCS denies there are any conservation refugees, since 'no villages existed within the park when it was created.' But equally, some 2,000 Bongo pygmy people who lived outside the park lost their ancestral rights to harvest its resources when the park was created. Curran concedes that definitions about environmental refugees differ. But he says critics of conservation are still misleading – especially when reports by Schmidt-Soltau and others are littered with pejorative phrases such as 'brutal eviction'.

In recent years, a new generation of conservationists in WWF and elsewhere has tried to limit the damage to indigenous people, eliminating expulsions, and finding ways for them to benefit directly from conservation. They say this is both ethical and more likely to deliver successful environmental results. The end of Rupert's rule at WWF helped this trend. So did the 1992 Earth Summit, which urged a new era of 'sustainable development'. But has the talk turned into successful projects? Chris Sandbrook of Britain's University of Cambridge found 'a startling lack of data'.

Whatever their sustainability rhetoric, very few conservation projects trouble to 'measure the impacts of their work for either conservation or poverty alleviation'. Curran admits that 'to date there have been few long-term studies of the effectiveness of protected areas for biodiversity conservation, nor their impact on local societies.' With billions of dollars spent over many decades on thousands of biodiversity projects covering millions of hectares and affecting the lives of millions of people, this is an alarming admission.

But greens are impatient. As David Kaimowitz, a forest specialist at the Ford Foundation, puts it: 'Some conservationists feel that time is too short to negotiate every intervention. While they doubtless regret the hardships local people experience, their main concern is to save species.' Twenty years after the Earth Summit, Kaimowitz detects a move back to 'pure' conservation. Back to the 'fortress conservation' philosophy of Rupert and Prince Bernhard and, before them, of Huxley and Grzimek. In truth, the big money in conservation has always been directed towards schemes that exclude locals in the name of conservation, and attract the top dollars that can be earned from selling environmental spectacle. Hence the dozens of huge, privately owned parks and conservancies around the world. From Patagonia to Tanzania.

Buying your own slice of Eden is certainly a growing trend around the world. The American Prairies Foundation, a spinoff from WWF, is on a shopping spree for the bison ranges of the American West, with a huge slab of Montana already on its books. Swedish-born businessman Johan Eliasch, head of sports goods manufacturer Head and a forest adviser to former British prime minister Gordon Brown, bought 160,000 hectares of the Amazon rainforest. Virgin boss Richard Branson has turned one of the islands he owns in the tax haven of the British Virgin Islands into a zoo for ring-tailed lemurs that he has imported from Madagascar.

And nowhere is this trend towards the privatization of nature seen more than in Rupert's old stomping ground of South Africa. Across the country, many large, mostly white-owned ranches are giving up livestock in favour of wildlife ranching. According to a study by Dhoya Snijders of the VU University of Amsterdam, a staggering 17 per cent of South Africa has been given over to private wildlife reserves.

Big-ticket billionaires have moved in. The 23,000-hectare Phinda game reserve in KwaZulu Natal, north of Durban, is owned by Tara and Jessica Getty, heirs to the Getty legacy. Virgin boss Branson – yes, him again – owns the 10,000-hectare Sabi Sands, one of nine private game reserves that circle the two-million-hectare Kruger National Park, sharing its wildlife. Nicky Oppenheimer, chairman of the De Beers diamond empire founded by Cecil Rhodes, who once dreamed of an African land grab from the Cape to Cairo, has spent some of his $3 billion fortune on the 100,000-hectare Tswalu Kalahari game reserve, South Africa's largest, in the north of the country. And, in case you thought we could get through a chapter without mentioning a Gulf investor, the 25,000-hectare Shamwari game reserve in the south, near Port Elizabeth, is owned by Dubai World, a real-estate-grabbing arm of the government of Dubai, which also has luxury beach resorts in Djibouti, Zanzibar and the tiny Indian Ocean island nation of Comoros. The sheikhs bought Shamwari from Adrian Gardiner, whose Mantis Group created the reserve from former farmland, and has an empire of 40 game reserves and luxury boutique hotels across Africa. That's green grab.

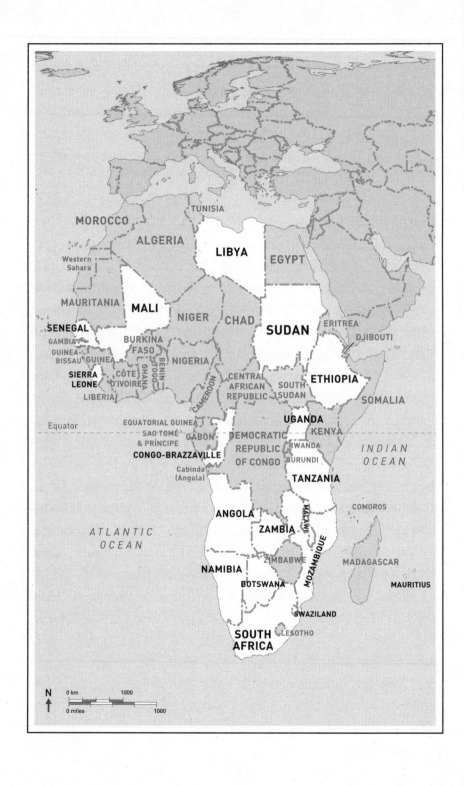

21

AFRICA
The second great trek

They are calling it the second great trek. Almost two centuries ago, the descendants of Dutch settlers in the British-run Cape of Good Hope hitched their wagons to oxen and headed inland to establish new republics in the Transvaal and Orange Free State that eventually became the heartland of South Africa. Now they are on the move again. This time the destination of the 'white tribe' is the whole of the African continent. Boer farmers are now being courted by black nations to the north.

As I travelled across the continent for this book, I constantly met white South Africans managing new plantations, as well as running mines and tourism ventures. They are often the technicians and foot soldiers of the African land grab. But they are also buying on their own behalf. Since the end of white rule in South Africa, there have been sporadic moves north by Boer farmers. Some felt unwanted at home. Others felt the tug of new adventures. Most went to near neighbours like Mozambique, Botswana and Zambia. But there is now an organized migration further afield, with approval and assistance from governments at both ends.

The men in khaki shorts and Springbok rugby caps are being offered millions of hectares, some of it 'virgin' bush and some of it already cultivated by smallholders and state farms, or grazed by herders. The hope is that their undoubted agricultural know-how can kick-start an agrarian revolution across Africa. Whatever else, it is a dramatic reversal of the ostracism the Boers suffered in the days of apartheid.

The travel agent for these Boers with itchy feet is Agri South Africa, the post-apartheid successor to the old South African Agricultural Union, which was formed in 1904 to represent white farmers. Agri-SA has some 70,000 members today, including some black farmers. Its deputy president, Theo de Jaeger, says he has received offers of land for his members from 22 countries in all parts of Africa. By mid-2011, formal government-backed deals to cement the relationships were in place for Congo-Brazzaville and Mozambique, with more to follow.

The incentives from would-be hosts are considerable. Along with free land come tax holidays, promises of new roads and power lines, and freedom to export produce and profits. Such sugar-coating often angers local peasant farmers who have never enjoyed such benefits. In the South African capital, Pretoria, assisting the farmers to move is also government policy. In 2010, ministers set aside $450 million to support South African farmers outside the country's borders – in recognition of the fact that some 30 per cent of South Africa's white-owned farmland is due to be transferred to black owners by 2014.

Agriculture minister Tina Joemat-Pettersson told the annual congress of Agri-SA in 2009: 'If we can't find opportunities for white South African farmers in this country, we must do it elsewhere in the continent.' But she also sees the second great trek in a strategic context, pointing out that the Chinese, Brazilians and others are moving in on African farmland. In 2011, she said: 'Africa has almost 60 per cent of the global arable land that is under utilized. It is imperative that the South African government works together with the private sector and civil society to champion the South African foreign policy agenda in the continent.' If there is a land grab going on, then South Africa should not be left out.

The biggest offer so far is from Congo-Brazzaville. This is the smaller and more northerly of the two adjoining Congo states. Plagued by internal conflict for decades, the oil- and timber-rich but probity-poor former French colony has languished on the international sidelines. Its long-time leader, Denis Sassou Nguesso, who was born in a remote village in the north of his country, is no stranger to international land deals. He has his own lucrative real estate on the French Riviera. And he is keen for South Africans to take some of his homeland: up to 10 million hectares, an area not much smaller than England.

Sassou Nguesso's government says the Boers are being offered 'vacant land'. The first arrivals are taking over a huge former state farm in the fertile Niari Valley, which is in the heavily populated southwest, along the railway that connects the capital, Brazzaville, and the coastal second city, Pointe-Noire, with neighbouring Gabon. According to de Jaeger, the farm has been abandoned for more than a decade. 'The bulk of the property remains in good condition. The farmers will move into the houses on the property.' They hope. For since the state gave up the farm a decade ago, the former occupiers of the land have returned, and now grow manioc and peanuts there.

Ruth Hall and Gaynor Paradza of the Institute for Poverty, Land and Agrarian Studies at the University of the Western Cape in South Africa paid a visit to the proposed 'vacant land' in late 2011, just ahead of the arrival of the first convoy of South African farmers. 'There are people living there,' Paradza told me on her return. 'At least five settlements will be affected by the land transfer. In one of the villages, Malolo 2, there was something that passed for con-sultation, culminating in an elder symbolically spitting palm wine on the ground, which the ministry official took as indicating community consent.' In another village, Dehese, the local chief told her he had not been consulted at all. But he feared the worst. South African farmers had been to the village, putting pegs into the ground in the school yard and around village water sources.

Hall said there was no published map of the land allocated to the South Africans. 'I met the ministers of land affairs and agriculture personally, but they had different stories. Nobody even knew how long the leases would be.' Problems evidently lie ahead.

In March 2011, land affairs minister Pierre Mabiala said that his people expected 'abundant food' from the colonists. Agri-SA promised its hosts that the newcomers will first plant staples like maize. And they 'will do skill transfer to the people of Congo to educate them to become successful farmers themselves'. But back home, de Jaeger has been selling prospective pioneers the idea of growing more profitable tropical fruit like avocados and bananas, and even biofuels for export to Europe. Whatever the promises to local ministers, he believes the contracts give the Boer farmers the right to grow what they want, to take a five-year tax holiday, not to pay any rent, and to repatriate all their profits.

Next up is Mozambique. There is some inauspicious history here. In 1996, an agreement between South African president Nelson Mandela and his Mozambique counterpart Joaquim Chissano gave South African farmers the chance to take up 50-year leases to farm up to 200,000 hectares of old Portuguese cotton farms. The land was in the Lugenda river valley in the country's least populated, most forested and most northerly province of Niassa, bordering Tanzania. The land was along one of the few roads through the province, close to the large Niassa National Park, one of Africa's best lion sanctuaries.

The scheme was dubbed the 'promised land', but the plans drawn up in South Africa were also widely criticized for recreating an apartheid-style society. Absentee white landlords would employ what the South African high commissioner in Maputo called 'tame

Kafirs' from back home, to supervise local labourers living in 'rural townships'. In any event, the plan failed. The South African Chamber for Agricultural Development, an agency set up by Mandela to manage the migration, couldn't find the promised funding for the promised land. By 1999, only 13 South African farmers of the anticipated 500 had actually moved in. At the last count, only five remained.

Undeterred, the Mozambique government has now offered a further million hectares. This time, the deal looks more enticing. The farms are in the southern province of Gaza, less than 500 kilometres by road from Pretoria. The new inter-government arrangement was set up by white farmer Charl Senekal, a close associate of the new South African president, Jacob Zuma. Senekal was declared South Africa's 'farmer of the year' in 2003 for building a 45-hectare enterprise into a highly profitable 18,000-hectare sugar and game estate.

The deal was sealed in May 2011, at a ceremony at Agri-SA's office in Centurion, near Pretoria, where the farmers' union called it 'a platform to consolidate South African commercial farming interests in Mozambique'. Rich soils, combined with water from the Limpopo River, are expected to make Gaza the future granary of Mozambique. Hundreds of South African farmers will most likely move into the area.

Other countries are enticing itinerant Boer sons of the soil. Zambia wants them to grow maize on two new farm blocks totalling 300,000 hectares. Sudan offers land and irrigation water to grow sugar cane along the Nile. The vast arid nation of Namibia, which only got rid of South African occupiers in 1988, now wants them back to irrigate fields on the banks of the Orange and Kunene rivers. Angola has offered two farms totalling 140,000 hectares, and Uganda hints at 170,000 hectares. Another deal, on hold at the time of writing, may yet see them growing grapes and olives on 35,000 hectares of Libya.

Despite the success of Agri-SA in opening up Africa to Boer farmers, a new travel agent has emerged with a different trek in mind. The ultra-conservative Transvaal Agricultural Union refused to embrace the post-apartheid South Africa, and still represents almost exclusively white farmers. So it is spurning offers from African governments in favour of a proposal from the post-Soviet – and eminently white – state of Georgia. It wants to take Caucasians to the Caucasus.

In early 2011, prospective Boer settlers made a tour of inspection. They were dined by the first lady of Georgia, who was born in the Netherlands and reportedly chatted to her guests in their ancestral Dutch. The Transvaal Agricultural Union has set up a Georgia website, www.boers.ge, full of images of the mountain idyll and links to farms up for purchase. The largest on offer when I checked was 360 hectares of mountain pasture in Dedoplistskaro, amid the vineyards of the far east of the country. It was tiny by South African standards, and, in comparison with the free land on offer in Africa, rather expensive at £237 a hectare.

While governments are keen to help South African farmers relocate, so are banks and investment funds. The new trek is attracting support from, among others, the Johannesburg-based Standard Bank, which now describes itself as a 'pan-African bank'; the home-grown Phatisa Group investment fund; and Emergent Asset Management, the joint UK–South Africa fund run by former Goldman Sachs high-flyer Susan Payne (see Chapter Eight).

Not everyone is happy, however. The 'exodus' has provoked scary headlines in South Africa. 'The last of the white farmers are about to depart for greener pastures,' said one. Nonsense, of course. But there is a political subtext here. The alarm is being whipped up to inflame opposition from rural Boer heartlands to the country's land reforms, which are intended to end a land apartheid that has persisted after political apartheid ended. Ruth Hall says the trek really just represents a recognition of the market value of South African farmers in an era of land grab. The most telling fact is that most farmers are not fleeing South Africa at all. The great majority are planning to maintain their farms in South Africa while working elsewhere. They are hedging their bets rather than cutting their ties. 'This is not racial flight or South African imperialism,' says Hall. 'They are going not to feed either South Africa or their hosts. They are finding cheap land, water and labour. This is global capitalism.'

If global capitalism has been hot for South African farmers on the move, it has been doubly hot for farming corporations that specialize in growing sugar. Booming demand for our favourite sweetener, plus rising biofuels production, pushed sugar prices to record levels in 2011. Big sugar-processing companies were buying land to keep up with orders.

One of the buyers is Associated British Foods. There are few blander corporate names. But behind the anonymous face, ABF is among other things the world's second-biggest sugar producer, through its ownership of British Sugar. British Sugar has long been a fixture at home, consuming the entire output of Britain's 4,000 sugar beet farmers. Its brand, Silver Spoon, is part of British life. But recently it has carved out a whole new sugar empire in Africa, through the purchase of a controlling interest in the rapidly expanding South African sugar juggernaut Illovo.

And that makes British Sugar and ABF's owners – the secretive Weston family from Canada, headed by the company's current chief executive, George Weston – major African landgrabbers. Oh, and water grabbers, too. Sugar cane requires prodigious amounts of water to grow. It requires fields to be flooded to a depth of more than two metres during a typical year. That is twice as much as required by other water-guzzling crops like rice or cotton. Across the world, sugar cane empties rivers and wrecks underground water reserves.

Illovo emerged from some restructuring of old South African apartheid companies in the 1990s. It has escaped from its homeland to buy up farms in Malawi, Mauritius, Zambia, Tanzania and Mozambique. It owns some 120,000 foreign hectares, and counting. African commodities buccaneer Tiny Rowland was once big in sugar, and several of his plantations have ended up in Illovo's hands. Now Illovo's purchase by British Sugar gives it improved access to markets in the European Union, where it supplies a third of all imports.

Africa is a great place for people with large chunks of land and access to water to grow sugar cane. Sugar yields in Africa, unlike those for many other crops, are at least as good as those in the world's top producers like India, Brazil, Thailand and Australia. So Illovo is heading north, grabbing land as fast as it can.

An early Illovo acquisition was Zambia Sugar. Its main plantation, the Nakambala estate, covers 15,000 hectares of the Kafue Flats, a huge area of drained wetland beside the River Kafue, a major tributary of the mighty Zambezi River. White settlers annexed the estate from local farmers and herders long ago. Its fences stopped cattle from reaching their old grazing grounds on the Kafue Flats, reputedly once the best in Zambia. Meanwhile, dams built to generate hydroelectricity and irrigate Nakambala sugar have flooded out thousands of people and destroyed wildlife habitat for millions of birds and antelope, including the rare Kafue lechwe.

The Nakambala estate was nationalized after independence, but then privatized, ending up in Illovo's hands in 2001 – in effect a reversion to settler colonialism. The company has bought a neighbouring 10,000-hectare cattle ranch. South African president Jacob Zuma came personally to open the new sugar fields. The combined estates are now the biggest farm in Zambia, and the second-biggest sugar farm in Africa. Illovo provides a tenth of all the 'formal' jobs in Zambia, many of them for cane-cutting migrants. But the gradual annexing of the Kafue Flats over decades, and the estates' demand for water, have damaged ecosystems and wrecked the farming and herding livelihoods of thousands of people. There have been protests and arrests, and cane fields have been burned.

Illovo's great trek is taking it next to Mali, in order to irrigate 14,000 hectares of cane fields. Some 1,600 people will be cleared off the land by the Mali government to make way. But, as we shall see in Chapter Twenty-five, the biggest threat to the locals may come from its water take. It will suck as much as half a cubic kilometre of water a year from the River Niger, the region's lifeblood.

Illovo has rivals for its status as Africa's sugar daddy. Two contenders are shaping up for a tussle in Senegal in West Africa, on the banks of the River Senegal. The current sugar monopolist there is a Swiss-domiciled French banker named Jean-Claude Mimran. His father got rich logging Côte D'Ivoire and Madagascar. But Jean-Claude is the long-time owner of the Compagnie Sucrière Sénégalaise, which cultivates some 8,000 hectares of sugar, and is expanding into bio-fuels production for sale to Europe.

Mimran's monopoly is being challenged by the Nigerian sugar and soft drinks baron Aliko Dangote. Dangote, an influential political sponsor back home, recently toppled the Saudi-Ethiopian landgrabber in Gambella, Sheikh Mohammed Hussein Ali Al Amoudi, as the world's richest man of African descent. In 2011, Dangote was reported to have obtained 40,000 hectares from the Senegal government to pursue his sugar dreams. But more sugar estates on the banks of the River Senegal will inevitably deprive herders of their grazing grounds and farmers of irrigation water. Especially given the similar grabs for land being made by Arab investors in rice production (see Chapter Three).

The world has a sweet tooth. But demand for sugar is being accentuated by its emergence as the feedstock of choice for making ethanol to burn in cars. Brazil, which pioneered the sugar-to-ethanol business back in the 1970s, continues to expand its huge plantations, often with foreign capital. Americans are piling in, led by investors George Soros, Goldman Sachs, Merrill Lynch and Sun Microsystems. So are foreign energy companies like BP and Shell. But Brazilian sugar producers are inncreasingly eyeing Africa, where land is cheaper than at home. The country's third-biggest producer, Açúcar Guarani, recently bought Mozambique's Sena Holdings, which has 14,000 hectares of sugar plantations.

Joining them, Singapore's ubiquitous commodities giant Olam said in 2010 it was looking for somewhere to plant 10,000 hectares of sugar cane in Africa. And Swiss-based Addax Bioenergy has secured 10,000 hectares of savannah grassland in central Sierra Leone to grow the stuff. 'Some isolated settlements may be asked to move,' it says. But there won't be many jobs for cane-cutters, because the company has opted for mechanical harvesting. The water will come from damming the nearby Rokel River.

The world's largest sugar farm remains Sudan's flagship Kenana sugar plantation. It covers 84,000 hectares of desert on the banks of the White Nile, 250 kilometres south of Khartoum, and is easily spotted by Europeans on flights to and from East Africa. It has its own desert city of 60,000 people to tend it.

Kenana was the brainchild of Tiny Rowland back in the 1970s. But its dominant shareholders today are the Kuwait Investment Authority and the government of Saudi Arabia. The farm meets all Sudan's sugar needs and exports across the Middle East and North Africa, India and Europe. Its irrigated desert fields require a staggering three cubic kilometres of water a year – roughly 4 per cent of the entire annual flow of the Nile, the world's longest river. It is probably the biggest single agricultural water user in the world. Its thirst may soon increase further. An Egyptian private equity fund called Beltone, which won big in the real estate boom during the Mubarak era, has decided to invest a billion dollars in Kenana to help Sudan double its sugar output by 2014.

The sheer scale of sugar production often makes it a social and environmental menace. In the eighteenth century, its cultivation in the Caribbean was the economic driver of the slave trade. It helped enrich British slave ports like Bristol and Liverpool, on the backs of Africans forcibly shipped across the Atlantic to cut cane in Jamaica and Barbados. Rainforests, wetlands and rich pastures have all been cleared for the crop, and rivers emptied. In seven countries, its cultivation once covered more than half the entire land area. Numbers are down now, but it still covers around 40 per cent of Mauritius.

And sugar still warps societies. Sugar accounts for almost two-thirds of the agricultural output of Swaziland, a small landlocked kingdom in southern Africa. The country produces more than four tonnes of cane a year for every inhabitant. Sugar generates a fifth of Swaziland's meagre GDP, and directly or indirectly employs most of the adult population. But the industry locks up land and labour so tightly that few other enterprises get a look in.

Illovo is there, with some 8,000 hectares of cane fields. But the dominant producer, and the nation's main employer, remains the Royal Swaziland Sugar Corporation, a company that is the personal property of UK-educated King Mswati III – Africa's last absolute monarch. The king's corporation is also, in effect, the country's government, buying farm produce, providing the only clinics and schools, employing its own police force and building roads and power lines. Most of its sugar output goes either to South Africa or to the Tate & Lyle factory on the Thames estuary, the world's largest sugar refinery, now owned by American Sugar.

The country is an economic slave to sugar, maintained at the whim of an absolute monarch – and of Illovo's owners, the Weston family.

22

MOZAMBIQUE
The biofuels bubble

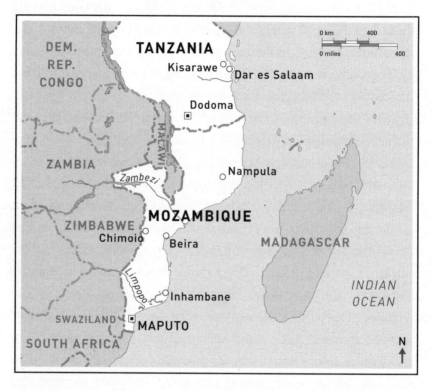

Richard Morgan was a happy man in mid-2011. After four years of planning, his company shipped its first batch of oil made from the seeds of a toxic African weed called jatropha, grown on a former tobacco plantation in Mozambique. Sun Biofuels' first client was Lufthansa, the German airline. Morgan had invested no less than $9 million, and employed over a thousand people cultivating 3,000 hectares of land, to get those 30 tonnes on the boat at Beira. It looked like a breakthrough in turning Africa into a hub for saving the planet from climate change through the production of green biofuels.

Lufthansa had just won permission from airline regulators to fly planes powered by kerosene containing jatropha juice. For now it was one engine on a regular flight from Frankfurt to Hamburg, but the company had 700 aircraft. 'Lufthansa alone is seeking 400 million litres of biofuels every year,' Morgan's local boss Luis Gouveia told excited media in Mozambique. Well, that was the story, anyhow. But three months later, Sun Biofuels was bust and in administration. The cash had run out. Investors had taken flight faster than a Lufthansa jet, and Richard Morgan was nowhere to be found.

Sun Biofuels had looked like one of the brightest stars in the biofuels firmament. It was backed by some big names in the City of London, including boutique investor Simon Shaw and his EEA Fund Management, a carbon trading outfit. Morgan told me in 2011 that by 2015 he would be cultivating 10,000 hectares of jatropha, producing 20,000 tonnes of oil a year. There was, he admitted, a lot of technical stuff to get right first. When I found Morgan in his modest office on the fourth floor of a block above an estate agent in Kensington, he was on the phone to Mozambique, deep in con-versation about the relative merits of heavy and light pruning of jatropha bushes. For, while there may have been a wave of enthusiasm among financiers for jatropha, the would-be wonder-fuel was still an experimental crop. The best way to grow and harvest it remained work in progress, he told me.

Morgan was also dealing with some flak from NGOs keen, he believed, to shut down his operation. One charge, of course, was landgrabbing. He felt that was unfair. After all, his Mozambique plantation was largely made up from eleven old tobacco farms that dotted the area west of the town of Chimoio on the road to Zimbabwe. The farms had been abandoned by Alliance One

Tobacco, a merchant based in North Carolina. A thousand-strong workforce had been laid off for two years, till Morgan began planting. 'When we returned, there were 700 people waiting at the gate,' he remembered. 'They had gone back to subsistence farming in the meantime. To the bush, essentially.'

The Mozambique operation was Sun Biofuels' showcase. Britain's international development minister Stephen O'Brien toured it in early 2011. The local governor was so pleased at how things were going that he offered Morgan another old tobacco farm. But there were problems elsewhere.

At the start, in 2005, the company's first land grab was in Ethiopia. The government there gave it communal pasture in Benishangul Gumuz, north of Gambella near the remote border with Sudan. The company established jatropha nurseries and planted some 5,000 hectares. With an option on another 80,000 hectares, and talk of taking more land in Tigray and elsewhere, it was shaping up to be a big operation. Then the company thought better of it and began to pull back. Remoteness seems to have been one factor, but clearly the crop wasn't doing well, either. Sun Biofuels effectively pulled out of Ethiopia.

Sun Biofuels next set up in Kisarawe, central Tanzania, on 8,000 hectares of what the company called 'severely degraded coastal forest . . . devastated by charcoal burners and firewood collectors'. From the start, it was in trouble with the locals. Morgan dismissed the charcoal burners. They were squatters and would be moved out, he told me. But there were several villages in the plantation area, too. Nobody had farmed the plantation land, but they had used it for grazing and foraging for fruit, firewood and other materials. 'We spent two years talking to the villagers, 11,000 people altogether. We spoke to everyone we could find. The villagers decided what land we should have, and we paid compensation for what we took.' So he played it by the book.

But, he added, 'Yes, sometimes small people do get trampled on.'

I appreciated his candour. Some didn't. Friends of the Earth, in a report in 2010, simply said he had 'cheated villagers of their land'. That made him angry. 'They are sitting at their desks in London, having never visited the farm, and criticizing us for land-grabbing. Why aren't they pleased that we are protecting the forests from the charcoal burners?' Oxfam waded in, too. At least they visited the site, Morgan says. 'But they were pathetic. They went to Mtamba, one of five villages that didn't contribute any land – and found they didn't get any compensation. The people who did lose land have all been compensated, and the money was paid to the individuals concerned. The people at Mtamba were actually cross because we *hadn't* taken their land, so they missed out on compensation.'

These early forays happened before Morgan arrived in 2007. The legacy clearly embarrassed him. He admitted to me that 'The founding shareholders weren't pleasant people. They wanted a quick in and out.' They imagined there were quick profits to be made. 'But a lot of the early claims have been debunked now.' He saw success just round the corner. 'We can see much more clearly what will work and what will not. I worked for New Britain Palm Oil in Papua New Guinea. They are like a military camp. Really efficient. We'd like to be like that.' He told me he thought his investors were in it for the long haul, with no profits likely before 2015. 'We are well funded, with [Shaw] willing to keep spending. And we have been prudent.' I admit I was convinced.

But months later, it had all collapsed. The company talked of a drought in Tanzania upsetting production. But if Morgan had been right about his investors, it would not have mattered. In reality, they had got cold feet as quickly as their predecessors had. The leases were sold on – in the case of Mozambique to British hedge fund managers at Highbury Finance. But for the time being at least, the farms were untended. This is one of the problems when the corporate and financial worlds move in on the peasant world. If things go wrong, the big shots can move on and make their profits elsewhere. But they often leave behind broken promises and angry and disappointed locals with a mess to clean up.

Sun Biofuels has joined a growing list of companies that tried and failed to make it big from the world's sudden enthusiasm for biofuels in the first decade of the twenty-first century. Some might have succeeded. Others always looked like buccaneering bad boys.

Energem was a Canadian company owned by a South African, Tony Teixeira. Previously known as DiamondWorks, it had a well-documented involvement with people who were trading 'blood diamonds' from Angola and Sierra Leone. It had links to London mercenaries, and at one point employed Simon Mann, a former SAS officer who was later convicted in Equatorial Guinea for trying to organize a coup there. Allegations that Teixeira was aiding gun-runners supplying South Africa-backed UNITA fighters in Angola led to his being dubbed a 'merchant of death' by British foreign minister Peter Hain in 2000.

Under its new name, Energem embraced the new century by pitching into the biofuels boom, buying an ethanol plant at Kisumu in Kenya from the family of Raila Odinga, the current Kenyan prime minister, and winning a listing on the London Alternative Investment Market in 2007. On the back of that, it won a 60,000-hectare concession to grow jatropha on grazing land in the Mozambique province of Gaza. It planted some 2,000 hectares. But in mid-2010 Energem suddenly stopped paying salaries at the farm, and in early 2011 the Daily Telegraph reported that it had gone bankrupt 'without telling shareholders'. The bankruptcy had happened, the paper said, 'after it could not recover $54 million owed by companies linked to its deputy executive chairman [and owner] Tony Teixeira'. This was not surprising. The debtor companies, it turned out, were mainly connected with Teixeira's motor-racing enterprise A1 Grand Prix, which went into liquidation in 2009. Energem was notorious in Africa for having bought an executive jet from another business controlled by Teixeira. The plane was needed, Energem said at the time, to ferry its management to 'any location in Africa at short notice'. Quite so.

At its height, the biofuels boom was popular among a number of figures in the minerals world. Some 600 kilometres south of Sun Biofuels' Mozambique plantation lies the detritus left behind by another band of minerals entrepreneurs who got into biofuels. Whether, in Morgan's words, they were 'pleasant' or not, they and their investors certainly seem to have wanted 'a quick in and out'. Their failure left a bad taste in the mouths of thousands of Mozambicans.

A lot of people who know nothing of finance or even biofuels will have heard of one of the group. He was Phil Edmonds, once one of the stars of English cricket. He played 51 Tests. I rather admired him back then. A spin bowler of guile and courage, he was described by the cricketers' bible, *Wisden*, as 'a throwback to an earlier time . . . with his aristocratic manner'. Maybe all that guile, courage and aristocratic manner helped him carve out a controversial career in financing mining deals that frightened off others. Maybe it also helped his company, Procana, secure 30,000 hectares of Massingir district in Mozambique, close to the South African border.

Edmonds owned Procana with a Zimbabwean friend called Andrew Groves and a South African, Izac Molthausen. They promised to raise $500 million to clear the land and grow sugar cane for ethanol production and sale in South Africa. But the company quickly got into disputes. First, the local agencies running the Great Limpopo Transfrontier Park – Anton Rupert's first 'peace park' – claimed the Procana concession took half of the land earmarked for resettling people made homeless by the park. Then local farmers said the company destroyed some of their fields during early clearing, and unnecessarily cut them off from vital sources of water along the Elefant River. Tihovene village, one of six involved, said Procana had taken most of its fields and grazing land without their consent, while land they had offered was ignored.

The trio of biofuels musketeers seemed both high-handed and inept. But in any event, the money was never raised, few of the promised 7,000 jobs were ever created, only 800 hectares were ever cleared, and they pulled out without even telling the Mozambique government, which cancelled the lease when it found out.

There is no trace of Procana now. The three men went back to their mining deals. They have since acquired 60 per cent of minerals exploration rights to 530 square kilometres of the Kpo mountains in Liberia and are pursuing coal-mine interests in Zimbabwe and Botswana. But they did not entirely give up on farming. Edmonds and Groves are now chairman and chief executive of a new company, Agriterra, which has a 20,000-hectare beef ranch under development in Mozambique. They promise investors that by 2013, they will have 10,000 animals grazing new pastures at a small town called Dombe, which the government has recently cleared of both land mines and tsetse flies. It is, coincidentally, just down the road from the abandoned fields of Sun Biofuels.

Many biofuels projects have collapsed across Africa. In Tanzania a Dutch jatropha plantation company called Bioshape, which claimed 81,000 hectares, went bankrupt. As did a scheme run by a Swedish clean energy company called Sekab. Others limp on. Take the fate of Flora EcoPower. In 2007, the Munich-based company joined up with two Israeli brothers, Alon and Ayal Hovev, to operate two big concessions they had won in Ethiopia and Madagascar. The idea was to grow castor beans, from which to extract oil to make biodiesel for Europe.

In Ethiopia, their 50-year lease covered 56,000 hectares of land an hour's drive from Harar, a town east of Addis Ababa known for its mosques. Satellite images commissioned by the company suggested the land was empty. But in fact there were pastoralists. And environmentalists said the forests they cleared were inhabited by elephants and black-maned lions, the Ethiopian national symbol. The plan went ahead, nonetheless. A processing plant was built. In 2008, the first castor beans were produced. Things looked good. The company reportedly planned another 72,000 hectares and a large outgrower network. Prime minister Meles Zenawi paid a visit. But in April 2009, the Hovev brothers disappeared. Employees were left without five months' wages, and banks with debts.

At almost exactly the same time, the same thing happened at the other joint project in the Mangrare valley in Madagascar. The company had 40,000 hectares and had begun trial planting in 2008. According to local academic Barry Ferguson, 'The Israelis bugged out in March 2009.' Ferguson claims that they first 'commandeered all the company assets, including a couple of tractors, before they left'. Again, there were staff left unpaid. One of Ferguson's students, an intern working there, was left stranded.

The shareholders of Flora EcoPower changed the company's name to Acazis, paid up the outstanding bills, resumed business in Ethiopia (though not in Madagascar) and declined to answer my questions about what happened in the Hovev days. In Ethiopia at the end of 2010, the new CEO, Patrick Bigger, blamed his former Israeli managers for the debacle. 'It was discovered that they were not managers, and not even farmers,' he told a local interviewer. When last heard of, the Hovevs were in Tanzania, as director and head agriculturalist at a company called Tendaji Agro, which says it is trying to recreate in East Africa the Israeli kibbutz system of co-operative farming. Ferguson said that in late 2011 the Madagascan site was 'completely dormant'.

Who is next? The Tana River delta is Kenya's largest coastal wetland, rich in wildlife and home to some 25,000 traditional pastoralists. There, Bedford Biofuels, a company run by an ebullient Canadian businessman called David McClure, has acquired a 45-year lease on 160,000 hectares. The Alberta-based company wants to grow jatropha. It claims the 'underutilized land' provides 'some of the best conditions for growing jatropha in the world'. It plans to 'employ thousands of workers . . . within the first three years of development'. In July 2011, Bedford Biofuels announced that 'after three years of fund-raising' it was 'breaking ground' on land leased to the company by Orma pastoralists. But there is a long history of acrimonious disputes in the delta. Herders there say they have been sold out by elders living in Nairobi. But they are not giving up. And prominent environmental NGOs, such as Birdlife International, have sided with those trying to prevent development of the wetland. They have won past battles. They may win again.

Across the continent, the West African state of Ghana briefly emerged as a major centre for jatropha production. More than twenty companies obtained more than a million hectares of land to grow the crop. Stavanger-based Scanfarm for a while cultivated jatropha on the lands of the Agogo people, part of the Ashanti tribe, close to the city of Kusami. But yields were poor and it switched to growing maize on part of the 13,000 hectares it had acquired (not the 400,000 hectares that has sometimes been claimed). Italy's Agroils, with its local subsidiary Smart Oil, planted jatropha on some of its 105,000 hectares beside Lake Volta. Israel's Galten Global Alternative Energy claimed 10,000 hectares near Kadima. And Canada's Kimminic Corporation had 65,000 hectares in central Ghana.

Many of these numbers were fanciful. Britain's Jatropha Africa operates from a suburban house in south London, and claims to have a lease on 50,000 hectares and an option on an additional

70,000 hectares. But despite being on the ground since 2006 it had by 2011 only planted 100 hectares, and exported just 10 tonnes – to a biofuels company in Japan. As its CEO Clive Coker told me: 'Having access to vast areas of scrubland is one thing, having the resources to turn that land into a jatropha farm is another.'

If you believe its claims, the biggest land grab in Ghana may be by Gold Star Farms, a small US company that thinks big and boasts of operating in 15 countries. It claims to have been promised two million hectares, though it has never revealed where this land is and only 5,700 hectares have been planted. Gold Star's owner, Jack Holden, whose Ghanaian subsidiary is owned by his Ghanaian wife Diana Holden, says it shares profits with landowners, employs workers year-round, pays good wages and supplies medical insurance to workers.

How did all these deals happen? In Ghana, traditional chiefs still have a lot of power. Activists in other countries often say local power is the key to making sure communities are not trampled by governments when landgrabbers come calling. But Ghana suggests it doesn't always work out like that. Ghanaian forest researcher Eric Nutakor and George Schoneveld and Laura German of the Indonesia-based Centre for International Forestry Research investigated land deals in the country. They found that large areas 'were easily obtained by foreign companies through direct negotiations with traditional authorities, often through opaque, non-participatory and partially documented negotiations . . . locking up large tracts of land for periods of up to 50 years'.

Chiefs dispensed their thumbprints carelessly. They received 'drink money', which some critics regard as a bribe but is a customary practice recognized by the government. But whether bribed, confused, or simply acting out of ignorance, the chiefs and the people whose livelihoods hinge on the decisions they made were getting bad deals. Many households did not even get compensation for their lost land. The researchers concluded that greater government scrutiny could improve things. For it seems that 'only a small minority of foreign companies in Ghana registered at the appropriate government agencies' before getting those thumbprints.

The biofuels business went crazy in about 2007. The European Union's decision to require biofuels to be added to all vehicle fuel meant there was a legally guaranteed market. Many governments were emboldened to get into biofuels after hearing George W. Bush call for a biofuels drive in his State of the Union address in January 2006. And financiers were seduced by a gung-ho prospectus for jatropha from Goldman Sachs. They saw big profits and major development opportunities.

Back then, Brazil was talking about replacing a tenth of the world's fossil fuels with sugar ethanol. Malaysia and Indonesia both said they would set aside up to 40 per cent of future oil-palm plantations for biodiesel. Even oil companies joined in. Chevron claimed to have 400,000 hectares of land set aside for biofuels in the US. And Western entrepreneurs headed for Africa, in search of cheap land to grow old-style vegetable oils, sugar for ethanol, or new wonder-crops like jatropha. NGOs counted more than a hundred biofuels projects in Africa, operated by 50 companies in 20 countries. At one stage it was estimated that such projects covered as much as 11 million hectares.

There was a bubble. The bubble has been partly deflated by the practical problems, by the discovery that quick profits are unlikely, by anger about the mess left by some of the early arrivals, and also by a new environmental realism that questions the simple belief that biofuels automatically cut global carbon emissions. Africa will be living with the consequences for decades to come as dubiously obtained leases play out.

Some mourn the bursting of the bubble, and hope that it may

prove only a temporary setback. But before we are seduced by the benefits of biofuels, it is worth asking what they are supposed to deliver.

The original environmental case was this. Like any other carbon-based fuel, when biofuels are burned, they release the greenhouse gas carbon dioxide into the atmosphere. But if the fuel comes from a crop, then growing the plant will absorb the same amount of carbon dioxide from the air as is eventually released by the burning. Carbon in; carbon out. A cycle is created, in which growing new plants neutralizes the emissions. The logic is impeccable, but it leaves out two things. First, there is the carbon 'footprint' of growing, transporting and processing the crop. And second, the question of what else might have happened on that land and what its carbon consequences would be.

The first can be calculated. The maths makes growing maize for ethanol look dumb. The large amount of energy needed to manufacture fertilizer to grow the maize, and then to process that maize into ethanol, often means it would be more climate-friendly to stick with regular fossil oil. Other ethanol crops, such as sugar cane, look better because they need less fertilizer and less processing. Most of the vegetable oils slated to replace diesel look quite good, because processing is easy. You just squeeze. If it grows well, jatropha can deliver a two-thirds emissions saving, for instance. Soya looks sensible, and oil palm even better. These are the calculations used to justify both growing biofuels and the EU laws requiring mixing biofuels with regular fuel. Biofuels, the regulators say, don't eliminate emissions, but they do reduce them.

But what about the second issue? Biofuels require land. The calculation above only works if nothing else would have grown on the land in question. Usually, that is not the situation. Not many biofuels grow in deserts. If biofuels replace something else, whether a crop or natural vegetation, that has to be taken into account. The most dramatic example is oil palm. It is often grown on land formerly occupied by rainforest and carbon-rich peat bogs. Clearing the forests and draining the peat bogs will create a huge carbon footprint. Taking that into account, the overall carbon footprint of biodiesel from palm oil is often much greater than fossil oil.

More often, biofuels are grown on former pastures, in which case we need to know how much carbon the grass would have absorbed. Or they might be grown on fields that once grew food. Assuming the food now has to be grown somewhere else, we then need to know where it is grown, and what the carbon footprint of the food crop is. Maybe someone somewhere chopped down a forest to keep people fed. Or added extra fertilizer to another field to increase yields. Making fertilizer is an extremely energy-intensive, carbon-producing activity.

Very often, answering this chain of questions may reveal that biofuels come at a carbon cost greater than the fossil fuels they replace. It seems rather obvious. You might presume that the carbon calculators had taken this into account. But no. Tim Searchinger of Princeton University, who has campaigned among scientists for answers to these questions, says the land issue is still not being assessed by most regulators plotting our route to a low-carbon future. And it is true. Regulators I have spoken to say they have left the land bit out because it is too hard to calculate. Quite so. But until this carbon accounting error is fixed, regulators often simply don't know if, or when, biofuels are worth it.

23

ZIMBABWE

On the fast track

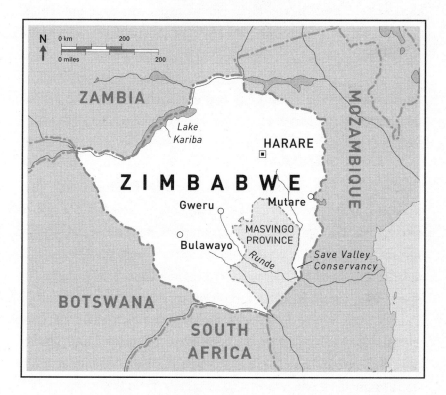

One of the most notorious land grabs of the new century was not by foreign corporations or sovereign funds or speculators. It was an old-fashioned state land grab – by Robert Mugabe's Zanu-PF party and the war veterans of Zimbabwe. Many of the 'veterans' were too young to have fought in the long war to liberate Zimbabwe from a white supremacist government which had ruled the country in defiance of British attempts to grant independence. But they regarded themselves as completing that war by taking over land still occupied by whites.

The chaotic and often violent land reform – much of which was ruled illegal by the country's supreme court – was played out in graphic detail on TV a decade ago. Many of the outcomes have been disastrous. Many of the new settlers had neither the know-how nor the means to maintain productivity on the land. Agricultural output from large farms collapsed. There followed an economic crisis, growing poverty and hunger. But, says Ian Scoones of the Institute of Development Studies at the University of Sussex, it was not all bad.

Scoones and a team of Zimbabwean colleagues have pieced together what happened in the southeast of the country, Masvingo province, in the decade after the reforms. The resulting book, *Zimbabwe's Land Reforms: Myths and Realities*, is a remarkable piece of sustained on-the-ground research, conducted under often difficult conditions. Their findings may not be typical of the whole country, but they do reveal a more nuanced story than is normally told. In some areas, especially where the previous landowners had run private ranches and plantations largely devoid of people, the gains from new settlements have been important.

What everyone agrees is that, following independence, land reform was needed. Foreigners, particularly the British government, had promised to fund it. But in the first twenty years of independence, up to 1999, the old landed elite of some 6,000 mostly white commercial farmers, along with some organizations like churches, had clung on. They had cut their holdings only marginally, from 15 million hectares to 12 million hectares. They still had 30 per cent of the country. Progress on redistribution was slowing as the British and Zimbabwean authorities failed to agree on how to do it. Something had to give.

President Mugabe decided not to wait any longer, or to bother with legal niceties. After 1999, his 'fast track' land reform resulted in seven million hectares changing hands – some by government decree, and some through freelance invasions by 'war veterans'. As the big farms succumbed, established domestic markets in commodities like wheat, tobacco and coffee collapsed. Around 150,000 workers on the large commercial farms lost their jobs, and often their homes, as the veterans invaded white-owned property. But Scoones and his colleagues examined what happened next. While war veterans and political cronies undoubtedly got more than their fair share of the redistributed land, some 180,000 smallholders also benefited, often acquiring land for the first time. Some older people went back to land they remembered as children, before they were evicted to make way for commercial farmers.

In the wake of Mugabe's land reforms, much of the country's economy collapsed, because of the destruction of its mainly exporting agribusinesses, and because of chronic mismanagement of the escalating crisis by central government, including the money-printing that created hyper-inflation. Only foreign exchange had any value. With shops empty and trading almost impossible, people turned to subsistence and barter. But there was another side. As the war veterans and other settlers took over parcels of land on the vast estates, production and informal trade in farm commodities boomed. Small grains like sorghum, the traditional produce of dry-land African farms, did well. Cotton production, another smallholder crop, flourished, says Scoones. And, despite the collapse of the big ranches, livestock prospered and the country probably ended up with as many cattle, pigs and sheep as before the reforms. The research team found that 'half of the 400 households sampled were accumulating and investing, often employing labour and increasing their farming operations ... agriculture has not collapsed'.

The most obvious gains, says Scoones, came from the takeover of the big white-owned ranches. Typical was Edenvale cattle ranch, which had covered 18,000 hectares but employed just 40 herders to look after 4,000 cattle. The same land now supports 18 villages, each with several hundred inhabitants. These new settlements created growth in the rest of the local economy at a time when the government was broke and riddled with corruption, and when aid agencies were largely absent. Some smallholder farms diversified into brick-making and craftwork, fishing and retailing. Since the economy stabilized in 2009, new commercial centres have developed in the occupied lands.

But today, the land reforms have moved to a new and darker phase, rather more like the land grabs in other countries. Powerful politicians, military figures and their friends are now capturing land for their own purposes. Mostly, the new elites are not trying to take the farms occupied by large numbers of smallholders. That would be too obvious a betrayal of the reforms. But the new landgrabbers are moving in on the remaining large white holdings that, whether by accident or design, survived the original reforms.

The takeovers include sugar estates such as Hippo Valley and Triangle, and a network of wildlife ranches in the southeast of the country. Mugabe and his wife are said to own 14 farms covering 16,000 hectares. Widely reported claims that party loyalists and leading military and police figures have between them grabbed some 5 million hectares are 'grossly exaggerated', says Scoones. But there is nonetheless a real danger that one landed elite is being replaced by another.

One convoluted case concerns the 350,000-hectare Nuanetsi ranch in Masvingo. It was owned by the Imperial Cold Storage Company of South Africa until being bought in 1989 by the Development Trust of Zimbabwe, an organization set up by Joshua Nkomo, Zimbabwean vice-president and a famous and respected political leader in the fight for independence. Profits from the Trust's many commercial activities were intended to develop the economy of his native Matabeleland. Nkomo died in 1999, as the land reforms got under way. And soon after, a new figure emerged on the Trust's board – a white Zimbabwean businessman called Billy Rautenbach with strong links to Mugabe.

It has been alleged that Mugabe's ministers secured substantial sections of the Nkomo estate for Rautenbach in return for financial support and other favours for his party. The opposition Movement for Democratic Change accused Rautenbach of hounding its officials. Rautenbach, who has been banned from entering both Britain and the US since 2008 because of his links to Mugabe, had also been a business partner in the metals exploits of Phil Edmonds (see Chapter Twenty-two). Under his influence, the Development Trust of Zimbabwe has joined up with Zimbabwe Bio-Energy for what the latter calls a billion-dollar development of the estate that will include growing sugar cane, installing a quarter of a million reptiles on a crocodile farm, cattle ranching, and moving a thousand buffalo from a national park to create a game reserve.

Game is the big new thing. Bigger than biofuels.

The big survivors of the original reforms were wildlife ranches in the Lowveld of southern Zimbabwe. Former cattle ranches, they linked up in the 1990s to create a series of wildlife 'conservancies' protected by high-security electric fences. They extend in an arc across the country from the Bubye Valley Conservancy in the west through Save Valley Conservancy to the Chipinge Safari Area near the Mozambique border. The Save Valley Conservancy claims to be the largest private conservancy in the world, covering 340,000 hectares. Though the Save conservancy combines 26 ranches, its heart is the huge Devuli Ranch, originally created by one of the great British imperial landgrabbers, Lucas Bridges, with land he bought in 1919 from the British South Africa Company, the creation of the African imperialist Cecil Rhodes who created Rhodesia (now

Zimbabwe) in his own name. (As we saw in Chapter Thirteen, Bridges also created the huge Chacabuco sheep ranch in Patagonia, later bought by American conservationists Doug and Kris Tompkins.)

Rhinos are the prime conservation interest in the Lowveld, though the conservancies also play host to passing lions, elephants, cheetahs, wild dogs and antelopes. Rhino ranching has been a very whites-only business. One of the founders of the conservancy idea was a white Zimbabwean conservationist called Raoul du Toit, who formed the Lowveld Rhino Trust. The trust was funded by the Beit family trust, which had been created a century before by Alfred Beit, a friend of Rhodes.

In conservation terms, the idea has worked. The rhino ranches together now cover 500,000 hectares and have 80 per cent of the surviving rhinos in Zimbabwe. Behind the fences, the animals are generally safe from poachers. But the plan, back in the 1990s, was for tourists to pay the bills. And since the country's collapse into chaos, tourists have been thin on the ground. Even so, some rich entrepreneurs have moved in. Wall Street's Paul Tudor Jones, owner of the Grumeti game reserve in Tanzania's Serengeti, bought the 43,000-hectare Malilangwe Wildlife Reserve. 'He has been a great source of help; he is paying to move rhinos around,' says du Toit.

But increasingly, the conservancies have caught the eyes of the country's political elite. Leading military and Zanu-PF figures have decided to complete the transfer of the country's land from white to black hands by grabbing for themselves a stake in what are, potentially at least, highly profitable 'joint ventures'. And they don't pay; they just turn up and insist on a slice of the action. Mafia-style, say the rhino ranchers.

In 2009, Masvingo's governor, Titus Maluleke, reportedly compelled safari operators within the Save Valley Conservancy to give 50 per cent shares to local bigwigs as 'indigenous partners'.

Some of the press reports are contradictory, but it appears that Major General Engelbert Rugeje, the chief of staff of the Zimbabwe National Army, and the local MP, Ailess Baloyi, have a share in the Humani Safari Ranch. The country's attorney general and Mugabe loyalist Johannes Tomana was alleged to have taken the Malingani ranch from its white owner, Kenned Hood. Hood said he had been 'chased off' his property, which was also home to 10 giraffes, 60 antelopes, 30 buffaloes, five lions and two cheetahs. Paul Mangwana, former minister of empowerment, was said to have taken control of the Wanezi block ranch, while local senator and former governor Josiah Hungwe took Mwenezi ranch. WikiLeaks later published US diplomatic cables repeating many of the assertions.

Early in 2011, the German government lodged a complaint alleging that one of its citizens had his land stolen. Willy Pabst was the owner of the Sango ranch on the Save Valley Conservancy. Berlin claimed that Maluleke had 'made it quite clear that he wanted a partnership without paying for it'. The complaint said Pabst's property was protected under the 1995 Bilateral Investment Promotion and Protection Agreement between the two countries. But Zanu-PF said it had recently revoked the agreement on the grounds that 'no foreigner should be allowed to own rural agricultural land in Zimbabwe'.

Zimbabwe's parks director Vitalis Chadenga called these conservancy grabs the 'unfinished business of the land reform programme'. But there was little sign that the ranches were being given to smallholders. Conservationists said that the new bosses were keen to sell hunting licences to safari companies from South Africa and Botswana.

In the light of all this, it may be no surprise that some white Zimbabwean farmers have been in search of pastures new. They remain less popular in Africa than the Boer trekkers, but their undoubted farming skills are in demand. In 2005, a group of them were welcomed in Nigeria. There, near the town of Shonga on the banks of the River Niger, they lead what Michael Mortimore, a British geographer who has visited them, calls 'a somewhat reclusive existence in the bush'. It is more than an hour to the nearest hairdresser's, one of their wives complained when a BBC film crew found them.

The group of 13 farmers were each given a 25-year lease on a thousand hectares by the governor of Kwara state. The land was not previously empty. The governor confiscated it from the inhabitants of 15 surrounding villages. He said it had not been permanently cultivated. True. But in what is a familiar African story, the villagers said it was vital for their herding and shifting cultivation. They seem to have been assuaged, however, by compensation payments, electricity lines and asphalt on their roads. Meanwhile the Zimbabwean settlers have received assistance in the form of a chicken abattoir, and milk- and cassava-processing facilities.

Mortimore says the results have been 'spectacular'. But he wonders whether this white Zimbabwean enclave in the middle of Nigeria will, as the state governor hopes, catalyse a new form of farming across the state. The farmers told the BBC they have not yet made a profit, and cannot find banks willing to invest in their farms. One rice farmer, John Sawyer, said that despite the state subsidies, he faced bankruptcy. The scheme did not look like a model for feeding Africa.

PART SIX

THE LAST ENCLOSURE

The world's commons are under siege. The biggest prizes for the landgrabbers are unfenced forests and pastures – and many governments are willing to sell out their inhabitants. It looks like the Earth's final round-up; the last enclosure. And with the land often comes water – a free resource being privatized. Millions of Malians suffer as their water is siphoned off for Chinese, South African and even Libyan farmers. The world's poor and hungry are losing their land and water in the name of development. Can this really be the way to feed the world?

24

CENTRAL AFRICA
Laws of the jungle

Vincent Bolloré is a friend of France's President Sarkozy, and a long-time neighbour of Sarkozy's wife, Carla Bruni, in the private Parisian mansion of Villa Montmorency. He has a personal fortune estimated at $2 billion. His Bolloré Group is as well connected in the former French colonies of central Africa as it is in the salons of Paris. For that is where its wealth comes from. In the region's capitals, Vincent Bolloré is nicknamed the 'last emperor'.

Bolloré is especially big in Cameroon, where his group runs the main port at Douala and the country's railway links to its neighbours, has trucking companies and pipelines, grows oil palm, sells cigarettes and taps rubber. And there are the timber concessions. In Cameroon, Bolloré owns a third of the logging rights.

His main rival in the convoluted forest politics of Cameroon is Hazim Hazim Chehade, Lebanon's long-standing consul to the country. Since the 1990s, Hazim has controlled some 150,000 hectares of Cameroon forest. His company, Société Forestière Hazim, has been accused repeatedly by government agencies and Greenpeace of illegal logging, both within his own concessions and in those of others. The colourful but slightly sinister presence of Bolloré and Hazim in the country seems straight out of a Graham Greene novel. But they are far from alone.

In the steamy forests of central Africa, foreign loggers control 40 times more land than local forest communities. Another French forester, Francis Rougier, oversees his family's million hectares in Cameroon and Gabon. That's an area the size of Northern Ireland. Much of Rougier's land in Gabon is accessed by the Trans-Gabon railway. Built in the 1980s, it runs through 700 kilometres of jungle from the coastal capital of Libreville deep into the interior to Franceville, Rougier's company town. Like the Bollorés, the Rougiers are close to Sarkozy. Before him, they were intimates of former presidents François Mitterrand and Jacques Chirac. In early 2010, Sarkozy visited Franceville with Rougier and Gabon's president, Ali Bongo. You have to pinch yourself to realize that the colonial era is over.

Hans-Joachim Danzer heads the Swiss-German Danzer family. They have specialized for half a century in producing veneers from hardwoods logged in Congo-Brazzaville and the Democratic Republic of Congo. Their combined concessions in the two Congos cover 3.3 million hectares, an area approaching the size of Switzerland.

DRC, the former Zaire, is Africa's second-largest country and the golden prize for loggers. Its huge swathes of jungle are the heart of the last great rainforest on Earth. Those forests have been largely spared from foreign loggers through recent decades of war and chaos. The roads have returned to bush and the chainsaws have fallen silent. Only Zimbabwe's military entered. A decade ago, its soldiers did a deal with Kinshasa and set up armed logging camps in what was for a while one of the world's largest and most militarized logging concessions. The generals reportedly harvested from 33 million hectares of forests around the mining region of Katanga in the south of the country.

As the country opens up, the Zimbabweans are gone, but the Danzers are still there. So is an American dynasty from Philadelphia. Daniel Blattner's family has for 50 years logged a concession of more than a million hectares around Kisangani, the trading town above Stanley Falls that was the model for Kurtz's 'inner station' in Joseph Conrad's *Heart of Darkness*.

The Danzers and Rougiers, Bollorés and Blattners are the old guard in central Africa, family firms whose logging concessions have persisted barely noticed by the outside world for half a century. But today many concessions are changing hands, and the pace of logging is increasing. In 2007, another French family company, Thanry, sold its 600,000-hectare concession in Gabon to the Swiss group Precious Woods, a neighbour of the Danzers in the tiny Swiss canton of Zug. The same year, Precious Woods also bought a minority interest in Liechtenstein-based Nordsudtimber, which controls four forestry companies in DRC. Precious said it was 'laying the foundation' for a greater presence there.

Mostly, however, the concession buyers are from the east now. Thanry was the largest logging company in Cameroon, with more than 700,000 hectares of logging rights until selling out a decade ago to the Hong Kong-based Vicwood Group, which specializes in plywoods. Vicwood also operates in Congo-Brazzaville and the Central African Republic. It has a total of 7 million hectares of forest awaiting its chainsaws.

Keeping up with who owns the Congolaise Industrielle des Bois (CIB) concession in Congo-Brazzaville is hard. CIB is the country's biggest employer; its holdings comprise 1.4 million hectares in the country's northern highlands. Its tenants include many pygmy hunters who in the past have been forced to become its labourers. Originally CIB was French-owned. It was taken over by the German Stoll family in 1968. The Stolls sold it in 2006 to the Danish Dalhoff Larsen & Horneman Group (DLH), a low-profile company that had become briefly notorious for receiving timber shipped by the arms traders who ran Liberia's forests during its long civil war. After timber prices collapsed during the global financial crisis of 2008, DLH sold to the fast-growing palm-oil-to-timber combine Olam International in January 2011.

Olam is Singapore-based, but has its origins twenty years ago as a cotton-growing offshoot of the Kewalram Chanrai Group set up by Indians in Nigeria. In January 2011, Olam bought another DLH concession in Gabon, giving it a total of 1.6 million hectares of hardwood forests in the two countries. Rimbunan Hijau, the giant Malaysian conglomerate owned by Tiong Hiew King, also has half a million hectares in Gabon.

Meanwhile, the French-German Isoroy group sold a 550,000-hectare concession in Gabon to China's Honest Timber in 2009. Honest Timber is one of 15 Chinese private logging companies operating in Gabon, with concessions covering 2.7 million hectares, a tenth of the country. Annually, they ship around a million tonnes of the highly prized Gabonese okoumé timber to Chinese plywood manufacturers. For the past decade, Gabon has been by far the largest African supplier of timber to China. Collectively, the Chinese concession holders are probably the country's largest employer.

China's unusual success in wooing the country is due to one man, Jean Ping, the son of a Chinese trader and a Gabonese clan chief's daughter. As the country's minister of foreign affairs in 1987, Ping stopped off during an official trip to China to invite a long-lost nephew and timber trader named Xu Gongde to set up a logging company in Gabon. Xu came and brought many after him.

As the logging concessions go east, a new generation of Western forest entrepreneurs is moving in. They want to make money from conserving carbon, either by planting new forests or by 'protecting' natural forests. Under international climate treaties, such initiatives can earn them carbon credits worth between ten and twenty dollars per tonne.

This is good news for the atmosphere, of course. But the danger is that, unless properly done, it could be bad news for the people whose land is taken. And the companies, whether their motives are altruistic or strictly commercial, can get caught in the middle. Take the case of the New Forests Company, a London-based company with leases on 27,000 hectares for planting forests in Uganda, Tanzania, Mozambique and Rwanda. In Uganda, it found itself taking over land cleared of people by the national government's Forestry Authority. The people and their farms were to be replaced with pine and eucalyptus trees. The company hoped to earn up to $2 million a year by selling the carbon credits under the Kyoto Protocol.

Oxfam, the aid charity, calculated that some 20,000 people were evicted to make way for the company in Uganda, mostly in 2010. Nobody much disagrees with that, but the government and New Forests insist the people were squatters who had no right to be there. That might legally be true, but some of the people interviewed by Oxfam said their grandfathers had been given the land in return for fighting for the British Army in Burma and Egypt during the Second World War. And the manner of their departures was hardly fitting. The company said it had been assured that all the evictions were 'legal, voluntary and peaceful'. But, confronted with evidence that villagers were forcibly moved and their homes were torched, government officials told the *New York Times* this may have happened. Surely, whatever the law may say, they deserved better?

The Kyoto Protocol gives carbon credits for planting trees. Its successor will give credits simply for protecting natural forests threatened with destruction. The UN's international climate talks on cutting industrial carbon emissions may have stalled since the 2009 debacle in Copenhagen, but progress has been faster on a global deal called Reduced Emissions from Deforestation and Forest Degradation, or REDD. It aims to pay the forests' owners to keep that carbon out of the atmosphere by protecting their trees. The cash will come from rich-world power companies and industrialists whose emissions are limited by law at home. Even without a UN deal, that includes most large companies in Europe, some US states, Australia and elsewhere.

Conservationists see REDD as a way to unlock billions of dollars for both fighting climate change and saving the rainforests. No wonder they are excited. But it raises tricky questions. Who exactly owns the forests? And where will the money end up? Will the beneficiaries be the forest dwellers, or governments, or a new generation of corporate carbon concession holders?

In Brazil, there are signs that forest dwellers can use their hard-won land rights to harvest international cash. In part of the Juma forest reserve in Amazonia, the state government has given every household a credit card account into which it deposits $50 each month as a payment in return for keeping the forest intact. The Surui tribe in Rondonia believes it can sell the carbon content of the trees in its own reserve, without the government acting as an intermediary.

But the danger is that, with governments and corporations dominating negotiations on the rules for REDD, most of the compensation will end up in national treasuries, or with corporate concession holders and the consultants who will advise them on how to meet REDD's complex rules. One recent analysis found that consultancy services and other external expertise for a single REDD pilot project typically cost around $30 million, almost ten times what was originally envisaged. In Indonesia, which has become a REDD pioneer and expects to reap billions of dollars a year from carbon conservation, the first 11 forest carbon projects set up by the government gave forest communities only a fifth of the revenue.

As in the early days of the biofuels boom, carbon cowboys are on the lookout for opportunities to make a quick killing out of REDD.

In 2009, something went badly wrong in Papua New Guinea, a country already well known for its duplicitous and sometimes corrupt treatment of forest dwellers. An agent for the Australian carbon trading company Carbon Planet called Kirk Roberts had been travelling to forest communities with genuine-looking carbon-offset certificates, purporting to be from REDD. Their authenticity seemed real since they were signed by the head of PNG's Office of Climate Change, Theo Yasause. Roberts had done deals with 40 communities, exchanging the certificates for the rights to sell carbon offsets from the villagers' forests.

But the Adelaide-based Carbon Planet director Dave Sag has since admitted the certificates were worthless 'props'. They have no value to the villagers. Yet if REDD becomes a reality, then the carbon rights that the company bought with the 'certificates' could one day become extremely valuable. Both Yasause and Roberts, a disqualified Australian horse trainer who once ran a cock-fighting business in the Philippines, left their posts under a cloud shortly afterwards. In 2011, Yasause was charged with the murder of a former national rugby league star, Aquila Emil, after a shooting incident outside a Port Moresby nightclub.

REDD's requirement to protect threatened forests could become a new reason to throw forest dwellers out of their forests. The argument will be that natives are destroying their forests, and that outsiders must be brought in to protect them – and harvest the carbon credits from doing so. Shifting cultivators are an obvious target. Conventional forest surveys blame them for destroying large areas. But usually their small forest clearings swiftly regenerate. Recent research suggests that, far from being jungle villains and deforesters, most forest communities are admirable custodians of their land. It is outsiders who cause the problems.

In a detailed study across the tropics, Ashwini Chhatre of the University of Illinois and Arun Agarwal of the University of Michigan found that forests under the control of local inhabitants usually stored more carbon than government-owned forests. For all their green talk, most governments licensed destructive logging, or simply failed to protect the forests from invaders. But locals had a long-term interest in ensuring their forests' survival, and most did just that. 'We can increase carbon sequestration simply by transferring ownership of forests from governments to communities,' they concluded.

But out in the rainforests, what is happening is mostly the opposite. 'There is a real fear that REDD will lead to dispossession of local communities [as] governments stake their claim on emissions reduction credits,' said Chhatre and Agarwal. 'Existing REDD action plans from the UN and World Bank do not identify communities as relevant agents for managing forests to sequester carbon. Instead they focus on national governments, replicating long histories of centralized control over forests.'

Frances Seymour, director of the Center for International

Forestry Research in Bogor, Indonesia, says this research reflects the findings of her own investigators: 'Poor people are usually too poor to do much damage.' Machetes rarely chop as much timber as chainsaws. Rather than snatching the forests from their inhabitants in a bogus effort to 'save' them, the world needs to tackle the real forest destroyers, she says. That means mothballing pulp mills in Sumatra, and rejecting proposals to convert forests into oil-palm plantations.

Will governments do that? She doubts it. They want to harvest carbon credits while continuing to harvest the timber and clear the land for commercial agriculture. To achieve that, they will perpetuate the mythology of forest-destroying peasants. They will continue to throw forest dwellers off their land, and will soon be cashing in REDD cheques for 'protecting' the forests. The losers will be the forests' traditional inhabitants – and the forests themselves. It is the most pernicious form of green grab yet.

25
INNER NIGER DELTA, MALI
West African water grab

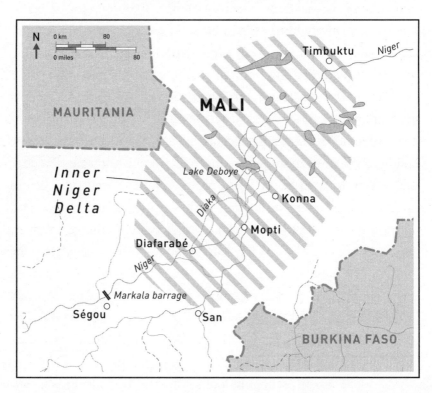

Daouda Sanankoua is an aquatic mayor, and proud of it. The elected boss of Deboye district in the West African state of Mali arrived for our meeting by overnight ferry through flooded forests and submerged banks of hippo grass. In the wet season, the majority of his district is flooded. Thank goodness. 'More water is good,' he said, waving a long elegant finger and peering at his foreign inquisitor over his glasses. 'Everything here depends on the water, but the government is taking our water. They are giving it to foreign farmers.'

Mali is a landlocked state on the fringes of the Sahara. Its 15 million people are among the poorest in the world, mainly dependent on irrigated agriculture and fishing. Much of this activity is sustained by the River Niger, which snakes through the country's populated south. The Malian government has decided that the best way to make the country richer is to bring in foreigners to boost productivity from its land by expanding irrigated agriculture. To do that, a major land grab is going on. But land means nothing in an arid place like this without water. So just as important is the simultaneous water grab, to irrigate that new farmland. And that is what is angering Daouda.

Daouda's district is in the centre of the inner Niger Delta, a wet-land the size of Belgium, where the great river spreads out, flooding the desert in a maze of lakes, waterways and wetlands, before gathering its waters again and heading on through Niger and Nigeria to the ocean. The delta is an immense smudge of green and blue on the edge of the Sahara, and a wintering ground for millions of birds migrating from Europe. During my journey through the delta, I constantly grabbed binoculars to spot kingfishers, marsh harriers, cormorants and purple herons. Out there too, though I did not spot any, are hippos, African manatees and the odd crocodile.

I spoke to the scholarly-looking mayor Daouda in the tiny schoolyard of Akka village, a few metres from the lapping waters of Lake Deboye in the heart of the delta. Women rushed around putting mats on the ground, bringing bowls of rice and then fish – all products of the lake. The headlines around the world that week brought news of flood disasters in Pakistan, Australia, Brazil and Sri Lanka. But Daouda and the various ethnic groups that inhabit the delta were grateful for their flood.

The waters nurture abundant fish for the Bozo people. Probably the area's original inhabitants, the Bozo punt and row and sail their six-seater pirogues from dawn to dusk, laying their nets and catching around 100,000 tonnes of fish each year. As the dry season approaches, the receding waters leave behind wet soils in which the Bambara people, founders of the great thirteenth-century Mali Empire, plant their millet and rice. The waters also nurture vast aquatic pastures of hippo grass, locally called *bourgou*, that sustain cattle and goats brought by nomadic Fulani herders from as far away as Mauritania and Burkina Faso. When everywhere else in the region is dry and dead, the delta still provides rich pastures.

I was there in January, as the floodwaters began to recede. I watched the arrival of the Fulani with their cattle to settle for a few months in their distinctive square mud homes on islands in the delta. I talked to Bozo fishing families as they packed up their homes – loading mats, bedding, bags of rice and sweet potatoes, firewood, cooking pots, chairs, sound systems, even TVs, into their boats – to set up temporary camps beside the deep-water pools where fish would concentrate in the weeks ahead. The rights to harvest the delta's fish, plant crops and graze pastures are based on long-standing custom neither known nor recognized beyond its borders. Land and water are inseparable. Different people use different resources at different times. Sustainability has no better model.

But this rare and magnificently productive ecosystem, on which a million inhabitants depend, is facing unprecedented threats from water grabs just upstream of the delta. Others want this water. Over a torch-lit evening meal of Nile perch, millet porridge and bananas – all fruits of the wetland – the mayor said that water abstractions were diverting water, drying out fields, damaging the *bourgou* pastures and upsetting fish breeding. Later in the year, an environmental disaster loomed as huge water abstractions for irrigation combined with a drought upstream to lower water levels in the wetland. People were leaving. Temporary outward migration is a traditional coping strategy here during droughts, but the exodus none-theless underlined the precarious state of this vast oasis in the desert.

This is not yet a dying ecosystem. But the people are having to adapt to the changes. So far they are doing this with some success. The next morning, I walked across caked and cracked soil, grazed by three desultory donkeys, with a large contingent of Akka's 300 women. They have created a small oasis on the edge of the village, where tiny amounts of water taken from the lake irrigate small plots of onions, chillies, aubergines and lettuces. They eat most of the produce in the village and sell the rest at the market in Youvarou, just across the water, or in Mopti, the big town on the edge of the delta. Meanwhile, men in the delta are starting to rear animals in pens rather than on pastures. Mayor Daouda said he had 10 sheep fattening in a pen at home, fed on *bourgou*.

Bourgou is vital here. Villagers call it 'starvation food'. They eat it when their millet crops fail. It tastes rather like couscous, and ferments to make a popular sweet beer. So, with wild *bourgou* in decline as the delta diminishes, they have begun cultivating it. On a short boat ride from Akka, I saw a 30-hectare stand that attracts fish – another benefit. The fish attracted birds. Thousands of cormorants and pelicans gathered round. I asked if the villagers were not con-cerned about the birds taking their fish. But they said the bird droppings made the water more productive. 'The more birds there are, the more fish we get,' said the haughty, purple-robed Alpha Fofana, who was in charge of the *bourgou* project.

That night in Akka, young women were watching French soap operas late into the evening on the village's only TV, powered by batteries recharged during the day from a photovoltaic panel on the school roof. Later still, a lone male motorcyclist rode up and down the shore for several hours. The delta and its people are changing. But they still understand their ecosystem.

*

The next morning I headed for Kakagna, a few hours south across the delta. It is a village on a small hill with myriad narrow alleys leading to minute domestic compounds and imposing mud mosques. The river bank at the tiny jetty was covered in the products of a thriving village pottery business. There were brightly painted clay pots for water and incense, for oil and cooking. Women ushered me to huts where they made the pots, turning them by hand in depressions on the mud floors, and baking them by covering them in straw and setting a fire.

Kakagna was dominated by women. Some were Bozo fishers and others Fulani, with traditional rings through their noses and cuts in their cheeks from initiation rites. Embarrassingly, both groups of women separately brought us food from their competing kitchen gardens – and then parting gifts of mats, pots and wooden models of boats. To augment the lake fisheries, they run a small aquaculture project. Every year, as the dry season approaches, they dredge a small channel to direct remaining water into ponds where they nurture fish. The women take their pots and surplus fish to market in Mopti. They also sell mats made from wetland grasses, as well as fish and birds netted on the wetland. Business is still good. Fish on sale in Mopti were being smoked, dried or packed up with ice for trucking in huge boxes throughout Mali and to Burkina Faso, Ghana and Côte d'Ivoire.

But behind all this effort to sustain livelihoods on the delta, there was no disguising the fact that the wetland ecosystem is not as wet as it was. Mayor Daouda blamed the government, and in particular its agency in charge of irrigation projects upstream of the delta, called the Office du Niger. 'We don't hear from the Office du Niger,' he said with a hard stare. 'They damage our fish, but they don't come and tell us their plans, and they don't listen to us. The government is not interested in our local concerns.' I left the delta to find out more. To investigate the water grab.

*

The Office du Niger is a geographical area as well as an administration. It was established by the French administrators in 1932 in a thinly populated desert region immediately upstream of the inner Niger Delta. They built a barrage on the river, dug irrigation canals and brought in hundreds of thousands of farmers to till the land. The administration was in effect a state within a state, and since independence in 1960 it has been answerable only to the president or prime minister.

Progress on meeting the government's dream of irrigating a million hectares of farmland here has been slow. The 816-metre Markala barrage, with its 488 sluices, was eventually completed in 1947. It is an impressive structure, controlling the flow of the mighty river and distributing its water down three giant canals to the irrigation zones. But more than half a century on, fewer than 100,000 hectares are irrigated, a tenth of the intended area. A large map of the Office du Niger's domain sits on the Niger bank by the barrage. It shows a few small areas painted green, because they are being irrigated, and a wide area still covered in peeling yellow paint, showing it is awaiting irrigation.

The government chose to grow thirsty crops here in the irrigated desert. First it concentrated on cotton, then since 1970 on rice, augmented recently with sugar cane. Most of the farming till now has been done by smallholders who pay rent in the form of water charges. Most of the irrigation equipment is dilapidated and very wasteful. Enough water is put into the canals to flood each hectare of fields to a depth of almost three metres during the course of a year – at least twice any sensible requirement for growing rice. As a result, the fields become waterlogged, while the standing waters attract malarial mosquitoes, harbour snails that cause bilharzia and spread cholera.

So in 2003, Mali began looking for foreign investors to

rehabilitate the system and speed up progress to its million-hectare target. In Ségou town, I went to the headquarters of the Office du Niger. With his president's portrait behind him and two mobile phones and a national flag on his desk, the then CEO, Kassoum Denon, was every inch the trusted bureaucrat. He told me his first task was to double irrigation to more than 200,000 hectares by 2020, 'but if private investors can help us go faster, we are open to working with them'. On the roads outside his office, the outcome of his ambition was obvious. Fulani men herding long lines of cattle to pastures on the wetland were fighting for space with trucks bringing in building materials and taking out rice.

The effort to 'go faster' and speed up economic development follows a familiar pattern of land grab. Some grabbers are local opportunists. Modibo Keïta, the boss of Grand Distributeur Céréalier du Mali, a major distributor of cereals, bullied villagers off 7,400 hectares of grazing land near the Markala barrage, where he wanted to grow wheat. When they were not encouraged to leave by gifts of soccer balls and jerseys, and promises to build a school, a hospital and even a windmill, he sent his engineers to dig a canal, dumping the mud on the villagers' millet fields. The standoff ended in a pitched battle between stick-wielding policemen and villagers armed with farm tools, in which children were beaten and two pregnant women miscarried.

Most of the big land allocations being made by the Office du Niger have been to foreigners, however. Four of the biggest, covering 156,000 hectares, went to developers from Libya, South Africa, China and the US. The land is not currently irrigated, but it has cattle pastures, some millet farms and orchards, and is crossed by cattle trails used by Fulani herders. The new occupiers will pay no rent, provided they invest.

Illovo, the British-owned South African-managed sugar giant, aims to join with government agencies to cultivate some 14,000 hectares of sugar cane, irrigated from 210 giant pivots (see Chapter Twenty-one). Thousands of jobs will be created at its $550-million Markala sugar project, Illovo says. But its contract stipulates that the Office du Niger must first remove the 1,600 people currently occupying the land, and that the project's water needs must be fully met before anyone else on the distribution canal can receive anything.

If there is any water left, that is. For sugar is one of the world's thirstiest crops. The project will take 20 cubic metres of water a second from the River Niger during the first phase alone. If an option of cultivating a further 17,000 hectares is taken up, the contract says the project can take 35 cubic metres a second. Since sugar requires year-round irrigation, that could amount to a billion cubic metres of water a year. Yet an assessment of environmental and social impacts published by the African Development Fund, another partner in the project, fails even to consider how this abstraction could impact water users downstream.

A second scheme, close by, is the 20,000-hectare N'Sukala sugar farm, in which the Mali government has a 40 per cent shareholding, and the remainder is held by the Chinese state-owned China Light Industrial Corporation for Foreign Economic and Technical Cooperation. Contract documents do not specify how much water will be required, but they do say that all water needs must be met before other takers get their supplies. It is likely to require at least as much water as the first phase of the Markala sugar project.

The US government's Millennium Challenge Corporation – which is trying to stimulate economic growth to achieve the UN's millennium development goals – has taken charge of 16,000 hectares along the Canal du Sahel, the largest distributor of water from the Markala barrage. Its $230-million Alatona Project is converting the land to rice cultivation and handing over five-hectare plots to thousands of local cattle herders. To help them become rice farmers, the herders will also receive starter kits, including ploughs, wagons, fertilizer and seeds, and the assistance of experts from MCC's American contractors, the non-profit development agency ACDI/VOCA, the product of a 1997 merger between Agricultural Cooperative Development International and Volunteers in Overseas Cooperative Assistance. The experts, says the agency, will train the herders 'in the practice of sedentary rice farming, irrigation system management, producer organization and agricultural credit management'.

US embassy representatives were on hand in June 2010 when the first water flowed to the relocated 800 former inhabitants of Beldenadji village, the first of 33 villages that, in the words of ACDI/VOCA, are being 'targeted to relocate to their new village site'. Will it work? Can American technical advisers turn cattle herders into capitalist rice farmers? Or will the herders, as some locals wearily suggest, end up selling the land to bigger landowners, including perhaps foreign investors, and returning to their cattle and goats? We shall see. But whatever the local benefits of the MCC's plan, it is another drain on the water resources of the river. The MCC's project includes drastically deepening the Canal du Sahel. Its current capacity of 100 cubic metres per second will be almost doubled to 190 cubic metres a second.

The largest and most controversial of the four foreign schemes is a Libyan enterprise slated to cover 100,000 hectares. The Malibya project was part of a grand plan by Libyan leader Colonel Muammar Gaddafi to make his desert nation self-sufficient in food through land deals with nearby countries. He signed a secret deal with Mali's president, Amadou Toumani Touré, under which the Libyans got a 50-year lease on the land, plus as much water as they need, in return for putting cash from Libya's sovereign investment fund, the Libya Africa Portfolio Fund for Investment, into the project.

Details are sketchy, and the whole project was on hold at the time of writing because of the fall of the Gaddafi regime. But if it goes ahead, the Malibya project is likely to grow rice, which will probably be trucked across the Sahara to Libya. There is no published social and environmental impact assessment of the project. But the terms require the land to be handed over to the Libyans free of occupants. It is far from clear how many families will lose their land if the project is completed, but the Office du Niger must find new land for those farmers. Meanwhile, the project could require more water than the other three big foreign projects put together.

The project was under way before the fall of Gaddafi. I saw contractors from the Chinese state-owned China Geo-Engineering Corporation constructing a large canal and road for the 40 kilometres from the river to the project area. They have already bulldozed orchards and fields, and divided villages in two. As I drove down the road, I noticed a family cultivating the thin strip of land between road and canal. They were growing onions to sell in the local village market. Children were watering the precious crop in the desert heat by bringing water in an endless succession of bowls and buckets dipped into the canal. 'Malibya took all our millet fields to build the canal,' their leader told me. 'They gave us compensation for knocking down our house, but we got nothing for the lost land. So we came here.' My guide, from the local branch of Office du Niger, frowned. He was in charge of compensation.

The Malibya canal is a monster. The canal's intake has the capacity to grab as much as 210 cubic metres a second, potentially more than doubling the amount of water taken from the river for irrigation. The director-general of Malibya, Abdalilah Youssef, boasted in 2008 that his new canal could supply up to four cubic kilometres of water a year to his project.

Why did Touré sign up for this? Local campaigners say the Mali government had become dependent on Libya and had little choice.

Many of its civil servants work in offices built by Libya. International visitors stay at Libyan-built hotels. Also, as Lamine Coulibaly, head of communications for the Mali small farmers' union, CNOP, told me when we met in one of those hotels: 'The government is so obsessed with getting investment for its agriculture that it cannot see when that investment will do more harm than good to its people. It will turn our farmers into agricultural labourers.'

During my visit, Mali's roads carried hundreds of billboards advertising 'Malibya Agriculture: Projet des 100,000 hectares à Macina'. There was relief in the delta a few weeks later, when the civil war in Libya cut off the cash and the bulldozers stopped. Malibya may collapse. But at the time of writing that was far from clear. The new administration in Tripoli may decide to revive the project in the interests of feeding its people.

Irrigation in the Office du Niger produces more than 300,000 tonnes of rice, 40 per cent of national consumption. It provides income for a claimed 280,000 people. None of this should be ignored. But the trouble is that for every winner in the rice fields there are four losers in the delta just downstream. The current water take from all the existing irrigation projects in the Office du Niger is 2.7 cubic kilometres a year, or just over 8 per cent of the typical total annual flow of the River Niger, according to the Office du Niger's records. Some years it is a much higher proportion. In the dry season, the irrigators remove up to 70 per cent of the flow.

The engineers at the Markala barrage are in charge of maintaining both river flow downstream to the delta and water diversions into the irrigation canals. They decide how much or how little is diverted. I asked them about the rules. 'The official minimum flow through the barrage is 40 cubic metres per second,' said Lansana Keita as we sat watching water running through the sluices. 'We do our best to release that much, but irrigation has the priority. Last year, the actual minimum was 38 cubic metres.'

According to Office du Niger data, since 2006, the barrage has regularly failed to deliver the official minimum discharge between January and May. There simply isn't enough water now. Yet the system is about to be asked to triple the amount diverted. The four foreign projects alone, if completed, have the potential to take some six cubic kilometres out of the River Niger each year. So what does that mean for the inner delta? Will this water grab leave the herders, fishers and farmers there high and dry?

Leo Zwarts, a hydrologist at the Dutch ministry of public works and water management, reckons that existing irrigation off-takes from the Markala dam have cut the area of the delta that is flooded by an average of 600 square kilometres, or between 3 and 7 per cent. Combined with the effects of drought, and changes in river flow caused by the Sélingué hydroelectric dam further upstream, this has killed several formerly flooded forests and at least half of the *bourgou* fields vital to grazing cattle. There are clear effects on fishing, too. A dramatic pair of graphs produced by Zwarts shows how the amount of fish sold in the market at Mopti goes up and down with the size of the delta inundation the previous year. In recent years, both have been going down. Water levels even correlate well with the breeding population of purple herons back in Europe.

Engineers are working hard on enlarging the three canals from the barrage, to ensure that the land grabs can have the water they need. The Canal du Sahel currently extracts 100 cubic metres a second, but the Millennium Challenge Corporation has promised to almost double that to 190 cubic metres a second. The smaller Canal Costes-Ingoiba has for many years extracted 13 cubic metres a second. But when I visited, it had recently been upgraded to 45 cubic metres a second, in order to supply the new Chinese sugar project, N'Sukala. But the biggest expansion is intended for the

Canal du Macina. Till recently this has been removing up to 75 cubic metres a second. But the massive new Malibya intake means it can now take up to 210 cubic metres a second.

Thus the plan is to almost triple the maximum amount of water that these three canals can extract from the river, from 188 to 445 cubic metres a second. That won't be possible just yet. The short waterway that connects the river to the point where the three canals begin is not big enough. It is currently being dredged to allow it to carry 300 cubic metres a second. The ambition is clear. Ever more water will be taken from the river.

Equally clear are the consequences. If all this goes ahead, perhaps 20 per cent of the wetland will dry out. There will be virtually no flow during the dry season. The *bourgou* grasses and flooded forests could all but disappear. And there would be drastic declines in fisheries across the delta. Mali may soon be awash with rice, but starved of fish.

Land with year-round sun and water for irrigation is an increasingly valuable commodity round the world. That's why the Libyans and Chinese and South Africans are in Mali. Water is now the limiting factor for agriculture on roughly a quarter of the world's fields. Yet nobody that I could find in government in Mali is thinking seriously about water as a limit on its own development. When I interviewed him at his office in Ségou, the then head of the Office du Niger, Kassoum Denon, was boasting that the president had just allocated him an extra 100,000 hectares – presumably to compensate for the 100,000 hectares taken out of his control by the Malibya deal. That means that the land theoretically allocated in the area for irrigation is now 1.1 million hectares. Where do they imagine the water will come from?

Kassoum and his president measure progress in terms of investment made in irrigation works, and in rice production. They see saving the wetland as an environmental luxury that must not divert them from their primary task. But out in the delta, the real economy is about fish and cattle and *bourgou* and bananas and firewood and millet. 'More people will lose than win from most irrigation projects in Mali,' says Jane Madgwick, CEO of Netherlands-based Wetlands International, with whom I travelled across the delta. 'These projects will decrease food security in Mali by damaging the livelihoods of those most vulnerable. What they are trying to do at the moment makes no sense because there is simply not enough water.'

Mali of course needs development. It is changing and so are the wants and needs of its people. Out in the delta, schools and clinics are starting to appear. Every fishing encampment has a TV antenna. There is sporadic mobile-phone coverage. I tuned in to several local radio stations. In Kakagna, the young village men broke the still wetland night with rap music on their car-battery-powered sound system. The fishing nets are now made of nylon and come from China. The kids wear Obama T-shirts and gear advertising European football teams like Chelsea and Barcelona. Motorbikes are starting to replace donkeys as the motive power of choice – though people still ride motorbikes as if they were donkeys, sitting far back on the seat and holding the handlebars like reins.

These days too, traditional lines of ethnicity and livelihood are blurred. I saw Fulani cattle herders going fishing, Bozo fishers harvesting grain, and Bambara millet farmers herding goats. But the fecundity of the delta remains the basis of their survival in one of the poorest countries on Earth. And the most valuable resource here on the edge of the desert has no dollar signs attached, and does not appear in anyone's account book. It is a commonly owned but vital resource: the water of the River Niger.

As we left the heart of the wetland, our boat kept grounding on the bottom of the narrowing waterways. Macaques laughed as we waded into the shallow water to find sufficient depth to resume our journey. The low water was simply a sign of the changing season, but it felt like an omen for the wetland.

26

BADIA, JORDAN

On the commons

Mohammed is a modern Bedouin from the Badia, the arid 'outback' of eastern Jordan. He exchanged his camels years ago for a truck and a big motorized water tanker. For much of the year, he lives a sedentary life in his village in the Tafila district in southern Jordan. He keeps his sheep close by, nourished on subsidized feed. But in spring, he phones his friends to discover where the rains have fallen and the grass is lush, then loads his flock into trucks, fills his water tanker and heads for distant pastures. This part-time nomadism is at the centre of a debate that could determine the future of both the Bedouin and the Badia. And could help determine the fate of Mohammed's fellow pastoralists worldwide.

A generation ago, the Bedouin and their camels roamed the deserts of the Middle East. It wasn't a free-for-all. Rights of owner-ship and access were tightly negotiated and policed, but without fences, formal laws or national boundaries. Mohammed's fore-fathers, members of the Anizzah tribe, travelled between the River Jordan and the Euphrates, a thousand kilometres across the desert, and south into Arabia. They lived a largely self-contained, nomadic existence. Today, they are stuck behind the national boundaries of Jordan, Syria, Iraq, Israel and Saudi Arabia. The camels are dis-appearing. In the northern Badia, less than 1 per cent of households own camels, once a sign of nobility among the Bedouin. But 99 per cent own sheep, which they rear for the cash that their meat, wool and milk will earn.

The Bedouin are settling down to a less noble but more profitable existence. Most have a family home in a village. Their children go to school and take jobs in business or government. Only a minority of households now depend on livestock for their main income, and many hire others to look after their flocks for much of the year. Even so, a quarter of families in the Badia still migrate hundreds of kilometres each year to find grazing pastures. Though Mohammed can no longer pass unhindered into neighbouring countries, his sheep can. Many Bedouin sell their animals across the border for a season to a fellow tribe member, and then buy them back later.

The Badia, the back yard of Jordan, remains the country's main region for livestock production. But the contrast between the old life and the new is often bizarre. Desert tents made of exquisite woollen fabric are patched with old fertilizer bags. Trucks bump across the

Badia delivering barrels of water. Shepherds follow their flocks on donkeys before driving into Safawi, a truckstop on the road to Iraq, to hear the latest gossip. Farmers, new settlements, roads and other infrastructure are all invading the pastures. In the villages, vegetables grow under plastic. The Badia has become a market garden for Amman, and for export.

The Jordanian government would like more permanent settlements and more farmers. Many claim that people like Mohammed are over-grazing the pastures, destroying the fragile grasslands and creating new desert. But the evidence for permanent ecological decline is scant. Many ecologists say the Badia is alive and well in the hands of the Bedouin, and that it is the development plans that could destroy it. If true, that leaves Mohammed, with his feedlots and his phone calls, as the unlikely ecological hero of the Badia. Jordan's semi-nomadic shepherds may just turn out to be the wise men.

The story of the Badia is being played out across the world. Pastoralists often flourish where they are allowed to do so. The world has hundreds of millions of them, and probably another billion people who combine farming with keeping livestock that graze on common pastures. By some estimates, they occupy 45 per cent of the planet's land surface – approaching four times more than farmers who till the soil.

The grass may not always be green, but the pastures are certainly productive. The livestock of Mongolia are responsible for a third of that country's GDP. In Morocco they deliver 25 per cent. In Sudan and Senegal, 80 per cent of agricultural productivity comes from pastures. The herds of alpaca, vicuña, llama and guanaco in the Andes provide food, fuel, clothing and transportation. Cashmere goats are money-spinners in Tibet. Cattle dung is the main fuel and fertilizer in rural India. Yaks feed millions in central Asia. The global market for camel milk is $10 billion. While minding their animals, pastoralists tend trees producing gum arabic that turns up in everything from Coca-Cola to paint; they harvest thousands of tonnes of medicinal plants and honey by the tanker-load; they escort desert tourists and guard wildlife. Oh, and they produce meat – the most popular foodstuff on Earth.

Pastoralism's PR is dreadful. Stories of over-grazing and 'desertification' spread around the world, often told by farmers who want the pastoralists' land. Pastoralists are seen as the big villains in the environmentalists' narrative of the 'tragedy of the commons', in which the American ecologist Garrett Hardin posited that sharing the environment doesn't work. According to Hardin, in the case of common pastures, those with the most animals will make the most profit, while everyone, however many or few animals they have, will share in the suffering as the pasture is over-grazed. The only rational response is therefore to graze as many animals as you can till the pasture turns to dust. Remedy: privatize the lot. The tragedy of the commons is a landgrabbers' charter.

Nice theory; shame about the facts. First, herders have long traditions of collectively managing their pastures. Whatever it may look like to the outsider, there is no free-for-all. And second, ecologists now realize that reports of desertification are greatly exaggerated. In fact, in most places, cattle and other animals grazing the grasses and browsing the bush are, as a recent report from the International Union for the Conservation of Nature put it, 'vital for ecosystem health and productivity'. Far from wrecking the land, pastoralists and their animals have for thousands of years conserved biodiversity, held back the desert, stored carbon and prevented erosion. Pastoralism is the best way of using the fickle climate of the dry grasslands of Africa and elsewhere. If future climate is going to be less reliable, perhaps even drier, then the skills and knowledge of pastoralists will be of even greater value.

In places like the Badia, it is the spread of the plough – especially in the hands of outsiders – that is the real threat, both because it obliterates the natural grasslands and because it hems in cattle herders and shepherds. Pastoralists need to be as flexible as the ecosystem they inhabit. They need to react quickly to changing circumstances, altering the sizes of their herds and migrating to areas where the vegetation is best that year, unencumbered by rules of individual land ownership and unfettered by state boundaries.

Ethiopia is just one country where pastoralists are being systematically marginalized, demonized as environmental destroyers while their economic contribution goes largely unrecognized. Pastoralists make up a tenth of Ethiopia's population and still occupy a third of its land, which they consider to be their ancestral territories. In return, they raise 40 per cent of the country's cattle, 75 per cent of its goats, a quarter of its sheep and all its camels. Leather production in Ethiopia, the country's second-largest foreign exchange earner, comes largely from pastoral herds on common land. But pastoralists are losing their land fast, to the plough and sometimes to misguided conservation schemes.

Take the Oromo, the largest ethnic group in Ethiopia, with some 30 million members. Their main pastures east of the capital Addis Ababa have come under sustained attack. In 1961, the government fenced off 75,000 hectares to create the Awash National Park. Then a Dutch company took over 15,000 hectares to create the Metehara sugar estate. Big ranches moved in next, taking a further 34,000 hectares. 'The community, the original owners of the land, were not consulted when the land was illegally taken from them,' says Eyasu Elias of the Ethiopian Institute of Agricultural Research and Wageningen University in the Netherlands. 'Instead they are charged huge fees for their cattle to be allowed access to the ranches during extended drought.'

Most recently, in 2008, the Ethiopian government gave an

Indian company, Chadha Agro, 22,000 hectares to grow yet more sugar in Oromia, in return for Indian investment in a sugar refinery. The new sugar estate 'took some of the best dry season grazing areas along the Awash River', says Elias. After armed protests from the Oromo, the Ethiopian government nationalized the farm and brought in soldiers to protect it.

Altogether, the Oromo have lost 60 per cent of their land. As a result, they have been over-grazing some of their remaining pastures. And they have fought over land with the Afar people, who live on the other side of the Awash park. In despair, some are giving up their animals and switching to farming, charcoal burning and smuggling. Others are heading for Addis, which is less than three hours away by bus. But not all. As I write this, Reuters is reporting that the Ethiopian police have arrested 29 people, 'for plotting to carry out bomb attacks'. All allegedly 'had links with the Oromo Liberation Front, a secessionist group Addis Ababa blacklisted as terrorists last year'.

From Afghanistan to West Africa, the revenge of the pastoralists looks like it is becoming an important political issue. Go west from Oromia to Niger and Mali, and there are plenty of Tuareg tribesmen who have been progressively deprived of their pastures by farmers. Some have joined Al Qaeda, and begun kidnapping and murdering foreigners across the Sahel from Mauritania to Burkina Faso. In Mali, tourist trips to the fabled Dogon highlands effectively ended in 2011, due to kidnappings. Aid agencies I met in Mopti told me they had recently abandoned driving to Timbuktu because of armed car-jackings. We can pay a heavy price for ignoring pastoralists.

To discuss all this, I flew to Kenya and met Liz Alden Wily in the Village Market. Despite its name, the Village Market is a giant shopping mall in northern Nairobi – the new Kenya masquerading as the old. The only Maasai people there were selling trinkets in the shops. We drank coffee for hours as she discussed Africa, customary land rights and the fate of pastoralists. Alden Wily is a political economist and land reform expert in demand around the world. And she tells a story not often heard, about some of the world's most marginalized and persecuted people. About people that even old Africa hands don't often see – until perhaps they hit the headlines wielding a Kalashnikov or a rocket launcher.

Pastoralists, along with forest dwellers, occupy many of the planet's surviving commons. Those who pursue their traditional lives mostly spend their time far from towns or even roads, ignoring national laws and even national boundaries. Most African politicians I have met were brought up in such places, but now have the zeal of newcomers to city life. They believe that the people of the commons are historical leftovers, wild people who need to be tamed and settled, brought within national laws and norms. For their good and for ours. They should shop in the Village Market, not a real village market.

Alden Wily calls this dangerous nonsense.

Most places have commons. They vary in size from English village greens to the world's largest rainforests. But only in Africa is most of the land in some form of common ownership. About four-fifths of the continent's 2.4 billion hectares is not formally owned by anyone other than the state. There is no legal title, but rural inhabitants regard it as theirs. As Alden Wily began one of her trenchant papers on the topic: 'Whether recognized by statutory law or not, African rural communities consider themselves to be the traditional owners of not just their house plots and farms, but also the forests, pastures and other naturally collective resources which fall within their domains.'

That's the rub. For what we are talking about is the land that the World Bank calls 'the world's last great reserve of underused land'. These are the supposedly empty plains of Africa that governments want to give to landgrabbers in the cause of economic development. Again as I write, Mozambique has declared six million hectares of this 'empty' land open to foreign investors on 50-year leases at an annual rent of $23 a hectare, and 40 fellow Portuguese-speaking Brazilian soya farmers are about to go over and take a look.

But to equate uncultivated with unused or un-owned is a bad mistake, says Alden Wily. 'In fact, virtually every inch of the continent is owned under customary norms and used in accordance with custom, for shifting cultivation, grazing, hunting, wood and non-wood extraction or as spare land for expanding farming when needed.' Common lands are also where domesticated livestock and wildlife have co-existed for thousands of years. They are the conservationists' 'Pleistocene landscapes'.

Africa is the last great stronghold of the commons, though the customary rights they entail often exist in parallel with, or in defiance of, formal law. European colonists never accepted them, though they mostly left the pastoralists to their own devices. Post-independence African states either expunged the customary rights or overrode them by nationalizing the common pastures and forests, in the name of socialism. Socialism is out of favour today. So the great sell-off has begun. In the name of economic development. Parcel it all out and all will be well.

Alden Wily wants neither state control nor privatization. Instead she wants a renaissance for customary land tenure, by enshrining it in national laws. That is no panacea. As we saw in Ghana, tribal chiefs can be as venal as government ministers when a foreigner comes calling with a chequebook. But without some change to vest land rights in the community, she believes that most of the commons are doomed. 'Half a billion Africans will remain tenants of a state that can perfectly legally sell or lease their farms and commons from beneath their feet.'

From Gambella to Mozambique, and South Sudan to Liberia, the great pastures and forests today are the only surviving places on the planet that 'provide the scale of contiguous and intact estates sought by large-scale investors'. That is why they are under attack as never before. The current land rush, she says, 'is a tipping point in the penetration of capital into agrarian societies'. We could be witnessing the beginning of the final enclosure of the world's unfenced lands, and with it the 'final extinction of customary land rights'.

It need not happen. In the rich world, some indigenous cultures in remote regions have beaten back the tide and successfully claimed their right to hold and manage large areas of land according to their own ways – whether the Inuit of Canada, the Sami of Scandinavia, the Aborigines of Australia or the Native Americans in their reservations. Alden Wily will, she says, 'not rest until the four billion hectares of customary land are legally entrenched in the hands of their rightful owners, the world's two billion rural poor'.

Brave words. For hundreds of millions of people across the planet – from Omot on his waterbuck skin in Gambella, to Mohammed with his water tanker in the Jordanian Badia – the results of her battle will define their lives, and those of future generations. There are few more important issues for the twenty-first century than the fate of the world's commons.

27
LONDON, ENGLAND
Feeding the world

The spectre of Malthusian famines has returned to haunt the world. The British government's chief scientist, Sir John Beddington, forecasts a 'perfect storm' – a combination of climate change, rising world population, disintegrating ecosystems and land and water shortages. The storm will trigger a global food crisis that could see hundreds of millions starve. 'We are at a unique moment in history,' he says. 'We have 20 years to deliver 40 per cent more food . . . this is really urgent.'

Who will deliver that food? The answer, according to Beddington, is agribusiness. 'Small scale is not going to feed the world.' And he is part of a chorus of Western experts arguing that it is only by handing over the world's farmland to the landgrabbers that the world can be fed. The World Bank's former research director, Paul Collier, author of influential books like *The Bottom Billion* and *The Plundered Planet*, says that 'peasant farming is not well suited to innovation and investment' and that the 'most realistic way' of bringing down world food prices 'is to replicate the Brazilian model of large, technologically sophisticated agro-companies'. There are, he says, 'still many areas of the world – including large swathes of Africa – that have good land that could be used far more productively if it were properly managed by large companies'.

Investors are keen. The perfect storm is a perfect opportunity for landgrabbers, says Richard Ferguson, head of global agriculture at the investment bank Renaissance Capital, and a cheerleader for mechanized, globalized agricultural giantism. 'The latest great industrialization process is under way. Farms will get much bigger and more industrial,' he says. 'A free market with transparent pricing, enforceable property rights and liberalized trade would solve just about every agricultural problem under the sun.' Ferguson predicts that Africa and its food future will be transformed by 'industrial-sized farms of a million hectares'.

Let's pick all this apart, starting with Beddington's planetary threats. They are real, but need to be seen in perspective. The actual outcomes of climate change are far from certain. It could cut farm yields in some parts of Africa by 50 per cent by mid-century, and trigger monsoon failures in south Asia. But other regions, particularly the northern hemisphere outside the tropics, could see increased yields. Much will also depend on how cleverly farmers respond to changing weather by switching crops, and how good science is at developing more heat- and drought-tolerant varieties. World population will probably stabilize by mid-century at 9 billion or so people. That is still two billion more than today, and sub-Saharan Africa's population may double. But the headcounts in many countries outside Africa will probably be contracting by then, including most of Europe and much of Asia, including China.

Water shortages are worsening. Farms use most of our water, especially in the drier places. Many rivers tapped for irrigation are running dry. Cities are also demanding ever more. Water grabs could trigger water wars. But the potential for using water more efficiently, and for recycling urban wastewater for irrigation, is immense. Ecosystems, especially forests, underpin much agriculture by maintaining climate, river flows, soils and coastlines, and by providing more esoteric services such as pollinating insects. But the impact of their local degradation is hard to predict.

Finally, good new land fit for the plough is running short in some countries. But we won't 'run out' of land. Only 12 per cent of the world's land is currently used for cultivation, much of it at very low yields. Most agree we need to protect forests and wetlands from encroachment. But a critical question is how much of our unfenced and commonly owned grasslands and grazing pastures we want to, or can safely, give up. That, of course, has huge ramifications for the land grab debate, as we saw in the previous chapter. But there are choices. So what choices should we make? Do we need to hand over those commons, along with millions of cultivated smallholdings, to agribusiness in order to feed the world? Or is that part of the mythology behind the land grab?

For modernists such as Collier and Beddington, feeding a world of nine billion or more requires an urgent revolution in the way the world grows its food. That revolution must harness Western markets and technology, especially in Africa. Efficiency is the watchword – in production and trade.

Take trade first. 'Food security is best served by fair and fully functioning markets,' Beddington wrote in a report, *The Future of Food and Farming*, published by his government think tank in early 2011. The 2008 food price spike happened because of restrictions placed on exports by food producers. So 'Greater powers need to be given to international institutions to prevent trade restrictions at times of crisis.' In an aside, he agreed that 'empirical evidence' does not allow him to assess the importance of market speculators in pushing up prices during those dangerous months. But he absolves them anyway, by concluding that 'improving the functioning of commodity markets can reduce the element of volatility that does not reflect underlying market fundamentals'.

As we saw in Chapter Two, not many people in the financial

markets seem to agree with the professor's sanguine assessment of how more and freer international trade will stabilize prices and feed the world. Several said so in their responses to Beddington's report. 'In reality, open markets do not necessarily deliver either affordability or balance to the market for food,' said Nick Tapp, the head of agribusiness at Bidwells, the London-based international property consultants. 'The rapid price movements of early 2011 suggest an altogether more volatile market going forwards, as market pricing responds increasingly to the daily signals and sentiments flashed across newswires.' Hitching the food business more tightly to global financial markets will, as it did in 2008 and 2011, pump up price fluctuations and decrease food security. 'Periods of shortage and related hunger are endemic to a laissez-faire approach to markets,' he added.

If the modernists' enthusiasm for unfettered markets seems questionable, how about their assessment of the relative merits of peasants and agribusiness? Do we need to turn independent peasant farmers into agricultural labourers as fast as we can? Many experts strongly disagree with the bleak assessment of Collier and others about peasant agriculture's potential. 'There is a cultural prejudice against peasants,' says Olivier De Schutter, UN special rapporteur on the right to food. 'They are seen as backward, not worthy partners. These ideas are self-fulfilling.' One of Beddington's co-authors told me that the chief scientist's planned revolution stands a good chance of making the poor poorer. Big farms and big investment risk exacerbating the trends that bring hunger amid plenty. We could have both more food and more famines.

And that view seems to be shared by Sir Robert (Bob) Watson, a former chief scientist at the World Bank. He must have had some interesting conversations with Collier. In 2008, Watson chaired an international study of the future of the world's farming. The 2,500-page report of the International Assessment of Agricultural

Knowledge, Science and Technology for Development (IAASTD) reached rather different conclusions from Collier and Beddington. It proposed 'strengthening food security' by 'making the small-scale farming sector profitable', rather than by dismantling it. Far from embracing unfettered global markets, Watson warned that 'opening national agricultural markets to international competition . . . can undermine the agricultural sector, with long-term negative effects for poverty, food security and the environment.' Watson warned that extending the power of markets and agribusiness 'would mean the earth's haves and have-nots splitting further apart'.

Some will say Beddington and Collier are cold-eyed realists, while Watson and De Schutter are befuddled victims of political correctness. Collier says the latter are guilty of a 'retreat into romanticism'. But the prescription depends on the diagnosis.

Beddington and Collier see feeding the world as, in large measure, a matter of growing more food. And to do that they want to unleash commercial agriculture. To fill the grain hoppers, and improve Cargill's turnover. So they support ploughing up African pastures, and grabbing the smallholdings of millions of peasant farmers to create large, more 'efficient' farms. Watson, on the other hand, sees the biggest problems as poverty, lack of development in poor rural communities, and the uneven distribution of food. After all, he points out, we produce enough food now to feed the world, but still one billion people go hungry. He says the agribusiness prescription could kill the patient.

Half the world's undernourished people, and three-quarters of Africa's undernourished children, live on small farms. Watson says the best way to feed them is to help them feed themselves and their communities, by 'empowering the small farmer'. Beddington wants to take away their land in order 'to make agriculture more efficient'. But Watson asks: more efficient for whom? Are we most interested in the efficient use of capital or labour? In the efficient

347

delivery of food to markets or to the poor? In healthy bottom lines or healthy children? If these different efficiencies have different requirements, then Beddington's efficient farms may not solve the problem as he hopes.

There is no doubting that much peasant farming is in a mess, and nowhere more than in Africa. Per-capita food production in Africa has only recently returned to the levels of the early 1960s – whereas it has doubled in Asia and risen by 60 per cent in Latin America. But while a repeat of the dramatic success of Brazil in transforming the *cerrado* into a high-tech prairie might suit investors keen to profit from Africa's newfound reputation as the 'last frontier' for agribusiness, it may not suit Africans so well. As Raj Patel of the University of California at Berkeley put it for *Foreign Policy*, 'Big agriculture tends to work most lucratively with large-scale plantations and operations to which small farmers are little more than an impediment.'

There is another blueprint. It rejects Beddington's notions of 'efficiency', Collier's Brazilian aspiration and Ferguson's dreams of giantism. It holds that the idea of uprooting half a billion peasants, who grow 90 per cent of Africa's food, is a global capitalist version of the disastrous socialist experiments attempted by Stalin, Mao and Pol Pot. According to this blueprint, mixed farming systems operated by most of the world's smallholders have at least as much productive potential as big farms with their monocultures. As Patel said, 'If you're keen to make the world's poorest people better off, it's smarter to invest in their farms . . . than to send them packing to the cities.'

Simple measures of tonnes of grain per hectare may suggest big is best. But small farmers bring many other things to the kitchen table. Official statistics often ignore the fact that they use every corner of their plots, planting kitchen gardens where mechanized farms have vehicle yards. They gather fruits from the hedgerows.

They have chickens running in the yard. They feed animals on farm waste and apply the animals' manure to their fields. They raise fish in their flooded paddies. Big farmers may have access to more capital. But ultimately their purpose is to generate returns for that capital – to please their investors, rather than to feed families.

'There can be a green revolution in Africa,' said Gordon Conway, former president of the Rockefeller Foundation, launching his Montpellier Panel report on African agriculture in 2010. 'But it will be driven by smallholders – the 33 million smallholders in Africa with less than two hectares. The people from whom that continent gets 90 per cent of its food. It is their productivity we have to improve.'

Dig into the literature and you find that this view is widely held among many experts on world agriculture, even those working for organizations more associated with gung-ho agri-capitalism. The World Bank's *2008 World Development Report* concluded that investment in peasant farming was among the most efficient and effective ways of raising people out of poverty. Its 2009 study on 'awakening Africa's sleeping giant' is widely claimed to be a manifesto for big farming and land grabs. But even a cursory reading suggests not. The report notes, for instance, that 'Despite recent efforts, mainly by foreign investors, to launch large-scale agribusiness ventures in Africa, there is little evidence that the large-scale farming model is either necessary or even particularly promising for Africa.'

Asia's green revolution is often cited as a triumph for agribusiness. But a 2011 study by Diana Hunt and Michael Lipton at London's Chatham House, *Green Revolutions for Sub-Saharan Africa?*, says the real Asian lesson for Africa is that 'employment-intensive, small-scale farming [is] both more efficient and more pro-poor'. Vietnam, a country with a booming economy and fast-rising population, has gone from running a regular food deficit to being a major food exporter by investing in smallholder farming.

Big farms hollow out communities, while investment in small farms sustains and improves them, says a 2007 study by the Washington DC-based International Food Policy Research Institute. 'When small farm households spend their incomes, they tend to spend them on locally produced goods and services, thereby stimulating the rural non-farm economy and creating additional jobs,' says IFPRI's Peter Hazell. Small farms also nurture local agricultural know-how, and networks of marketing and other expertise. Such 'social capital' underpins wider development, but could never emerge from turning smallholders into labourers for corporate farms. 'Unless key policymakers adopt a more assertive agenda towards small-farm agriculture, there is a growing risk that rural poverty will rise dramatically,' says Hazell.

Pretending that big commercial farming can, or even wants to, feed the world, is dangerous, according to a 2010 report from the International Livestock Research Institute in Nairobi. 'It is not big efficient farms on high-potential lands but rather one billion small family farms, tending rice paddies or cultivating maize and beans while raising a few chickens and pigs, a herd of goats or a cow or two . . . who feed most of the world's poor people today,' write Susan MacMillan and Carlos Seré in *Back to the Future*. Small farms are good for the planet, too. They 'make up the biggest and most environmentally sustainable agricultural system in the world'. The world needs more of them, since 'this same group is likely to play the biggest role in global food security over the next several decades . . . Governments and researchers are mistaken to continue looking to high-potential lands and single commodity farming systems as the answer to world hunger.' Hooray to that.

But we can't just leave the peasants to get on with it. An important reason why smallholder farming has stagnated, in many parts of Africa in particular, is because even the most basic state help has been stripped away. The collapse of support for peasant farmers in Africa has been a continent-wide tragedy and a global disgrace, because it has often been carried out in the name of free markets, and demanded by structural adjustment programmes.

For decades, African governments have turned their backs on the countryside, putting their money into airlines, industrial enterprises and urban infrastructure, and starving smallholders of seeds, fertilizer and rural roads. The state marketing agencies that once underpinned local economies by buying crops at stable prices have been abolished. Extension services that once spread best practice have shrivelled. Research budgets have been slashed. Even the roads in many rural areas are more potholes than tarmac.

In 2003, African leaders pledged to raise the proportion of their budgets allocated to agriculture from an average of 3.5 per cent to 10 per cent. With agriculture responsible for typically two-thirds of their GDP, that still seems a small figure. But only seven nations, representing just 15 per cent of the continent's one billion people, have yet achieved it. Government spending still averages less than $20 per year per rural inhabitant. Compare that to the huge subsidies, handouts and tax waivers – not to mention free land – now being offered to foreign investors. Donors too have taken their eyes off this ball. Agricultural aid was halved between the mid-1980s and the millennium, bottoming out at 3.4 per cent of total aid. It has only recently begun to recover.

More spending will only make sense if it is used wisely, of course. But the good news is that there are innumerable examples of what can be done. The recent poster-child has been Malawi. Since 2005, the small southern African country has radically raised maize yields by distributing coupons that farmers can exchange for cheap fertilizer and maize seed. More than 1.5 million Malawi farmers benefit. The subsidy costs more than 6 per cent of Malawi's GDP, and absorbs 60 per cent of the budget of the Ministry of Agriculture.

But since the programme began, Malawi has gone from being a food importer to a food exporter. Economic growth is up and there are more jobs.

The system isn't perfect. Some parts of Malawi still lack food at certain times of the year; three-quarters of the vouchers end up in the hands of men, even though most of the farmwork is done by women; and environmental critics say a concentration on maize fed by chemical fertilizer will degrade the country's soils in the long run. But other countries, such as Zambia, are copying this model. Development expert Jeffrey Sachs of Columbia University claims Malawi's success could be replicated across the whole of Africa for $10 billion a year.

Much else can be done besides raining fertilizer across the continent. I have seen numerous and diverse success stories on my travels. I visited a research station on the mosquito-ridden shores of Lake Victoria in Kenya, where they have developed a simple system for banishing the stem borer, a common and destructive pest in maize fields, without expensive chemicals. Tens of thousands of maize farmers in East Africa now cultivate a common weed called napier grass on their field edges. The grass attracts the stem borer and leaves the field free of the pest. They call it the push-pull system. Farmers have discovered they can also harvest the napier grass to feed their dairy cattle.

In Mali, on the edge of the Sahara desert, I saw farmers stabilizing their soils and increasing crop yields by planting trees. This was a reversal of the advice from foreign agronomists who told them trees reduce yields and should be removed. The new practice had spread from neighbouring Niger, where Chris Reij, a Dutch geographer who first spotted the trend, reckons 200 million trees have been planted in a largely unremarked 're-greening' of the Sahel region.

More surprising still, because it slays some environmental

myths as well as undermining prejudice against peasant farmers, is the story of the Akamba people in Machakos, Kenya. Half a century ago, colonial administrators wrote off the 'overpopulated' and deforested district as destined for desertification, and the Akamba for destitution. But since then, Akamba farmers have increased output fivefold, while reducing soil erosion, increasing tree cover – and tripling their population. Desertification has been put into reverse. Malthus has been stood on his head. And all without outside assistance. Their trick has been to manage their land better, by terracing hillsides, capturing rainwater and planting trees. And they have been finding new markets for high-value produce. The Akamba still work small family plots, but they are selling vegetables and milk to Nairobi, mangoes and oranges to the Middle East, avocados to France and green beans to British supermarkets. Researchers call this the 'Machakos miracle'.

I also visited the dusty desert margins of northern Nigeria, around the ancient caravan city of Kano. The area is as densely populated as Belgium. Rainfall is declining. An incompetent government cannot keep chemical fertilizers in the stores. Only the richest farmers can afford high-yielding grain varieties or irrigation. The poor make do by cultivating almost every scrap of the sandy soil that they can find. Surely, you would say, those fields should be turning to desert? Yet the roadsides between the closely spaced villages are busy with fruit and vegetable stalls, and behind them the fields grow black-eyed peas, in rotation with grains.

I met Ado, who tended a two-hectare plot on the outskirts of Badume village, 50 kilometres northwest of Kano. He took me behind the high mud walls of his small compound, to an inner sanctum where a dozen sheep were munching away on waste straw he had cut from his fields. The sheep deposited manure that Ado scooped up to return to the fields as fertilizer. This simple nutrient recycling had tripled his pea harvest. And since the pea plants were legumes, they were adding more nitrogen to the soil and improving his sorghum and millet crops, too. The extra crops were transforming Ado's life. 'Now I can send my three children to school,' he said. 'The boys will become farmers, but I want my daughter to become a doctor.'

His neighbour, Galadima, was doing the same thing. 'Crops grow much better with manure,' he told me. 'I don't use chemical fertilizer at all now.' His two wives and 18 children came running out of the house and lined up for a family photo. 'We can double yields here easily and improve the environment at the same time,' said agricultural scientist B. B. Singh, who had advised the farmers as head of the Kano office of the International Institute of Tropical Agriculture. 'And this is nothing unusual. We can do it all over Africa.' So simple, but so effective.

In many places, new communications technology is helping smallholders. Mobile phones have revolutionized the ability of small farmers to access markets and check prices. In outgrower schemes for fresh vegetables – such as the Homegrown operation I watched in Machakos, which airfreights produce to Britain – farmers take orders by phone for the day's delivery while working in their fields.

Africans can learn from each other, but also from elsewhere. Well-organized milk markets are still rare in Africa. But Indian milk production has gone from 78th in the world to number one, almost entirely through the work of farmer-owned cooperative dairies. The knowledge that a truck will be collecting milk from the local village every morning has done wonders for the productivity of even the smallest Indian farmers. I met Jitbhai Chowdhury, who cultivates two hectares of irrigated alfalfa in Kushkal village in northern Gujarat. He feeds the alfalfa to half a dozen cattle. Every morning, he milks the cows and carries two churns containing 25 litres of milk to a village collecting point. From there, a tanker takes it to the modern Amul dairy in Anand, Gujarat, which supplies dairy products across India. Co-ops currently collect from 10 million Indian farmers in more than 80,000 villages.

Urban markets are creating new opportunities for rural smallholders. Nairobi's consumers have been an important part of the Machakos miracle. In Ethiopia, the bulk of the milk and honey sold in the capital, Addis Ababa, comes not from large commercial enterprises but from informal markets supplying the output of smallholders. But city dwellers also grow their own food – on a huge scale.

As much as a tenth of the world's food is grown within cities. Most of it comes from small farmers – micro-farmers, even – cultivating roadside verges and wastelands, rooftops and military bases, garbage dumps and parks, gardens and greenhouses, railway yards and university campuses, and scraps of land beneath bridges or beside canals. Urban farms are a major source of leafy vegetables. In Haiti, people grow vegetables in old truck tyres and even kettles. And they even supply meat. In Lima, Peru, they raise guinea pigs in squatter settlements. In Nairobi, chickens fatten in coops bolted to apartment walls. Sheep graze the roadside verges of the Armenian capital, Yerevan.

Urban agriculture is usually high-efficiency agriculture. According to the late Jac Smit, president of the Urban Agriculture Network of the UN Development Programme, city-grown vegetables typically use only a fifth as much irrigation water, and a sixth as much land, as mechanized rural cultivation. Hundreds of millions of urban dwellers get some of their food and part of their income from urban agriculture. They include professionals as well as the landless, and at least as many women as men. In a world where more and more of us live in cities, more and more of our food will come from cities, too. And when supermarket shelves empty or income falters, in times of drought or conflict, cities will feed themselves.

Of course, urban agriculture will only ever be a small part of the story. But, especially in Africa, it shows the dynamism and innovation of which small farmers are capable, given the right circumstances and a ready market for their produce. Whatever Collier may believe, they are often the true innovators. 'There is much that is working well in Africa, working much better than many appreciate,' says Jules Pretty of the University of Essex, one of Beddington's team of experts. Smallholder farming is the solution rather than the problem, he says, a success story waiting to happen. Small farms have great potential to increase their output – but also to raise the incomes and improve the livelihoods and skills of their operators.

Few small farmers in Africa can abandon subsistence food production. Nor should they. But successful cash crops turn African smallholder farming from, at best, an 'old man's business' into something young adults seek out, even when they have the chance to go and work in factories or offices. Perhaps that is the biggest challenge of all. If the young don't want to till the soil, then as Ben White of Erasmus University, Rotterdam, as staunch a supporter of smallholders as you will find, admits: 'We will have no argument against the corporations growing the world's food, because there will be nobody else to do it.'

NOTES ON SOURCES

The following is a far from complete listing of sources used in preparing this book. Many of the news items I used were first accessed from the website http://farmlandgrab.org, which is maintained by GRAIN, an NGO. Among the academic sources are papers at the International Conference on Global Land Grabbing held in Brighton, England, in April 2011, available at http://www.future-agricultures.org. Below I refer to this event as 'the Brighton conference'.

Mostly I have cited material available online. I am happy to provide further references where required. Contact me at pearcefred1@hotmail.co.uk.

Introduction
Siggs's quotes are from his presentation 'Can Africa be the world's bread basket?' at the Agriculture Investment Summit Europe in London, in June 2011: http://www.feronia.com/investors/news-and-events/feronia-presents-at-the-agriculture-investment-summit-europe-2011. Davies was speaking at the Brighton conference.

Chapter 1: Gambella, Ethiopia
I visited Gambella in February 2011. I thank Omot Agwa Okway and others for their hospitality. I consulted media and other reports on the Anuak community online at http://www.anyuakmedia.com. The

villagization plan appears at http://www.anuakjustice.org/downloads/ VillagizationProgramActionPlan(2003).pdf. Shiferaw is quoted in 'Ministry says ongoing resettlement in Gambella state key to improving livelihoods', 2010, at http://www.anyuakmedia.com/ Ethionews_temp_10_11_3.html.

For Karuturi, see 'Karuturi Global eyes East African markets', 2010, http://www.bloomberg.com; and 'Karuturi and the conquest of the African mind space', 2011, http://www.financialexpress.com. For Saudi Star, see Davison's 'Saudi billionaire's company will invest $2.5 billion in Ethiopia rice farm', 2011, http://search1.bloomberg.com; and 'Silence over Ethiopian land grab broken' at http://farmlandgrab.org. Contract terms appear at http://www.anyuakmedia.com/ Obang_SMNE_11_5_11.html and http://www.solidaritymovement.org/ 110510EthiopianAgriculturalPortal.php.

Government responds in 'Land deals in Ethiopia bring food self-sufficiency and prosperity', 2011, http://www.guardian.co.uk and 'Come and farm our virgin lands, Ethiopia tells India', 2011, http://www. thehindu.com. But read 'Targeting the Anuak', 2005, http://www.hrw.org; UNICEF 'Livelihoods & Vulnerabilities Study: Gambella region of Ethiopia', 2006, http://www.genocidewatch.org; and 'Gambella Journal: A river washes away Ethiopia's tensions for a moment', 2004, http://www.nytimes.com.

Resource politics is discussed by Dereje Feyissa in *Africa Development* (vol. XXXI, pp. 243–60), http://www.codesria.org/IMG/pdf/ 10_feyissa.pdf and his book *Playing Different Games* (Berghahn Books, 2011). On wildlife, see my 'Agribusiness boom threatens key African wildlife migration', 2011, http://e360.yale.edu. I quote from Cherie Enawgaw's 'Recent survey results and status of potential wildlife sites in Gambella national park', Ethiopian Wildlife Conservation Authority, December 2010.

Chapter 2: Chicago, USA
I visited the Chicago Board of Trade in the summer of 2010. Kaufman's 2010 piece in *Harper's* is at http://frederickkaufman.typepad.com. For

the 2008 global food crisis, see the *Guardian's* coverage at
http://www.guardian.co.uk/environment/series/global-food-crisis. Also
'Food price rises threaten global security – UN', 'Food prices could swing
future UK elections', and 'Poor go hungry while rich fill their tanks' – all
at http://www.guardian.co.uk.

Sheeran is quoted in 'Food crisis sparking conflict', 2008,
http://www.opendemocracy.net. Masters's senate testimony appears at
http://hsgac.senate.gov/public/files/052008Masters.pdf. American
economists warn in 'Economists support regulation of commodities
futures markets in the reconciliation of the Financial Reform Bill', 2010,
http://ourfinancialsecurity.org. Schutter's briefing on 'Food commodities
speculation and food price crises' is at http://www.srfood.org/index.php/
en/component/content/article/894-food-commodities-speculation-and-
food-price-crises. The World Development Movement fingers speculation
in 'The great hunger lottery', 2010.

Goldman Sachs is quoted at http://www.thomhartmann.com; Soros in
'We are in the midst of the worst financial crisis in 30 years', 2008,
http://www.stern.de; and Ghosh at http://www.pacificfreepress.
com/news/1/6154-a-global-food-bubble.pdf. Munden and Fischler were
speaking at meetings I attended in 2011. The 2011 UNCTAD report is
'Price formation in financialized commodity markets' at http://www.
unctad.org. Mid-2011 prices are from 'High food prices are here to stay –
and here's why' in http://www.guardian.co.uk.

Chapter 3: Saudi Arabia
I visited Saudi Arabia for the Saudi Water and Power Forum in 2009. Al
Safi farm is in 'Creature comforts help dairy cows thrive in the desert',
2003, http://www.worldvet.org. McGuckian is profiled in 'Dairy tycoon
brings music to our ears', 2005, http://business.timesonline.co.uk. For
water issues see 'Camels don't fly, deserts don't bloom', 2004,
http://www.soas.ac.uk/water/publications/papers/file38391.pdf, and my
book *When the Rivers Run Dry* (Eden Project Books, 2006).

Saudi land grabs are discussed in 'Kingdom plans agriculture investment
in 27 countries', 2011, http://arabnews.com; 'Transnational land deals in

Mindanao', presented at the Brighton conference; 'Indonesia sees rice crop up, seeks Gulf farm investment' at http://farmlandgrab.org/13670; 'Saudi-based partners launch Africa rice farming plan', 2010, http://af.reuters.com; and 'Saudi investors poised to take control of rice production in Senegal and Mali?' 2010, http://www.grain.org. Rajhi's story begins with 'Green grow the deserts O' (*The Economist*, 6 April 1985) through 'Saudi farms turn soil for seeds of change', 2009, to 'New Saudi company leases Asia land for rice', 2010, both at http://www.ft.com.

For Gulf agriculture strategy see 'Bridging the food gap' by NCB Capital 2010, http://farmlandgrab.org, and '$53b food basket', 2011, http://www.zawya.com. UAE Pakistani purchases are in 'Foreign land deals and human rights', http://www.chrgj.org. King Abdullah gets his medal at http://www.fao.org/news/story/en/item/45133/icode.

Qatar's London holdings are at 'Qataris enjoy rich pickings in London property', 2011, http://www.guardian.co.uk. 'Qatar in talks to buy Argentina, Ukraine farmland' and 'Hassad to buy sugar project in Brazil', both 2010, are at http://af.reuters.com. Sarawak's deal is at 'Tanjung Manis eyes investments worth RM650 million from Mideast', 2011, http://www.bernama.com. See Qatar's Australian ambitions in 'Nation feeds Gulf's appetite for ownership', 2011, http://www.smh.com.au; and 'Qatar plans 70 per cent food self-sufficiency by 2023', 2011, http://farmlandgrab.org/post/view/19016.

Woertz discusses 'Potential for GCC Agro-Investments in Africa and Central Asia', 2008, at http://www.grc.ae. I discussed Agrisol's plans with a PR man from Burson-Marsteller. Read also 'Iowan Rastetter leads Tanzanian ag project', 2011, http://farmlandgrab.org/post/view/18802, and *Understanding Land Investment Deals in Africa*, 2011, at http://media.oaklandinstitute.org.

For food prices and the Arab Spring, see 'Egypt and Tunisia: rocked by the global food crisis', 2011, http://www.newscientist.com , and 'Global warming and Arab spring', 2011, in *Survival* (vol. 53, pp. 11–17), http://www.iiss.org.

Chapter 4: South Sudan

Find Jarch at http://www.jarchcapital.com. And Heilberg in *Rolling Stone's* 'Will global warming, overpopulation, floods, droughts and food riots make this man rich?', 2010, http://news.haverford.edu/blogs/ ourschool/files/2010/06/Capitalists-of-Chaos-Mckenzie-Funk.pdf. Also his *Fortune* quote in 'Betting the Farm', June 2009, and 'South Sudan looking into US land deal', 2009, http://af.reuters.com. Read on Mayom mayhem in 'Bul Community in Diaspora Challenge the Wisdom of Abysmal SPLM Leadership in Unity State', 2011, http://allafrica.com. See also 'The scramble for the South', *Africa Confidential* (vol. 52, No. 7, p. 8).

I discussed Nile Trading with Eugene Douglas and quote from his un-published correspondence with Oxfam and others. Meet his team at http://kinyeti.com. See also 'Mokaya Payam leaders reject 600,000 he land lease', 2011, http://www.gurtong.net. I also spoke with David Deng, author of *The New Frontier,* at http://www.npaid.org, and 'Land belongs to the community: demystifying the global land grab in Southern Sudan' at the Brighton conference. Also hear the BBC 2011 report at http:// audioprospector.appspot.com/programme/p00hn7ll.

Al Ain's mystery Boma enterprise emerged in 'An odd deal over land', 2009, http://www.economist.com. Also see 'Al Ain zoo makes room for luxury', 2010, http://www.thenational.ae. The Canadians are at http://www.cedas.org; Green Resources at http://www.greenresources.no and Citadel at 'Egyptian companies look beyond borders', 2010, http://www.ft.com.

Chapter 5: Yala Swamp, Kenya

I visited Dominion Farm in February 2011, and interviewed Burgess both before and after the visit. I thank him as well as Leonard Oriaro and Chris Owalla. See http://www.dominion-farms.org and http://dominionfarmskenya.blogspot.com. NGO output includes 'Yala swamp – a living museum of biodiversity' at http://www.culturalsurvival.org, and 'Land grabbing in Kenya and Mozambique', 2010, http://www.fian.org. Kenya Wetlands Forum's 'Rapid

assessment of the Yala swamp wetlands', 2006, is at
http://www.kenyawetlandsforum.org. The Darwin Initiative draft
conservation plan, 'Yala Swamp Important Bird Area Conservation
Management Plan', 2009, is at http://darwin.defra.gov.uk/documents/
EIDPO029/21535/EIDPO029%20AR1%20Ann18-
%20Draft%20Yala%20Swamp%20IBA%20Management%20plan%20_v1
_.pdf.

See also 'Dominion farms chief fears for his life', 2011, http://
www.menafn.com and 'Obasanjo leads prospective American investors to
Taraba', 2011, http://www.vanguardngr.com.

Chapter 6: Liberia
I visited Liberia in November 2010. 'Timber, Taylor, Soldier, Spy', 2005,
is at http://www.globalwitness.org. See also SAMFU Foundation's
'Plunder: the silent destruction of Liberia's rainforest', 2000,
http://www.forestsmonitor.org; 'Conflict timber and Liberia's war', 2005,
http://www.etfrn.org/etfrn/newsletter/news4344/articles/2_2_Blundell.pdf;
and 'How a tyrant's logs of war bring terror to West Africa', 2001, at
http://www.guardian.co.uk. Also Mr Gus in 'New trial for Dutch "arms
smuggler" ', 2010, http://news.bbc.co.uk.

Time wrote on 'Rebuilding Liberia', 2009, at http://www.time.com.
Liberia's EU deal was signed in 2011, http://www.efi.int/files/attachments/
euflegt/efi_liberia_press_release_-_en_-_final.pdf. Problems with new
logging licences are discussed in 'The Hunter's whistle', 2009,
http://www.illegal-logging.info.

Firestone is here: http://www.firestonenaturalrubber.com, and some of its
critics here: http://www.stopfirestone.org/history.shtml. Read more in
'The Heavy Load', 2009, http://www.laborrights.org, and *A Critical
Examination of Firestone's Operations in Liberia* by Tarnue Johnson
(AuthorHouse, 2010). Goll's Town is in 'Understanding diversity: a study
of livelihoods and forest landscapes in Liberia', 2009, http://iucn.org.
LAC's history is in 'Human rights in Liberia's rubber plantations: tapping
into the future', 2006, http://unmil.org. Buchanan is at
http://www.buchananrenewables.com.

Gbalin is showcased in 'Building business as a way out of poverty for women in Liberia', http://www.oxfam.org.uk. The Libyans are exposed in 'Libyan funded agriculture project vanished', 2011, http://www. liberiawebs.com. Green Advocates is at http://www.greenadvocates.org. Brownell has written on 'Land grabbing and land reform in the new Liberia', 2007, http://www.pacweb.org. See also Liz Alden Wily's 'Whose Land Is It?' 2008, http://www.rightsandresources.org.

Chapter 7: Palm Bay, Liberia

I visited EPO at Palm Bay in November 2010. See also http://www.epoil.co.uk. Sime Darby's troubles appear in 'Grim prospects for Sime Darby in Bomi', 2011, http://www.liberianobserver.com, and 'Halt Sime Darby plantation expansion', 2011, http://allafrica.com. See 'Recycling the past: rehabilitation of Congo's colonial palm and rubber plantations', 2006, http://news.mongabay.com, and 'Oil palm in Africa: past, present and future scenarios', 2010, http://wrm.org.uy.

The Blattners are at http://www.gbedrc.com; and in 'Kinshasa Journal: Getting rich in Zaire: an American, 33, tells how', 1989, http://www.nytimes.com. The Roundtable on Sustainable Palm Oil is at http://www.rspo.org. For new African arrivals, 'Olam invests US$1.5b in Gabon', 2010, http://www.channelnewsasia.com; 'The plunder of Africa continues', 2010, http://www.wrm.org.uy/bulletin/158/Africa.html; 'Congo: un agro-industriel malaisien va investir 300 millions de dollars', 2010, http://www.afp.com; 'Chinese agribusiness company in DR Congo to offer thousands of jobs for locals', 2009, http://www.xinhuanet.com; and 'A huge oil palm plantation puts African rainforests at risk', 2011, http://e360.yale.edu. Sierra Leone's 2010 pitch to investors is at http://www.slideshare.net/kizuki/sl-sugar-investment-opportunity-150210-compatibility-mode. Feronia is at http://www.feronia.com.

Chapter 8: London, England

Emergent and Envest both had a critique from the Oakland Institute in its *Understanding Land Investment Deals in Africa*, 2011, http://media. oaklandinstitute.org. See also http://www.emvest.com and http://www. emergentasset.com. Payne's Kondratiev cycles are in 'African Land Fund:

Breaking new ground in Africa', a presentation by her on 3 December 2009. See also the company's website and Murrin's book, *Breaking the Code of History* (Apollo Analysis, 2011).

Read 'McKinsey on Africa: a continent on the move', 2010, http://www. mckinseyonsociety.com. Rothschild is profiled in 'Lunch with the FT: Jacob Rothschild', 2010, http://www.ft.com. Bramdean is at http://www.bramdean.com, and 'Horlick and Tchenguiz do battle', 2009, http://www.guardian.co.uk. *The Wall Street Journal* on private equity in 2010 is at http://farmlandgrab.org/16790. Greenleaf is at http://www.greenleaf-global.com; Agricapital makes promises at http://www.agricapital.info; and GreenWorld is at http:// www.greenworldbvi.com.

Nigel Woodhouse discussed Farm Lands of Guinea with me. See also 'Investment in Farm Lands of Guinea Inc', http://investegate.info, and company profiles at http://www.hotstocked.com/8-k/–356410.html. See 'Pension funds: key players in the global farmland grab', 2011, http://www.grain.org; and TIAA-CREF's investment is analysed, 2010, at http://farmlandgrab.org/14063. SilverStreet is at http://www. silverstreetcapital.com and 'SilverStreet raises $198m from PKA and OPIC', 2010, at http://www.privateequityafrica.com.

Standard Bank on 'Financing Land Investment in Africa' is dated 8 April 2011 and summarized at http://www.afribiz.info/content/investors-must-tread-carefully-in-new-rush-for-land-in-africa-warns-standard-bank-press-release. Read about the 'Tanganyika groundnut scheme' at http://en.wikipedia.org.

Chapter 9: Ukraine
Spinks headlined in the *Wall Street Journal's* 'Richard Spinks of Landkom snaps up Ukraine plots to cash in on high crop prices', 2008, http:// farmlandgrab.org, and in *Farmers' Weekly*, 'Farming in Ukraine', 2007, http://www.fwi.co.uk. Landkom is at http://www.landkom.net and its 2011 crisis is in 'Poor rapeseed crop sends Landkom shares plunging' at http://www.agrimoney.com.

Mark Rachkevych writes in the *Kyiv Post*. For instance, 'Agribusiness giants may become kings of farming', 2011, http://www.farmlandgrab.org and 'Investing in Ukraine: Top 10 picks of 2010', 2010, http://www. farmlandgrab.org. Beigbeider is at 'Agrogeneration exploitera plus de 100.000 hectares de terre d'ici 2012', 2010, http://www.farmlandgrab. The Maharishi is in 'Organic Agriculture venture set decades backward by Pinchuk's Fund' at http://www.investukraine.net.

'Land grabbing in post-Soviet Eurasia', 2011, is examined by Oane Visser and Max Spoor in the *Journal of Peasant Studies* (vol. 38, pp. 299–323). Trigon Agri is at http://www.trigonagri.com. I wrote about Greenfield in 'Biofuels could clean up Chernobyl badlands', 2009, http://www. newscientist.com. Mettetal is in 'Ukraine, Russia grain export curbs deter investors', 2011, http://www.usubc.org; Tleubayev in 'The new gold rush', 2008, http://farmindustrynews.com; and Rozinov in 'Ivolga puts world's biggest farm up for sale', 2011, http://www.telegraph.co.uk.

Black Earth Farming is at http://blackearthfarming.com, and Richard Ferguson's http://farmlandgrab.org/wp-content/uploads/2009/05/20081027-agriculture-richard-ferguson.pdf. Orlov is in 'Russia's collective farms: hot capitalist property', 2008, http://www.nytimes.com and 'Agriculture: the battle to bring more land into production', 2008, http://www.ft.com. Alpcot Agro is at http://www.alpcotagro.com.

Chapter 10: Western Bahia, Brazil
I travelled to Western Bahia in March 2011 with Conservation International. Thanks to Gabriela Michelotti and her colleagues. For agribusiness in the *cerrado*, see http://www.agbrazil.com, and http://farmlandgrab.org/wp-content/uploads/2009/05/20081027-agriculture-richard-ferguson.pdf. For soya, Cargill and the Amazon, see 'Eating up the Amazon', 2006, http://www.greenpeace.org. Also 'Agrarian structure, foreign land ownership and land value in Brazil' by Sergio Sauer at the Brighton conference. Try too 'The great Brazilian land grab', 2005, http://www.forbes.com; 'The miracle of the cerrado', 2010, http://www.economist.com; and 'How Brazil outfarmed the American farmer', 2008, http://money.cnn.com. Laura Graham wrote 'The tractor

invasion', 2009, http://www.culturalsurvival.org. Maggi is quoted in 'Relentless Foe of the Amazon Jungle: Soybeans', 2003, http://www.nytimes.com.

Agrifirma is at http://agrifirma-brazil.com. See 'Soros-Backed Adecoagro Raises $314 Million in IPO', 2011, http://www.bloomberg.com, and http://www.adecoagro.com.br. Levinsohn is analysed at 'Farm Bang collects labor and environmental crimes', http://www.reporterbrasil. com.br. See 'Conservation in Brazil: The forgotten ecosystem', 2005, http://www.nature.com; and 'Brazil loosens restrictions on Amazon land use', 2011, http://www.guardian.co.uk.

Mitsui is at http://www.mitsui.com, and 'Mitsui to boost Brazil soya exports', 2011, at http://www.bloomberg.com. 'Chongqing Grain Group to Build an Industrial Complex in Brazil', 2011, is at http://www.investin.com.cn and 'China will invest USD 10 billion in soybean production in Brazil', 2011, at http://en.mercopress.com.

Chapter 11: Chaco, Paraguay

I visited Paraguay in March 2011 with Roger Wilson from World Land Trust (http://www.worldlandtrust.org) and the staff of Guyra Paraguay (http://www.guyra.org.py). I wrote 'Battle of the Chaco: who will win the wilderness?' 2011, http://www.newscientist.com. 'The green hell becomes home: Mennonites in Paraguay' is at http://www.anabaptistwiki.org; the Filadelfia museum is at http://www.faunaparaguay.com/jakobunger.html; and 'Paraguay Mennonites find success a mixed blessing', 2003, at http://www.nytimes.com.

Read 'The case of the Ayoreo', 2010, at http://www.iwgia.org. The New Tribes Mission is at http://usa.ntm.org. Land reclaims are in the 'Chaco 2010 Programme Report' of http://www.cwslac.org. I wrote about Yaguarete Porã in 'Brazilian beef barons are greenwashing to preserve their place on your plate', 2010, http://www.guardian.co.uk. And see 'Ranchers caught red-handed from space', 2011, http://www. survivalinternational.org.

Check 'What are the Moonies up to?' at http://www.thetablet.co.uk and

'Paraguay and the Moonies – a town owned by a cult seeks liberation', 2005, http://www.economist.com. Scimitar Oryx is at http://www. scimitarpartners.com; Fric's story in 'Alberto Vojtěch Frič – Part I – The story of a Czech adventurer & ethnologist who brought a South American Indian to Prague', 2010, http://www.radio.cz; and Casaccia presented on 'Deforestation in the Paraguayan Chaco' in London, 2009, http://www.sas.ac.uk/750.html.

Chapter 12: Latin America

Vestey lost out in 'Lord Spam to lose Venezuelan farm', 2010, http://www.telegraph.co.uk. The story of United Fruit is in Peter Chapman's *Jungle Capitalists* (Canongate, 2006), and http://www. unitedfruit.org. The State Department report on Guatemala, 2010, is at http://www.state.gov/documents/organization/137411.pdf. See also 'Ranchers and Drug Barons Threaten Rain Forest', 2010, http://www.nytimes.com.

'The process of land concentration in Peru', 2011, is at http://www. landcoalition.org. Bolivia's Santa Cruz problem is in Mackey's 'Legitimating foreignization in Bolivia' from the Brighton conference, and 'Bolivia: Un millón de hectáreas de tierra en manos de extranjeros, según Tierra', 2011, is at http://farmlandgrab.org. See Ballvé's 'Territory by dispossession: decentralization, statehood and the narco land-grab in Colombia' from the Brighton conference, and his 'The dark side of Plan Colombia', 2009, http://www.thenation.com. Also 'Multinational invades sovereign Afro-Colombian territory', 2011, http://colombiareports.com.

Chapter 13: Patagonia

Doug Tompkins is profiled in 'Welcome to my world', 2009, http://www.guardian.co.uk and 'Back to nature in Patagonia', 2010, http://www.ft.com. The Tompkinses' trusts are at http://www. theconservationlandtrust.org and http://www.conservacionpatagonica.org. Their volcano is in 'Eruption in the back yard' at http://www.thecleanestline.com. Read the 'FARN Report: Benetton–Mapuche case', 2006, http://www.farn.org.ar, and Benetton's response at http://press.benettongroup.com/ben_en/about/facts/fact2. Also 'Leleque museum: Even Mapuche history appropriated by Benetton' at http://www.mapuche-nation.org.

For Patagonia overviews, see 'The end of the world is for sale', 2010, http://www.atimes.com and 'Mapuche: inhabitable land dwindles', 2007, http://www.unpo.org. See 'Warren Adams: Searching for profits and saving Patagonia' at http://management.fortune.cnn.com, and his http://patagoniasur.com. The Paulson story is in 'Treasury nominee Hank Paulson needs to answer some questions', 2006, http://www. humanevents.com.

Chapter 14: Australia

AAC's sale is in 'Iffco's investment Down Under shows vision', 2009, http://farmlandgrab.org/2914; and 'Cowboys won't beef up their stake in AACo', 2011, http://www.theaustralian.com.au. Packer is remembered at 'Kerry Packer: the Times obituary', 2005, http://www.timesonline.co.uk. His legacy is at http://www.terrafirma.com/cpc.html. 'MP Evans stokes Australia-US rivalry in beef', 2010, is at http://www.agrimoney.com. Also http://www.mpevans.co.uk. 'Nicole Kidman's family revealed to be one of the world's largest landowners', 2011, is at http://www.dailymail.co.uk. See Sara Henderson at http://www.bulloriver.com.

'Pastoral holdings remain a family affair', 2010, http://farmlandgrab.org, turned to 'Australia should look to its foods security', 2010, http://www.smh.com.au and 'Foreign ownership of Aussie land: the peril of selling the farm', 2011, http://www.crikey.com.au. Hassad features in 'Qatar land grab angers bush', 2011, http://www.theage.com.au. Read 'Investments pour in from far and wide', 2011, http://www.smh.com.au and 'That's what you call trying on a new hat', 2005, http://www. businessweek.com. 'Chinese company push for Western Australia farmland', 2011, at http://fw.farmonline.com.au.

In New Zealand, 'Crafar farm decision drags on', 2011, http://www.stuff.co.nz. And Greentree and Nicoletti were at 'Grain barons eye paddock to plate', 2009, http://www.countryman.com.au. And read how 'The Nature Conservancy and Partners Acquire Fish River Station in Northern Australia', 2011, http://www.nature.org.

Chapter 15: Sumatra, Indonesia

I visited Sumatra in late 2007, 'Bog barons: Indonesia's carbon catastrophe', at http://www.newscientist.com. My hosts were WWF's Yumiko Uryu, Afdhal Mahyuddin from Eyes on the Forest and APRIL's Neil Franklin. APRIL is at http://www.aprilasia.com; APP is at http://www.asiapulppaper.com.

'Eka Tjipta Widjaja, Indonesia's Richest Man', 2011, is at http://www.thejakartaglobe.com; APP's strategy is dissected in 'A forest falls in Cambodia', 2005, http://www.atimes.com. His rival is at http://www.sukantotanoto.net and http://en.wikipedia.org/wiki/Sukanto_Tanoto. Read on Arara Abadi in 'Without Remedy: human rights abuse and Indonesia's pulp and paper industry', 2003, http://www.hrw.org, and 'Indonesia: Investigate forcible destruction of homes by the police in Riau', 2008, http://www.amnesty.org.

See 'The financing of the Riau pulp producers' by Jan Willem van Gelder, 2005, http://www.jikalahari.or.id and William Sunderlin's 'Between danger and opportunity: Indonesia's forests in an era of economic crisis and political change', 1999, http://www.cgiar.org/cifor. Christopher Barr's 'Bob Hasan, the rise of Apkindo, and the shifting dynamics of control in Indonesia's timber sector', 1998, is at http://www.jstor.org/pss/3351402.

WWF summarized forest loss in 'Sumatra's forests, their wildlife and climate', 2010, http://assets.wwfid.panda.org. The corruption story surfaced in *Tempo* magazine's 'Road to Ruin', 17 September 2007, http://www.tempointeractive.com, and in 'How a $115b illegal logging probe was felled', 2011, http://www.thejakartaglobe.com.

Kampar draining is in 'EoF calls on SMG/APP and APRIL to keep their promises', 2010, http://eyesontheforest.or.id. APRIL's unpublished consultants' report was by UK-based ProForest. See also 'Indonesia: Communities reject APRIL's REDD plans on the Kampar Peninsula', 2009, http://www.redd-monitor.org. I reported on APP's greenwash in 'The deflowering of the EU's green logo', http://www.guardian.co.uk. See also 'Officeworks paper found to contain almost pure Indonesian rainforest', 2011, http://www.marketsforchange.org. Verchot is in 'Ban on new forest concessions in Indonesia is good news for climate change, but many challenges remain', 2011, http://www.cifor.org.

Chapter 16: Papua New Guinea

For deforestation in PNG, see 'Logging, Legality and Livelihoods in Papua New Guinea', 2006, http://www.forest-trends.org; 'Bulldozing progress: Human rights abuses and corruption in Papua New Guinea's large-scale logging industry', http://www.acfid.asn.au; and 'PNG: farewell to the forests', 2004, http://www.theage.com.au. Rimbunan Hijau was attacked in 'The untouchables', 2004, http://www.greenpeace.org. See also http://www.rhpng.com.pg.

Filer presented to the Brighton conference, 'The political construction of a land grab in Papua New Guinea', and published 'The new land grab in Papua New Guinea: A case study from New Ireland province', 2011, http://ips.cap.anu.edu.au. See also 'Lands department accused of corruption, negligence in Western province', 2010, http://malumnalu.blogspot.com; 'Controversy in land sales cited', 2011, http://www.postcourier.com.pg; and 'Papua New Guinea suspects controversial grants', 2011, http://news.mongabay.com.

Chapter 17: Cambodia

I visited Cambodia in March 2011, with assistance from David Pred at Bridges Across Borders Cambodia. His research on Ly Yong Phat appears in 'Bittersweet: A Briefing Paper on Industrial Sugar Production, Trade and Human Rights in Cambodia', 2010, http://babcambodia.org.

LYP is at http://www.lypgroup.com; 'Who is Ly Yong Phat?', 2010, is at http://australianetworknews.com; and see 'Eviction and land grabbing surges across Cambodia', 2010, and 'Land grabbing and poverty in Cambodia: the myth of development', 2009, both at http://www.licadho-cambodia.org.

'Economic Land Concessions in Cambodia: a human rights perspective', 2007, are discussed at http://cambodia.ohchr.org; and see 'World Bank land alert', 2010, http://farmlandgrab.org/15387. HLH is at http://www.hlh.com.sg; and see 'The end of the Suy people?' in 'The rights of indigenous people in Cambodia', 2010, http://www.iwgia.org. Also 'Chinese firm continues with evictions of Koh Kong villagers', and 'K Speu villager opposing land sale to stand trial', both in *Cambodia Daily*, 25 March 2011.

Mitr Phol is at http://www.mitrphol.com; Khon Kaen Sugar is at http://www.kslsugar.com/en. Everything-But-Arms is described at http://ec.europa.eu/trade/wider-agenda/development/generalised-system-of-preferences/everything-but-arms; and Cecilia Wikstrom is in 'Cambodian blood sugar condemned by EU parliament member', 2011, http://www.dw-world.de.

Chapter 18: Southeast Asia
Grey wrote 'China appropriates foreign and domestic land to build its rubber empire', 2009, http://farmlandgrab.org/post/view/2676. IUCN on the rubber invasion is in 'Rubber investments and market linkages in Lao PDR', 2009, http://cmsdata.iucn.org. See also 'Territorial affairs: turning battlefields into marketplaces in postwar Laos', 2010, http://erg.berkeley.edu/people/Student_Spotlight/Mike_Dwyer.shtml. Ziegler wrote 'The rubber juggernaut', 2009, http://www.sciencemag.org. Also 'China rubber demand stretches Laos', 2007, http://www.atimes.com, and 'Rubber: costs or benefits to the Lao PDR', 2009, http://www.sumernet.org. Doan Nguyen Duc is in 'Condo boss', 2009, at http://www.forbes.com.

'Farmland grabs by urban sprawl and their impacts on peasants' livelihood in China' is from the Brighton conference. Complant's Jamaica deal is in 'Gov't seals sugar deal with Complant', 2011, http://www.jamaicaobserver.com. Beidahuang's grabs are at 'China ups Argentine farmland purchases', 2011, http://www.lab.org.uk and 'China land deal causes unease in Argentina', 2011, http://www.guardian.co.uk, and 'New agricultural agreement in Argentina: a land grabbers' instruction manual', 2011, is at http://www.grain.org. 'Goldman Sachs buys Chinese poultry farms', 2008, at http://www.thepoultrysite.com.

China State Farms are assessed at 'China, Africa forge farming ties', 2010, http://www.chinadaily.com.cn. For Sino Cam Iko, see 'Chinese in

Cameroon: an agricultural misunderstanding', 2009, http://www.
afronline.org/?p=2908. Buckley's paper is 'Eating bitter to taste sweet',
presented at the Brighton conference. See also http://www.
chinaafricarealstory.com.

Korea's Daewoo plan was outlined at 'Daewoo's African dream', 2009,
http://www.koreatimes.co.kr and dashed with 'Madagascar scraps
Daewoo farm deal', 2009, http://www.ft.com. Hyundai in Russia is
'Hyundai Heavy Ind tests Russian investment', 2009, at
http://www.oilandgaseurasia.com. 'South Korea food security alarm',
2011, is at http://www.asiasentinel.com. Lee Woo-chang is in 'Corn on
the Cambodian cob suits Korean farmer', 2011, at http://cambodia-
business.blogspot.com.

Chapter 19: Maasailand, Tanzania
'Solitude in the Serengeti', 2007, is at http://www.telegraph.co.uk; and
see http://www.grumeti.com. Grumeti and Loliondo are 'In the shadow of
the Serengeti' at http://www.theinvestigativefund.org. See 'The brigadier's
shooting party', 1993, http://www.nytimes.com. Anaya probes 'United
Republic of Tanzania: Alleged forced removal of pastoralists', 2010,
at http://unsr.jamesanaya.org. Brittingham is at http://www.
tanzaniaquest.com; see Catherine Blampied's 'Tanzanian pastoralists
struggle for their rights' at http://www.global-politics.co.uk.

'Tourism is a curse to us', 2009, looked at Loliondo and Thomson's
Enashiva refuge at http://www.guardian.co.uk. Mara Goldman's 'Strangers
in their own land: Maasai and wildlife conservation in
northern Tanzania', 2011, is at http://www.conservationandsociety.org.
See also http://www.manyararanch.com.

Read about the Laikipians in 'The aristocratic class that owns huge tracts
of land in Kenya', 2004, http://www.africafiles.org; and 'The genesis of
land deals in Kenya and its implication on pastoralist livelihoods' at the
Brighton conference. See http://www.olpejetaconservancy.org;
http://www.sosian.com; Wildenstein's obituary at
http://www.telegraph.co.uk; and Cholmondeley interviewed in 'Curse of
happy valley', 2007, http://www.timesonline.co.uk. Note

http://www.lewa.org. Fascinating too is 'Sustainable inequalities: the case of Il Ngwesi group ranch', 2004, Ameyali Ramos Castillo's MSc thesis in the School of Geography at the University of Oxford.

Chapter 20: South Africa

I wrote a brief official history of WWF, *Treading Lightly*, in 2004. This chapter draws on some of that material. 'Conservation philanthropists, royalty and business elites in nature conservation in southern Africa' (*Antipode*, vol. 42, pp. 647–70, 2010) explores the Rupert/Bernhard relationship. Huxley's biography is *Peter Scott: painter and naturalist* (Faber, 1994). I wrote about Garamba in 'Rumble in the jungle', 1998, http://www.newscientist.com. Dublin is quoted from my feature 'Inventing Africa', 2000, http://www.newscientist.com. See 'Batwa land rights in Rwanda', 2003, http://www.minorityrights.org. Rights & Resources Initiative is in 'From needs to rights', 2009, http://www.care.dk.

I interviewed Vlissingen in 'Laird of Africa', 2005, at http://www. newscientist.com. The Africa Parks Foundation (now Network) is at http://african-parks.org. A study of the Peace Parks Foundation appears at http://www.geographie.hu-berlin.de. See also 'Breaking down the barricades', 1999, http://www.dur.ac.uk/resources/ibru/ publications/full/bsb7-3_warburton.pdf.

Schmidt-Soltau's 'Evictions from DRC's protected areas' is at http://www.fmreview.org/DRCongo/23.pdf. Curran and Schmidt-Soltau debate in 'Are Central Africa's protected areas displacing hundreds of thousands of rural poor?' and 'Is the displacement of people from parks only purported, or is it real?', 2009, http://www.conservationandsociety. org. See also *Nature Unbound: conservation, capitalism and the future of protected areas*, by Dan Brickington *et al* (Earthscan, 2008).

MacDonald's *Green Inc* is from Lyons Press, 2008. Kaimowitz wrote 'Conserving What and for Whom? Why Conservation Should Help Meet Basic Human Needs in the Tropics', 2007, Biotropica, http://www.cifor.org. Sandbrook wrote 'Linking conservation and poverty alleviation: the case of great apes', 2010, http://www.

povertyandconservation.info. Finally http://www.phinda.com, http://www.tswalu.com and http://www.mantiscollection.com.

Chapter 21: Africa

Ruth Hall spoke on 'The next great trek? South African commercial farmers move north' at the Brighton conference. See http://www.agrisa.co.za, and Joemat-Pettersson in 'Government drive to set up white SA farmers in Africa', 2009, http://www.businessday.co.za.

'Congo-Brazzaville: The South Africa-Congo Concession – exploitation or salvation?' 2010, is at http://allafrica.com, and see the Mozambique plan at http://www.agriallafrica.com/agrisamoz.html. 'Georgia – and Congo – on South African farmers' minds', 2011, is at http://mg.co.za. Also see http://boers.ge.

Illovo is at http://www.illovo.co.za. Ben Richardson examines 'Sugar cane in southern Africa: is it a sweet deal for the rural poor?' 2010, http://www.sucre-ethique.org. See Mimran versus Dangote in 'Expansion of sugar production in Africa', 2011, http://www.afriqueavenir.org. Addax is at http://www.addax-oryx.com. For Kenana see 'Beltone to launch $1bn Sudan agriculture fund', 2010, http://www.reuters.com; and 'Sudan: securing its future in sugar', 2005, http://www.new-ag.info. For Swaziland, http://www.rssc.co.sz.

Chapter 22: Mozambique

http://www.sunbiofuels.com no longer functions. 'Mozambique sells its first biofuel export to Lufthansa' at http://www.defenceweb.co.za. Oxfam discusses Kisarawe in 'Another inconvenient truth', 2008, http://www.oxfam.org.uk. Also 'Kisarawe villagers regret after leasing land to Sun Biofuels', 2010, http://allafrica.com; and 'Jatropha: money doesn't grow on trees', 2010, http://www.foei.org.

'Biofuels, land access and rural livelihoods in Tanzania', 2009, http://pubs.iied.org, covers both Sun Biofuels and Procana, whose problems emerge in 'Biofuels and land rights in Mozambique – the Procana case', 2009, http://pubs.iied.org/pdfs/12556IIED.pdf; and 'Mozambique: investors decided to pull out of Procana months ago',

2009, http://allafrica.com. See http://www.agriterra-ltd.com. 'Energem goes into bankruptcy without telling shareholders', 2011, at http://www.telegraph.co.uk.

Flora EcoPower suffered with 'Ethiopia: German biofuel company fails as employees abscond with assets', 2010, http://www.afrik-news.com; before 'Flora EcoPower resumes biofuel farm activities', 2010, http://www.capitalethiopia.com; and changed its name to Acazis, http://www.acazis.com.

Bedford Biofuels is at http://www.bedfordbiofuels.com. Environmentalists object in 'Tana River Delta', http://www.rspb.org.uk. See 'Biofuel land grabbing in Northern Ghana' at http://biofuelwatch.org.uk. ScanFuel is attacked in 'Norwegian land grabbers in Ghana – the case of ScanFuel', 2009, from Spire. And see Nukator and German's 'Towards sustainable biofuel development: assessing the local impacts of large-scale foreign land acquisitions in Ghana' at http://siteresources.worldbank.org. Searchinger summarized his case in 'Fixing a critical climate accounting error', 2009, http://www.sciencemag.org.

Chapter 23: Zimbabwe
The chapter draws on *Zimbabwe's Land Reform: myths and realities* by Ian Scoones *et al* (James Currey, 2011), and conversations with Scoones. See also 'Don't condemn Zimbabwe', 2011, at http://www.guardian.co.uk. This work is updated at http://www.zimbabweland.net.

For the Development Trust of Zimbabwe, see http://www.zwnews.com/ issuefull.cfm?ArticleID=85. For Nuanetsi and Rautenbach, see 'Party big-wigs locked in Nuanetsi ranch turf war', 2009, http://allafrica.com; 'Zimbabwe bio energy sets the record straight regarding Nuanetsi ranch', 2010, http://www.newstimeafrica.com; and 'Large-scale investment projects and land grabs in Zimbabwe: the case of Nuanetsi ranch bio-diesel project' from the Brighton conference. I interviewed Raoul du Toit in London in 2011. See also http://goldmanprize.org/2011/africa, and http:/savevalleyconservancy.org.

The Maluleke grabs are exposed in 'Safari operators enraged as Zanu-PF rewards the faithful', 2009, http://www.independent.co.uk; 'Zanu mafia in Lowveld land grab', 2009, http://www.thezimbabwean.co.uk; 'New land reforms – the death of wildlife tourism in Zimbabwe?' 2011, http://wildlife.co.uk; and 'New Zanu-PF land-grab exposed', 2011, http://www.thestandard.co.zw. The German aspect is in 'Zim, Germany argue over conservancy', 2011, http://www.financialgazette.co.zw. The 2011 US cable is at http://dazzlepod.com/cable/04HARARE2051.

I interviewed Mortimore at the Brighton conference, where he presented 'Land deals and commercial agriculture in Nigeria'. Also see 'Zimbabwean farmers working Nigerian land', 2011, http://www.bbc.co.uk.

Chapter 24: Central Africa
Much of the material on European loggers comes from unpublished WWF research. See Zimbabwe's logging of DRC in 'Branching out', 2002, http://www.globalwitness.org. And Blattner in 'The fight to save Congo's forests', 2007, http://www.thenation.com; and 'Sold down the river', 2007, http://www.guardian.co.uk.

'Chinese trade and investment and the forests of the Congo basin', 2011, is at http://www.cifor.org. Also see: 'From exclusion to ownership', 2008, http://www.rightsandresources.org, and 'Large acquisitions of rights on forest lands for tropical timber concessions', 2011, http://www.landcoalition.org.

'The New Forest Company and its Uganda plantations', 2011, is at http://www.oxfam.org, with 'In scramble for land, group says, company pushed Ugandans out', 2011, http://www.nytimes.com. Also see http://www.newforests.net. I reported on REDD in 'Save the climate by saving the trees', 2008. Chhatre's 'Trade-offs and synergies between carbon storage and livelihood benefits from forest commons' is at http://www.pnas.org.

The Carbon Planet scandal is in 'Australian firm linked to PNG's $100 million carbon trading scandal', 2009, http://www.smh.com. I interviewed Seymour in London in 2011.

Chapter 25: Inner Niger Delta, Mali

I visited Mali in January 2011 with Wetlands International's Jane Madgwick and Bakary Kone. Modibo Keita appears in 'Don't touch my land! Peasant resistance to land grabs in Mali', 2011, http://www.foodfirst.org. 'Assessing the contractual arrangements of large-scale land acquisitions in Mali with special attention to water rights', 2011, is at http://www.oicrf.org; Illovo's Markala project is profiled in 'Markala sugar project: appraisal report', 2010, http://www.afdb.org. See MCC in 'Turning African farmland over to big business', 2010, http://www.grain.org, and http://www.acdivoca.org/site/ ID/maliMCA-ASDA. For Malibya, see 'Libyan land grab of Mali's rice-producing land', 2009, http://www.viacampesina.org; 'Au Mali, des paysans réclament leurs terres vendues à Kadhafi', http://farmlandgrab.org; http://media.oaklandinstitute.org; and http://www.maliweb.net/category.php?NID=37605.

Zwarts's hydrology is at 'The Niger, a lifeline', 2005, http://www. altwym.nl , and 'Will the inner Niger delta shrivel up due to climate change and water use downstream?' 2009, http://www.wetlands.org.

Chapter 26: Badia, Jordan

I visited the Jordanian Badia in 1995 and wrote about the journey in 'Shepherds wise men', http://www.newscientist.com. Garrett Hardin's 'The tragedy of the commons', 1968, is at http://www.sciencemag.org. IUCN reports in 'Global review of the economics of pastoralism', 2006, http://cmsdata.iucn.org.

Oromia is discussed in 'Putting pastoralists on the policy agenda: land alienation in southern Ethiopia', 2010, http://pubs.iied.org; 'Pastoralists in southern Ethiopia', 2008, http://www.drylands-group.org; and 'Indian company given Oromia land twice the size of Singapore', 2011, http://www.jimmatimes.com.

Some of Liz Alden Wily's quotes come from 'The Law is to Blame: The Vulnerable Status of Common Property Rights in Sub-Saharan Africa' (*Development and Change*, vol. 42, pp. 733–57) at http:// onlinelibrary.wiley.com; 'Whose land are we giving away, Mr President?'

2010, http://siteresources.worldbank.org; and her paper at the Brighton conference, 'Nothing new under the sun or a new battle joined?'. 'Mozambique offers Brazilian farmers land to plant', 2011, is at http://farmlandgrab.org/post/view/19081.

Chapter 27: London, England

Beddington is quoted from 'Report: Urgent action needed to avert global hunger quotes', 2011, http://www.bbc.co.uk. His 'Foresight project on global food and farming futures' is at http://www.bis.gov.uk. Collier wrote 'Food shortages: think big', 2008, at http://www.timesonline.co.uk. Ferguson's 2008 report is at http://farmlandgrab.org/wp-content/uploads/2009/05/20081027-agriculture-richard-ferguson.pdf. Tapp's response to the Beddington report is at http://www.bidwells.co.uk. Watson's 'International assessment of agricultural knowledge, science and technology for development', 2008, is at http://www.agassessment.org.

Collier complains of romanticism in 'The politics of hunger', 2008, http://www.foreignaffairs.com. Raj Patel writes 'Can the world feed 10 billion people?' 2011, also at http://www.foreignpolicy.com. The World Bank's 'Awaking Africa's sleeping giant', 2009, is at http://siteresources.worldbank.org, and Hunt and Lipton's 'Green revolutions for sub-Saharan Africa?' 2011, at http://www.chathamhouse.org. Hazell's 'The future of small farms for poverty reduction and growth', 2007, is at http://www.ifpri.org, and ILRI's report, 'Back to the Future', 2010, at http://mahider.ilri.org.

See the Malawi experiment in 'The Malawi Agricultural Inputs Subsidy Programme, 2005/6 to 2008/9', 2011, http://siteresources.worldbank.org; and 'The Malawi fertilizer programme: politics and pragmatism', 2008, http://www.future-agricultures.org.

Read 'Push-pull technology: a conservation agriculture approach' in *International Journal of Agricultural Sustainability*, 2011, http://www.earthscan.co.uk/journals/ijas. Reij's stories of Sahel regreening appear at http://africa-regreening.blogspot.com.

Mortimore, Tiffen and Gichuki's book on Machakos, *More People, Less*

Erosion (John Wiley, 1994) is updated at http://www.drylandsresearch. org.uk. I have written about it in 'Out of the Demographic Trap: Hope for Feeding the World', 2010, at http://e360.yale.edu, and 'Desert harvest', 2001, http://www.newscientist.com. I wrote about Jitbhai Chowdhury in 'Earth: the parched planet', 2006, http://www. newscientist.com and in *When the Rivers Run Dry*. Smit wrote on urban agriculture at http://www.jacsmit.com. Pretty writes about 'Sustainable intensification in Africa' in *International Journal of Agricultural Sustainability*, 2011, http://www.earthscan.co.uk/journals/ijas.

INDEX

Fred Pearce is the environmental and development consultant for *New Scientist* and writes regularly for the *Guardian*. He has won many awards, including UK Environmental Journalist of the Year and the Association of British Science Writers' Lifetime Achievement Award. His previous books include *When the Rivers Run Dry* – voted among the all-time 'Top 50' books by Cambridge University's Programme for Sustainable Leadership, *The Last Generation*, *Confessions of an Eco-Sinner* – longlisted for the Samuel Johnson Prize – and *Peoplequake*.